## Praise for *Journey of*

*"Journey of the White Bear* is from the depth or the aution
teachings. This body of knowledge presented in their book is truly a moving art form for the generations. It is an honor to speak on behalf of the
White Bear, which was my mother Grace's [shi'ma's] totem. Gratitude to
both Robin and Sandy for gifting the world another round of inspiration.
May their journey be surrounded in beauty, above, below, before, behind.
Hozho Naasha and Lila Wopila Tanka."

—Sahn Nicole Hill, Navajo / Blackfoot,
Centre of Indigenous Arts, author of *A Discreet Medicine Story*

"Another teaching for others to grasp for a hopeful future that is needed at
this time. After reading the first book that Robin and Sandy wrote, *Path of
the White Wolf*, I felt they had started a journey that would take them and
their readers to different levels of living the medicine journey. Now after
reading *Journey of the White Bear*, the journey is continuing to foster new
teachings, and new levels of awareness that will support and create avenues
for personal growth and knowledge."

—Rhonda Aniquisi Meals, HD, PhD,
Cherokee / Chickasaw, author of *Dragon Moon Dancer*

"I've known Robin Tekwelus Youngblood for many years as a teacher,
healer, artist, and friend. I have a lot of respect for her and her work. I've
seen her work touch many people over the years, lifting people out of darkness and despair. This book will bring light and happiness to many."

—Johnny Moses, "Whis.stem.men.knee" (Walking Medicine Robe),
Tulalip traditional healer, spiritual leader, and storyteller

"I adopted Robin as a sister in ceremony in 2010 and gave her a Sacred Bundle of our traditional Rites to share. In our way, adoption is a sacred responsibility that crosses the veil between life and death. As well, I had the honor
of meeting Sandy, her sister friend, firekeeper and coauthor. These women
hold the fire of Regeneration. All life is reflected in this new book, *Journey
of the White Bear*. Anyone who wants to bring balance to themselves and the
world will want to read it."

—Grandfather Frank Settee, Okanagan / Ojibway / Lakota, Medicine Man

"This beautifully written book calls on each of us to pay attention to which Shaman's path we are called to walk, then gently guides us to it through the medicine of White Bear, and the authentic expert guidance of the two authors Robin and Sandy. This book will help you navigate your way home to your individual and collective magic. It is an ultimate guide that helps us heal our Earth, community, and selves."

—Omileye Achikeoi-Lewis, MEd, LCMHCA,
African-Caribbean, author of *My Heart Flies Open*

# JOURNEY *of the* WHITE BEAR

# About the Authors

© Gonda Postma / d'Raadgever

## *Robin Tekwelus Youngblood*

Robin Tekwelus Youngblood, Okanagan/Tsalagi, is a minister, teacher, author, artist, and a shamanic practitioner/healer. She has been a student of her heritage for many years. She has learned the sacred teachings of Indigenous elders from her own Native American tribes, along with Siberian, Polynesian, Aboriginal, and African elders. As a healing practitioner, Robin offers soul retrieval, aura cleansing, cord-cutting, crystal healing, and soul readings. Robin travels the world, offering Medicine Wheel, Wheel of Relationships, and Wheel of Co-creation workshops; Medicine Wheel Constellations; and Dance to Heal the Earth, as well as facilitating ceremonies such as Sweat Lodge and Vision Quest.

Robin is the co-author of *Path of the White Wolf, An Introduction to the Shaman's Way* with Sandy D'Entremont, published in the US (English) and sold worldwide, as well as in France (with a French translation), along with an accompanying meditation CD and several music CDs. She has been a member of the Seven Generations World Wisdom Council, which organized multicultural Wisdom Gatherings in several countries. She was a founding member of Grandmothers Circle the Earth, and still helps establish Grandmother Circles and Councils wherever she travels. In addition, she is a founding member of Sacred Earth Council, established to help us all move forward by sharing indigenous foundational teachings and healing ceremonies for these times. Robin has been using the COVID time to help humanity reset, sharing teachings on venues such as humanityrising .solutions, sacredearthcouncil.com, the World Water Law, worldunityweek .org, www.7days-of-rest.org, and returntoearth.land with Brooke Medicine Eagle.

Since 2012, Robin has circumnavigated the earth three times, sharing teachings and ceremonies. As a graduate of Barbara Marx Hubbard's "Agents of Conscious Evolution" training, Robin is a Guide for the Wheel of Co-creation, a method of working with others to co-create sustainable lifestyles. You can find Robin at www.churchoftheearth.org, a worldwide online congregation dedicated to serving Mother Earth and All Our Relatives. Robin founded Church of the Earth, a 501(c)(3) nonprofit, in 2006. It has currently expanded to a dozen working ministers all over the world. If you would like to be a member, please fill out the form at churchoftheearth.org. Robin also has several pages on Facebook.

For the last several years, Robin has taught online shamanic courses and shares onsite ceremonies, workshops, and events; if you are interested, please email her at whitewolfclanmother@yahoo.com.

© Caressa Weber

### Sandy D'Entremont

Sandy D'Entremont has been a student of earth-based spiritual practices for more than twenty-five years and blends the principles of many traditions into the Universal Medicine Wheel. Beyond her teaching and mentorship practice, Sandy's work in community focuses on supporting women's circles and women's ceremony, holding the container of the circle to foster initiation, transition, and transformation. She has been named sacred fire-keeper, ceremonial singer, intuitive seer, and healer. Sandy has taught drum-making, shamanic practices, and the Medicine Wheel Way in the Pacific Northwest, including the Women of Wisdom conference.

Holding the foundational belief that our relationship with the land is absolutely key to physical, emotional, mental, and spiritual health, Sandy also asserts that the land has its own influence in where and how we are called to live. An introvert by nature, Sandy shares a home with her fisherman husband and two adventurous Labrador retrievers, living at the very edge of the grid and counting mule deer, hawks, quail, ponderosa pines, and coyotes among her neighbors. Besides writing, she enjoys gardening, critter watching, and hiking, as well as the occasional weekend gathering of wild women friends in ceremony and sisterhood.

A graduate of the University of Washington–Bothell, Master of Fine Arts in Creative Writing & Poetics program, Sandy's creative work has appeared in *Clamor, Minerva Rising,* and *The Friendship Anthology.* She is the co-author of *Path of the White Wolf: An Introduction to the Shaman's Way* and the accompanying meditation CD with Robin Youngblood, published in the US (English) and sold worldwide, as well as in France (with a French translation). Sandy is currently finishing a coming-of-age novel series that features visionary and divination practices.

# JOURNEY *of the* WHITE BEAR

## A Path *to the* Center
## of Your Shaman's Heart

### ROBIN TEKWELUS YOUNGBLOOD
### SANDY D'ENTREMONT

Llewellyn Publications • Woodbury, Minnesota

*Journey of the White Bear: A Path to the Center of Your Shaman's Heart* © 2022 by Robin Tekwelus Youngblood and Sandy D'Entremont. All rights reserved. No part of this book may be used or reproduced in any manner whatsoever, including internet usage, without written permission from Llewellyn Publications, except in the case of brief quotations embodied in critical articles and reviews.

FIRST EDITION
First Printing, 2022

Book design by Valerie A. King
Cover design by Shira Atakpu
Interior illustrations by the Llewellyn Art Department

Llewellyn Publications is a registered trademark of Llewellyn Worldwide Ltd.

**Library of Congress Cataloging-in-Publication Data** (Pending)
ISBN: 978-0-7387-7180-9

Llewellyn Worldwide Ltd. does not participate in, endorse, or have any authority or responsibility concerning private business transactions between our authors and the public.

All mail addressed to the author is forwarded but the publisher cannot, unless specifically instructed by the author, give out an address or phone number.

Any internet references contained in this work are current at publication time, but the publisher cannot guarantee that a specific location will continue to be maintained. Please refer to the publisher's website for links to authors' websites and other sources.

Llewellyn Publications
A Division of Llewellyn Worldwide Ltd.
2143 Wooddale Drive
Woodbury, MN 55125-2989
www.llewellyn.com

Printed in the United States of America

# Other Books by Robin Tekwelus Youngblood
## and Sandy D'Entremont
*Path of the White Wolf: An Introduction to the Shaman's Way*

# Dedication

To All Our Relations, past and present,
from all Mother Earth's families, and to the
next generations who walk the trail yet to come.

*Great Mystery,*

*We speak to you as your daughters Robin and Sandy. We
thank you for our lives and for this day, and the opportunity
to do this work and share these teachings in the world. Thank
you for the beautiful abundance of our Mother Earth, she who
holds us always. And thank you for the boundless inspiration
of Father Sky and those who watch us always. Thank you for
our teachers, those who have touched our lives in both body
and spirit from all Earth's families, those who live on in our
hearts and whose messages we are honored to carry forward
with prayers for the Seventh Generation. And thank you for our
students, who teach us more than they could possibly imagine.
Thank you for our ancestors, who have given away so that
we can be here in this time and place on the Wheel of Life.
Thank you for our families, our partners, our children, and
grandchildren, those of blood and those of spirit, who bring
incredible love and joy into our lives, and who also catch us
when we falter, inspire us when we are disillusioned, encourage
us when we are tired, and love us anyway. And finally, Great
Mystery, from the bottom of our hearts, we thank you for
allowing us to share this earthwalk together, as sisters of
the wind, sisters of the heart, and for bringing us together to
dance in partnership on this Path. We do this work for All Our
Relations.*

*Aho Mitakuye Oyasin!*

# CONTENTS

———◆———

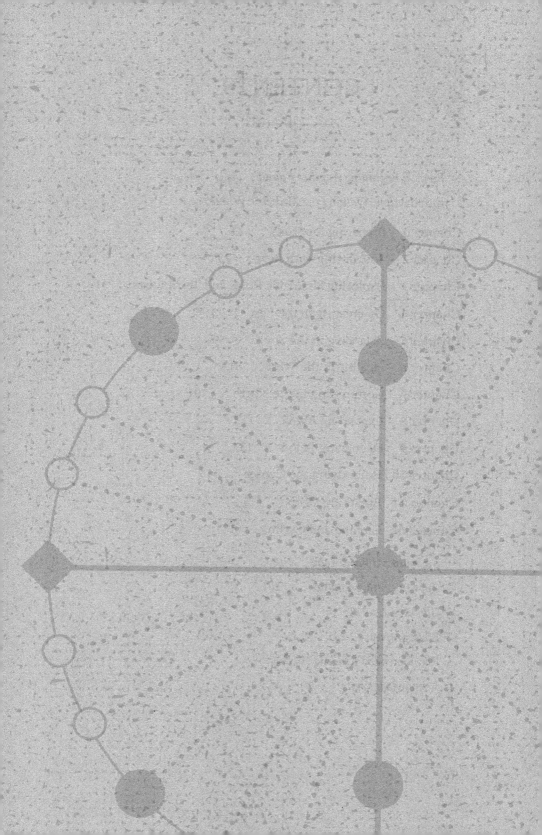

*Preface*

# BEGINNING
# ANOTHER ROUND

When Sandy and I wrote *Path of the White Wolf*, we were inspired to share a set of deep and meaningful teachings we had learned over many years. Sandy lived in the Seattle area and I lived in Haiku, Hawaii. We often say the book wrote itself, but as things progressed, we each wrote a chapter, then emailed it to the other to edit. Somehow, by the time we finished, even we couldn't tell who wrote what!

While the two of us live in closer proximity now, the process is still the same: write and email; edit and add or delete; return and revise. In between, Sandy and I have long discussions about the purpose of our work and this set of teachings; our challenging times; the immense paradigm shift that is absolutely imperative; and the ways that everything we've learned throughout our lives has dovetailed to bring us to this moment. This book. When we follow Spirit's guidance and the path set before us, we find the synchronicities are amazing, and the lessons are ever deeper.

We are passionate about this work. Committed to manifesting it and watching it fly. Compelled to do our small part in the next evolutionary leap our society—our planet—is poised to make.

And so ... Sandy and I write.

*Journey of the White Bear* marks the beginning of another round, the next cycle in the spiraling helix of our personal and collective evolution, a planetary evolution, which at its core asks us to develop spiritual adulthood, personal mastery, and a heart of service for All Our Relations.

In 2014, I survived a devastating mudslide that killed forty-three neighbors. As I surrendered to almost certain death, I heard Mother Earth screaming in pain and roaring with anger. Mother did not want that mountain to fall! She did not want to extinguish lives. Not just human lives, but also the lives of the resident eagles, bear, deer, heron, raccoon, salmon, and the entire plant and river ecosystem. Human error caused the mountain to fall. Nowadays, I tell people, "I'm a walking, dancing, singing miracle, and I know it!"

Within three months, through a series of serendipitous events, I was guided to start facilitating a worldwide ceremony called Dance to Heal the Earth, which has since been danced for four or more years in America, Asia, Africa, and Europe. Australia and New Zealand are next, if travel allows. Every year, I'm blessed to receive a message with the theme for the dance. The theme for 2021 was "Committed Spiritual Maturity: Individually and Collectively." The theme for 2022 (and beyond) is "Regeneration in Right Relationship to All Life." This is one of the many reasons the time for this book is NOW.

With global warming, civil wars, environmental disasters, famines, super storms, genetically modified food (GMOs), economic instability, and mass extinctions, the world we live in needs a huge course correction.

Today we have technologies we didn't even dream of when I was a child. Yet, one of the first shamanic teachings I received was that anything that can be manifested must first be envisioned. The second teaching is that we are responsible to, for, and with All Our Relations, unto the Seventh Generation and beyond. So we must be careful what we dream into existence, and thoughtful about how we perceive or imagine events.

There's an old story about a chief who had a gorgeous stallion he loved deeply. One morning, the village woke up and the chief's stallion was gone. "Oh, no," mourned the people. "This is awful! Your beautiful stallion is gone!" The chief answers, "I don't know if it's good or bad. I just know my stallion is gone." The next morning, the village rises, and the chief's stallion is back, and he has brought twenty brood mares with him. "Oh, Chief, this is wonderful!" shout the villagers. "Look—now you have a whole herd, and will have dozens of foals." The chief answers, "I don't know if this is good or bad. I only know my stallion is back and has brought all these mares." Next day, the chief's son tries to ride the stallion. The horse throws him, and the son breaks both legs. The villagers are shocked. "Oh, my chief! This is so terrible. Your son helps you with everything, and now he can't." The chief replies, "I don't know if this is good or bad. I just know my son has broken his legs." At dawn the next day, a messenger runs through the village shouting, "War, there's war! Every able-bodied man, grab your weapons!"... and the story goes on and on.

I don't know if all our technologies—all the things tipping the balance between humans and the environment these days—are good or bad. I only know they are. The Hopi say technology is neutral; it's how we use it that makes it good or not so good. We are all responsible for how we use the technologies we invent. I know that the way humanity is living now is not the way I want my children, grandchildren, and great-grandchildren to live. I feel an urgency to restore balance in any way I can, to ensure the earth is able to provide clean air, clean water, and food for the next seven generations, to protect the wild places and all earth's families.

And so... Sandy and I write. We pray that what you read here will help you in some way. For All Our Relations.

—Robin Tekwelus Youngblood
    May 2020

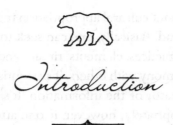

# Introduction

# WALKING THE
# MEDICINE WHEEL

And so you find yourself preparing to walk with White Spirit Bear on a journey to discover your Shaman's Heart. Where you travel on this quest will unfold in ways uniquely yours, shaped by your own perspectives and challenges, led and protected by your personal spirit guides and totems, guided by your higher and authentic self. What you encounter will be as diverse and powerful and beautiful as the Great Mystery itself. We cannot begin to predict what you will find, the new understandings you will gain, or the new teachers who may be guided to you. We invite you to place your foot on a trail many others have taken from time immemorial, a path of personal mastery in service to All Our Relations embracing the Shaman's Heart.

Studies of Jesus' life recount how he disappeared for three years before he began to follow his life mission. There's considerable speculation about where he was. Many believe he was studying with the Eastern masters during that time, and that part of the truths he taught afterward came from those studies. In *Journey of the White Bear*, you will follow a predominantly Native American path. Yet we have incorporated both modern and traditional teachings received from many other philosophies and indigenous teachers in these pages. We have been given permission to share these teachings in our own way, and we are always careful to credit those who have helped us learn.

1

There's much talk about cultural appropriation today. And it's an important concept to understand. Basically, one can seek to understand and learn
from another culture's practices, elements, rituals, and traditions. Before one
shares a teaching or ceremony with others, it's essential to ask for and receive
permission from the creator of the information. It's also essential that one
credit the teacher appropriately; however, if one attends a ceremony and,
having completed it, decides one now has the authority to offer the ceremony without asking permission and crediting the lineage they received
it from, that's called theft (i.e., cultural appropriation). It's also dangerous,
because if the person offering the ceremony hasn't lived or studied with the
people who know the protocols and traditions that keep participants safe, it
may not be. Please don't do that! This book is written for your personal use.
We cannot recommend you teach our methods to others unless you have
studied to become a credited teacher.

Everyone who has experienced a spiritual journey knows each journey
begins with a single step. You take that first step carrying your medicine bag
of experiences and teachings, after integrating the lessons learned in your
last cycle of learning. A spiritual path is often cyclical, circular, taking you
deeper, wider, and/or higher when you are ready. Consider the image of a
helix: each revolution brings you back to the same place on the spiral, but
at a slightly different level. We cycle the Medicine Wheel again and again as
we evolve, learning something new each time. Our very DNA demonstrates
this principle.

Spiritually, your next step starts, in essence, where your last journey
ended. And so, in the way of journeys, we begin this book with one of
Robin's stories, a vision that came to her many years ago when she was
taking pause after making a life-changing decision, both an ending and a
beginning.

> First, I saw myself walking through a mountain meadow
> in the snow. I was dressed in a beaded white doeskin dress
> with knee-high white moccasins and a fur-lined white buffalo
> parka. My friend Nahani, a white wolf, led me across the
> meadow. Suddenly, a huge white bear loomed over me. It wasn't
> aggressive; rather, it stood in a protective stance. After a few
> seconds both bear and wolf morphed into mountains, and I

*found myself standing between them. At that moment, a white raven flew over me and soared through the pass between the mountains. The white raven told me, "Go to where the white wolf and the white bear meet."*

*Much later I found out that there are two areas in North America where the white wolf and the white bear both lived. The Tsalagi (Cherokee) who lived in the Great Smoky Mountains, knew and held sacred both the white grizzly bear and the white wolf. And the origin of the Okanagan River and the Great Bear Rainforest in Canada are the two places in the world where the white spirit bear—the Kermode—is known to reside. (The Kermode is a subspecies of black bear. A recessive gene in both parents makes the black bear white or cream-colored. It's possible for a family to have white and black bear cubs at the same time!) And, of course, white wolves have lived in the area for centuries as well.*

In Robin's story, her teacher, White Wolf, led her to this vision, a vision that pointed her to the origins of both her parental lineages, as well as sources of wisdom. We do the same here in this book, guiding you to the white spirit bear who embodies the maturity of introspection, the Medicine of Dreaming, and protectiveness for All Our Relations.

## Returning to the Wheel

As you embark on this next cycle of learning, you begin with an understanding of how to use the Medicine Wheel's principles. You will see, with your vision in the east, that you incorporate the elements of trust, relationship, and purpose in the south, and that the north's wisdom becomes more meaningful when blended with healing work in the west. When you complete the cycle, pulling it deep within yourself, you'll recognize the important and essential step to connect to divine inspiration, the Great Mystery above, in order to better ground your manifestation below, on the Earth Mother's altar, and honor integration in the center or "within" direction. With this path, you'll come to completion standing fully present in the balanced center, holding tremendous power.

The foundation of the Medicine Wheel builds upon a set of teachings grounded in reverence for your connection to the Earth Mother. Accompanied by your teacher, White Bear, you will explore a new series of circular teachings, as each builds upon another. Bear shows you that within the wilderness of your heart, you are a divine spark from the Great Mystery, a treasured dream of your ancestors, capable of many things—perhaps more than you realize. In these teachings, as you *re-member* yourself to be a servant of creation and embrace responsibility for all that you are, you will continue to develop healing lifeways for yourself and bless and release what does not support your soul's purpose or is not in service to your heart's desire. You will embrace a more empowered way of being via spiritual adulthood. As well, you will live your life purpose more fully and passionately than has been possible before.

The spiral path we travel is designed to take you to the next level in transforming habits and dissolving blocks that inhibit your personal growth, as well as enhancing your ability to offer your medicine gifts to the world. These bad habits can include negative thought patterns, unsupported personal beliefs, unresolved emotional attachments, unhealthy or dysfunctional behaviors, and psychic wounds. You may find there are also dis-eases in multi-generational family patterns and ancestral patterns, and outdated cultural patterns that come to the forefront for your examination.

Under White Bear's guidance, in this book you will build upon your understanding of the Medicine Wheel, a foundation that integrates timeless philosophical concepts, as well as direct personal experiences, to help you embrace and bring forward your personal medicine. This integration furthers your spiritual evolutionary process and allows you to recognize and understand the lessons that Spirit gives you and apply them directly in your life. And, in turn, share them with others where appropriate.

The Spiral Path of the White Bear connects you with a powerful medicine teacher who encourages you to be fully yourself, yet at the same time to know that you are a member of Earth's family and fully connect with community, in service to All Our Relations. As Bear guides you along this path, skills and wisdom come to your attention in a new way, and you will discover you have senses you never experienced before.

# Traveling the Seven Sacred Directions

For those of you familiar with the Medicine Wheel, you know that each of the Seven Sacred Directions—east, south, west, north, above, below, and center—holds teachings that speak to us on a four-dimensional level: spiritual, physical, emotional, and mental. We must engage with all levels to move and build lesson to lesson, to learn something deeply and to transform. *Journey of the White Bear* dedicates one chapter to each of the Seven Sacred Directions (summarized briefly below) while also expanding on these foundational lessons to add additional concepts.

**East:** air/wind, the solo journey, the spiritual self, birth, spring, yellow, dawn, awareness and illumination, breath, voice, wind instruments, eagle and red-tailed hawk. Ceremony: Spring Equinox, Calling, Vision Quest

**South:** fire, partnership, the physical self, youth, summer, red, daytime, trust and innocence, rhythm, drums and dance, coyote and raven. Ceremony: Summer Solstice, Dancing the Fire, Making Relationship, Making Right

**West:** water, working with community, the emotional self, adulthood, fall, black, dusk, introspection and dreaming, balance and flow, harp, salmon and bear. Ceremony: Fall Equinox, Water is Life, Cleansing and Healing

**North:** stones and standing ones (tree people), world family, the mental self, elderhood, winter, white, midnight, ancestral wisdom and power, shakers (rattles, sticks, bones), buffalo and owl. Ceremony: Winter Solstice, Shaking Awake Dance, Blessing Ceremonies, Generational Healing

**Above:** space, multidimensional universe, the eternal self, indigo, timelessness, universal consciousness, divinity, sounding and overtones, star people. Ceremony: Creating Your Star Ancestor Wheel, Prayer with Pipe

**Below:** organic, compost and soil, yearly, moss green, night, surrender and acceptance, pregnancy of possibility, weeping tears, mycelium and subterraneans. Ceremony: Creating Your Secret Garden, Sweat Lodge/Purification, Earth Honoring/Constellations

**Center:** magic, etheric, now, rainbow, dreamtime, alchemy, knowingness and integrated connection, whale song, Those Who Come and Go (guides and helpers). Ceremony: Integration Movement, Rites of Passage

## Sacred Seven

The sacred number seven, the number of personal transformation, signifies contemplation, analysis, a search for personal truth and spiritual understanding, and completion gained from true insight. Ancient religions contain many references to Sacred Seven—seven sacraments, seven powers, seven virtues, seven sins, seven petitions, seven annual ceremonies, seven gifts of the spirit—implying that once you attain the seven, you are indeed transformed. As humans our energetic fields resonate with the energies of the seven chakras.

The number seven is associated with the moon, suggesting reflection (sunlight reflected from the moon) and the medicine of White Bear: introspection, intuition, and mystical spirituality. As we live within the construct of a seven-day week, the seventh day being a day of rest, when we rest, we pause and take stock, understand where we stand and how we stand, and identify what we've learned, in order to complete the cycle and step again on the path.

The number seven also relates to the law of octaves. The ancients knew and understood this law that determines the vibrations of sound and color, which emit wavelength vibrations of varying sizes that determine tone or hue. The law of octaves, as it applies to musical sound, is the use of seven sounds, repeating the first tone one octave higher, or seven notes with the eighth note repeating the tone of the first note, one generation above.

There are also seven hues, sometimes eight, visible in the rainbow: red, orange, yellow, green, blue, indigo, and violet. (Magenta is the eighth color and the hardest to see.) The same colors, usually invisible to the naked eye, are a part of the human aura, which can be photographed through a process called Kirlian photography.

# Reviewing the Medicine Wheel

*Journey of the White Bear* spirals around the Medicine Wheel, a representation of the Wheel of Life that encompasses all that is, and symbolizes the interconnection of all things, a foundational life compass.

Ancient medicine wheels—great circles of stone placed by native peoples eons ago on sacred ground—exist in the United States and Canada, in South America and Europe, in Asia and Africa, all around the world. The most ancient medicine wheel yet found is in South Africa. Medicine wheels empower ceremony and ritual. Our ancestors knew the medicine wheel's power to initiate change and generate healing. Often these stone circles were constructed in alignment with landmarks to designate yearly cycles such as solstices, equinoxes, and astrological events. Wheels can be designated for personal, clan, or tribal purposes; erected temporarily or more permanently; and can be of any size—as large as a mountaintop or as small as a desktop altar.

The Medicine Wheel aspects and concepts we present in this book help us view patterns and relationships, understand natural cycles, and help orient us as we spiral through experience. This Medicine Wheel has four outer quadrants representing the cardinal directions: east, south, west, and north; and three center or inner directions: above/sky, below/earth, and center/within.

The three inner directions, along with cross-directional lines that link directions, expand the wheel into three dimensions. The cross-directional line that links the east/west directions signifies the joining of spirit and matter, the Blue Road of spiritual attainment. The line that delineates the marriage of north and south symbolizes the union of creativity and wisdom, the Red Road of the physical plane. (Some practitioners position these in reversed fashion, but the significance remains.) The connecting line from the above/sky direction to the below/earth direction grounds inspiration, linking universal consciousness to the Earth plane of existence and uniting purpose with passion for manifestation. Together, the medicine of the circle and its intersecting crossroads offer a framework to hold the diversity of the universe.

To take this image one step further, if we visualize the cross-directional lines as infinity symbols or figure eights, with all three infinity symbols linked together in a firmly held center core, the wheel's image is that of a multidimensional flower—ever expanding, growing, blooming. When we sit at the center of the wheel and view the image holographically, our hearts *are* the connecting center, which allows us to unfold the integrated center direction. As expressed by many cultures, "As above, so below; as within, so without."

Imagining this multidimensional spherical construct, you can easily see how changes in one part effect changes in another. Similarly, changes in yourself as you use these teachings will transform your relationships at home, at work, in your community, and throughout all the worlds you touch, like ripples caused by a stone falling into a pond.

The Medicine Wheel attributes we present here originate primarily with the Okanagan peoples of southern British Columbia, Canada, and north-central Washington State. Some teachings presented are derived from other Native American and indigenous traditions, reflecting the lineages in our blood and our own medicine teachers. *Journey of the White Bear* integrates practices taught in Asia, Africa, Europe, Siberia, Polynesia, and Australia, and the teachings of the Mayan and Inca peoples of South America. With this inclusivity, we present a universal Medicine Wheel and a set of instructions for use in a global twenty-first century.

Our intention has always been to meld the best of past and present to form a full-spectrum learning cycle. The path around the Medicine Wheel is an ancient circular one. The wheel discussed in this book an earth-based system that takes us *within ourselves* to find knowledge and answers to dilemmas, whereas sun-based, astrological systems guide us in understanding influential forces *outside ourselves*.

As your familiarity with Medicine Wheel teachings expands, you'll find different peoples associate different aspects or teachings with the various directions. For instance, the element of air, one of the Four Winds of Powers, is in the east. Some teachers place fire in the east, which moves other directional aspects one quarter of the way around the wheel. Tribes in the Southern Hemisphere sometimes switch north and south because of the differences in directional energies. These adjustments present different perspectives of the wheel, and neither is more or less correct—simply a matter of your tradition. Even the four demarcation lines that define the four directional quadrants are seen differently. Robin defines the Blue Road as stretching between north and south, the Spirit Line that connects the ancestral wisdom to our personal purpose; and the Red Road as the line between east and west, which is the physical path we practice to maturation. Sandy sees the two lines north to south as the Red Road, and east to west as the Blue Road. Both ways work! While we ask you to use the wheel as we present it during your exploration of this book, we also encourage you to find and honor your inner Medicine Wheel.

Also, over the years of our individual and collective practices, we've both felt how the Medicine Wheel's aspects shift to best suit different situations, needs, groups and ceremonies, and to facilitate healing. As we've grown, so has our understanding, and our Medicine Wheel teachings have also similarly evolved, unfolding and expanding in ways beyond what we knew before. The Medicine Wheel concepts are fluid, meant to move, spiral, and flow with your understandings, just as it has moved us. That's part of its magic. Just as a story told to a five-year-old means something entirely different than the same story heard by a twenty-five- year-old, or a fifty-five-year-old, so it is with the Medicine Wheel.

Additionally, as you explore the direction chapters we present in this book, you'll find that each chapter embodies its own wheel, and you'll recognize areas where these wheels overlap. This "wheels within wheels" model is not new, and you may find other traditions represent this concept in a different way with different wheels. For *Journey of the White Bear*, we present the wheels we consider most important to this specific round of teaching toward spiritual adulthood, while recognizing that each chapter represents a substantial teaching or book in and of itself—and, in many cases, have been afforded this focus by other authors. We encourage further study to expand on the foundation we lay in these pages. As one of our beloved teachers always says, "Please take these teachings and run with them, further and farther and deeper than I did. With my blessing!"

## Preparing for Study, a Beginner's Mind

Just as you would prepare thoughtfully for any pilgrimage or sacred journey, you will ready yourself in specific ways to embark on the Journey of the White Bear. In the following chapter, and in the section titled Resources at the back of the book, you will find much of what you need to gather for the journey, including basic tools and checklists, as well as instructions for practices and ceremonies, explanations for key concepts, and a glossary.

Although we recognize many who come to this material may already be familiar with some of the terminology, tools, and practices, in the spirit of a beginner's mind, we encourage you to (re)familiarize yourself with some of these core concepts and teachings before and during your movement around the wheel. Refer to these sections for clarification and support to prepare for each set of lessons and the suggested ceremony.

Maintaining a journal to capture the information you receive in meditation or the journey world is *especially important* for this cycle of learning—as is a dream journal to chronicle teachings received from White Bear in the dreamtime.

To delve deeply into the medicine of each teaching, we suggest you spend as much time as you need on each chapter. When the lessons are completed consecutively, the course unfolds as a birthing process that culminates in the Medicine Shield ceremony in the final chapter.

## The Nature of Beginnings

Although there are many paths and many beginnings, on the spiral path we teach here you begin in the east, the place of new beginnings. What you will perceive and manifest, and what will remain in the realms of the undetectable and invisible, is determined by your individual evolutionary path. These spiral teachings embody the universal axiom—as within, so without—allowing you to follow the winding road around the wheel, then move through the above, below, and center (within) directions. As you complete a cycle of learning, you will move out again to the beginning position in the east, to a new and higher evolutionary education as is right for you.

Some of us remember the stories, or perhaps even the lifetimes, when human beings knew their oneness with all of creation. When none of Earth's families were placed above or below any other. When leaders functioned as servants of the people to fulfill the needs of community, rather than a select few. A time when humans respected all beings—plant, animal, mineral, swimmers or flyers, walkers or crawlers—and their unique gifts. All following their Original Instructions given to them by the Creator.

If we're to survive and thrive, we will need to reclaim the values the Old Ones held—those Original Instructions—even as we grow into new technologies and use more sustainable resources. The Hopi prophecies, which tell of these unprecedented times, tell us to grow our gardens, know our water sources, be close to our families and communities. They also tell us that technology is good, as long as it doesn't control us. These are all things we each need to reflect upon, individually and collectively, as we begin to co-create a new world. So we can make decisions according to whether those decisions would benefit or harm *the next seven generations and beyond,* our descendants.

Currently, we see many businesses and industries still continuing to develop technologies without having the foresight or planning to assess the consequences and the effects on all Earth's inhabitants. Imbalances caused by pollution, over-population, war, greed, and dissatisfaction continue to abound on our lovely planet, breaking natural law, threatening our very existence *and* that of Mother Earth. For those of us who recognize the disparity between exploiting our Earth Mother and developing lifeways to walk in balance with All Our Relations, it is time to find the way home, back into harmony. It is time to hold out our hands to help others find their way home as well.

*Journey of the White Bear* is a path that deepens and expands your relationship with yourself, while also teaching you additional skills to manifest your soul's purpose. You start by working on yourself to realize your individual potential, the way in which you perform the divine functions of creation and destruction, and come into alignment with natural law and your sacred purpose, your heart's desire. You will come to better learn how to allow the abundance of the universe to manifest through you and begin to trust and embrace that what the Creator—or Great Mystery—can add to your desires is bigger and better than anything you could possibly imagine. At the same time, you develop skills to help your brothers and sisters effect the same changes within themselves. As part of a consciousness that supports both personal and global spiritual evolution, you learn a simpler and more powerful way to walk gently upon the earth as you play your part in realizing the dream of peace for All Our Relations. These lessons will connect you more deeply to Spirit and move you into spiritual maturity to embody the Shaman's Heart, a heart of service.

As Robin likes to say, the time of the lone wolf is over; it's completed its purpose—to heal the individual. Now a different set of teachings stands on the shoulders of those that have come before, a set of teachings that underline a "we" instead of a "me." Teachings that ripple out and heal the collective, and by extension, the planet that sustains us all. Yet the foundational premise remains: peace, harmony, and wholeness begin at home, with the self. Because you cannot give away what you do not already possess.

So ... you now meet White Bear to take the next steps on your path, knowing that your evolution as one of Mother Earth's children holds great importance. You are an interconnected and interdependent student of the Great Mystery, brother/sister to all Earth's children. You have something to offer, something unique and priceless, something no one else can give our world. We honor that medicine in you and humbly ask you to bring it forward. *With the caterpillar-to-butterfly metamorphosis, caterpillar cells perish as imaginal cells begin to create the butterfly. Following the path of White Spirit Bear, know that you, too, will emerge transformed and ready to fly!*

We offer this work out of respect, reverence, and love for All Our Relations.

# Chapter 1

# PREPARING FOR STUDY

The way in which you prepare for any situation—be it a journey, a relationship, or a phase of life—is significant. The more conscious you are as you prepare, the more likely you are to be successful in your endeavor. Preparation for *Journey of the White Bear* includes familiarizing yourself with some practices to support your personal work. as well as gathering some tools. Consider approaching this preliminary work as a sacred act that connects you to the ageless wisdom of White Spirit Bear.

We imagine many readers may already possess a substantial foundation of knowledge gathered from previous cycles of learning and other teachings, if not other traditions. Yet, in our own teaching practices, we are continually surprised by how many have either skipped or set aside some of the basics. Embodying a beginner's mind, we encourage you to take a few minutes to (re)familiarize yourself with some of the core practices we present in this chapter before and during your movement around the wheel and the wheels within wheels. You may be surprised by learning some of these concepts in a slightly different way, or a deeper way. We've included these basics here for your convenience and to provide a common foundation for all readers. In addition, the resources section at the back of the book provides additional details on basic tools, practices for community ceremonies, and a glossary of terms.

## Setting Intention

Clarifying intention is sometimes the hardest part of finding our way in the world. Taking the time to slow down and identify what we really want in a particular situation or relationship. And yet, a clear intention can smooth your way and inform your expectations.

Whatever your intention in any situation, event, or in life, define it in your mind. Think about what you want to accomplish and what you most need to know. Ground your intention in the here and now by thinking about what you can do this hour, this day, this week, this month, to support this intention. You can view intention as a giving and receiving quotient: asking yourself what do I have to give; what would I like to receive? Or, what do I need to release; what would I like to bring into my life?

Leave room for Spirit to improvise and keep your intention simple. For example, intentions crafted with intricate detail can limit your experience. We find it useful to remind ourselves to say "This, or something better," and we are often pleasantly surprised at the outcome.

Bear in mind that thoughts *are* things. Karmic law states that what you give will return to you tenfold. Remember to affirm "harm to none."

## Using Prayer and Meditation

We communicate with Spirit—the Creator, Great Mystery, or whatever you choose to call the Divine—via prayer and meditation. In prayer we speak to our Divine Source. In meditation we empty ourselves of thought to listen and receive inspiration.

Prayer is simply speaking from your heart. You don't need elaborate verse or some ancient formula. It's just you and the Divine, the Great Mystery, Mother/Father God; speak honestly what you feel and think. Turn over your worries. Release your concerns to Spirit. Simple prayers like "Thank you" and "Please help me" are sometimes the most powerful. We often begin praying with speaking our gratitude for the blessings we have in our life, and then incorporate prayers for ourselves, loved ones, community, the world, and the earth. In these turbulent times, your prayers are sorely needed; there can never be too many or too often.

In meditation, you relax and empty your mind of conscious, distracting thoughts and images. It is often impossible to completely still the mind, especially when beginning this disciplined practice. So try simply watching thoughts flow through, like clouds in the sky, and you will find yourself detaching from the trails they tow you down, and any mental turmoil. Meditation is used to clear the path for receiving messages from Spirit, your higher self, or guides, and it is often a prelude to visualization and journeying. We find a regular meditation practice deepens your connection to the creative source and rejuvenates your energy field better than napping. Meditation can also help you release your attachment to outcome.

## Creating Sacred Space

Medicine work is best practiced in a space that is harmonious, clean, and quiet—especially for your private, personal work. A proper environment is essential to help you maintain focus, minimize interruptions, and support transformation. This dedicated space can be a clearing on your property, or a small corner of your apartment or home—any space consecrated to support your personal process.

In this private sacred space, you can set up an altar; store your tools, supplies, and journal; meditate, pray, and write; and perform sacred crafting and other practices. At times you may need uninterrupted privacy, so we recommend you make agreements with your cohabitants to facilitate that. We also recommend you consider wearing special comfortable clothes for your meditation, journeying, and ceremony practices, if not particular jewelry or a shawl or belt.

You'll want to locate both an indoor and an outdoor space—places where you know you are welcome and safe, have some level of privacy, and, in both spaces, can sense a strong connection with nature.

## Building Altars

For as long as humans have walked the earth, we have built altars to symbolize our connection to that which is greater than ourselves. Also called "faces of the earth," on this path altars symbolize aspects of the Great Mystery. These sacred shrines are created for specific reasons: for example, to honor sacred places or a particular deity, or for healing, prayer, and meditation. Altars are used for creating and holding sacred space, for intention, and for invocation.

Anyone can (and possibly, should) have at least one altar in their home. Medicine people build specific altars for each ceremony, as well as keeping a general altar for daily use, and often one for the ancestors. Usually, the altar holds something to honor each of the four elements: earth (i.e., stone); air (i.e., feather); water (i.e., small bowl of water); fire (i.e., candle). In addition, the altar will often contain items to honor the Four Directions (perhaps a small Medicine Wheel made of tiny stones), plus something that symbolizes the four ages of humankind (a rattle, a bone, a bell, a piece of hair). And living things are also included as offerings to the spirits—flowers, fruit, horsehair, etc., even occasionally alcohol, depending on the specific ceremony.

For your work with White Spirit Bear, we recommend you create a personal altar for your medicine work. This altar can be as simple as a small table adorned with a beautiful cloth. You may wish to place representations of each of the Seven Sacred Directions. The altar size is not important, but it will need to provide enough space to include something to represent the aspects we discuss in this book, as well as a representation of your spirit guides, ancestors, and Bear.

- East: air, spring, yellow, dawn, newness, eagle

- South: fire, summer, red, day, love, full moon, joy, coyote

- West: water, autumn, black, dusk, Bear Dreaming, balance

- North: stones, white, wisdom, ancestors, winter, buffalo, prayer

- Above: moon, sun, stars, the void, indigo

- Below: earth, nurturer, caves, rebirth, initiation, green

- Within: divinity, timelessness, rainbow, magic, guides and helpers

Your altar can become sacred art, incorporating objects and symbols you find beautiful and hold meaning for you. Feel free to change the altar with the seasons or with the work you are doing: the space will reflect your inner journey. Often, we include a colored candle for each cardinal direction to light during meditation or perform other inner work. May your altar be a place of light and healing.

# Grounding

Medicine work requires you be grounded and steady inside, so you can attune yourself to the voice within. This ability is developed over time with practice, including meditation, ceremony, and other rituals. Before you begin any spiritual work, we recommend you take a few moments to leave the outside world behind: breathe, and ground yourself, becoming fully present in what is happening now, undistracted by mundane concerns.

The quick exercise outlined below can help you ground. Eventually you will do this almost without thinking as soon as you arrive where you'll be doing the work.

1. Arrange your body in a comfortable position, either standing, sitting or lying down, and become still, but not rigid.

2. Take a few deep, relaxing breaths, and imagine the tension draining from your body with each out breath.

3. One breath at a time, begin to consciously relax parts of your body: feet, legs, hips, chest, arms, hands, throat, jaw, eyes, skin, internal organs, etc. We find it helpful to focus on each body part or organ, and to say "relax," silently, to that part of the body. Take as long as you need in each area. If you begin to think about other things, just disengage from the thoughts and gently bring yourself back to your body.

4. Once you feel fully present, relaxed, and calm, visualize yourself growing roots into Mother Earth (whatever that means for your physical situation). Feel the earth's solid support and loving presence and your connection to all that is.

5. Once grounded, center yourself by checking in with your emotions and releasing whatever feels worrisome, whatever might be getting in the way of your full attentive presence. Envelop yourself with your clear intention. Acknowledge yourself as a sacred being in sacred space ready to focus on the task at hand for All Your Relations.

# Smoke or Energy Clearing

Ritually cleansing sacred objects or spaces, such as ceremonial areas, a room, house, or land, using smoke (also called smudging) is a common practice in many traditions. To prepare for inner work or ceremony, you can also cleanse your personal energy field with smoke. A common technique is to use the smoke from herbs like sage, cedar, or sweetgrass. You can burn loose herbs in a fired earthen bowl or a shell, or as a tied bundle. The smoke cleanses your energy field as it touches the area around your torso, your back, legs and arms, the soles of your feet, and the space above your head. As you cleanse, focus on releasing negativity and distractions of all kinds; use a prayer or other words (silently, or aloud if you wish) to invoke your own power of protection.

There are many plant medicines that can be used for energy cleansing. Some are burned as we discuss above, but some are not. A plant "bundle" of sage and cedar can be burned to clear unwanted energy, entities, etc., and to bring healing to a particular person. Pinion pine and juniper are often used with sage in the Southwest. Copal and plant resins such as myrrh can be burned in a bowl and used with feathers to cleanse and bless a person or an area.

For those allergic to smoke, a plant bundle of laurel and bay leaves can be used. Swoosh the bundle about three inches from the body, just as you would with burning sage. Cedar can also be used to "bathe" someone's aura or physical body if they are physically ill in some way, using water rather than smoke. Tie cedar branches together, and dip in a bucket of water, then brush the branches gently over and around the body.

For sacred baths, cedar, juniper, sage, lavender, and sweetgrass can be used for certain ceremonies. Cedar, lavender, and rose petals are typically for women; juniper, sage, and pinion pine are usually for men. If one has a cold or the flu, powdered ginger in the bath is an excellent way to cleanse toxins in the skin and bloodstream. These plant medicines, plus cornmeal and sea salt, can be used for cleansing homes and ritual objects such as crystals. There are many other plants, crushed stones, and minerals used for other forms of cleansing, either psychic, spiritual, or physical.

Ritual cleansing can also include brushing the energy body with a feather, with or without smoke, in the same manner as described above. Some traditions use a candle flame to bring light into your energy field, moving your hand from the flame toward yourself with an upward motion. The simplest method is to use your hands to smooth and cleanse an energy field of interruptions, unwanted psychic debris, or outside energy forms.

## Calling the Circle

As you call upon the Seven Sacred Directions and the Great Mystery, your senses become more alive and sensitive to the ebbs and flows of energies within and outside yourself. Your entire being opens up. In the beginning, this experience may feel not only unfamiliar, but uncomfortable and at times a little scary. Remember, sacred space is your refuge, and can be protected by using special methods that cleanse and seal its energy. We use several techniques to do this. Primarily we use ritual cleansing, which is detailed above, and calling a circle.

To call or set a circle, assemble the tools you need, and follow the basic instructions included in the Tools for Ceremony checklist in the Resources section. As you become more familiar with this practice, you will expand it to fit your preferences and incorporate other elements. Some traditions refer to this practice as casting a circle.

## Connecting with Guides and Helpers from Other Realms

Often, we find that when you learn to journey, you connect with beings that seem to be watching over you and sharing wisdom with you. These helpers are called by many names: guardian angels, totem animals, personal guides, your own higher self, imaginary friends, relatives no longer of the Earth plane (ancestors), your own previous incarnations, nature deities, gods, or goddesses.

Sometimes these guides and helpers are with you long term; sometimes they appear for only a short time of need to impart a specific teaching or assist you through a transition. You instinctively know they mean you well, and you can sense their integrity. You can often also sense they are enlightened beings. On the shamanic path you will meet beings who can assist you during certain phases, bringing you information needed to progress in your cycle of learning. You can also ask them if they are here for a reason, season, or lifetime(s).

Occasionally you may meet nonphysical beings or entities (and also certain incarnate individuals on the Earth plane) who clearly do not mean you well. Remember to set your personal protection at all times so this is less likely to occur. If this does happen, call in your own guides again for protection, release the entity by sending it light, and seal yourself from it with your own protective light.

Infrequently, certain entities will not leave without outside intervention. In this case, we recommend you seek the services of a local medicine person or spiritual intuitive who can help discern what the entity is trying to fulfill through its attachment to you. This practitioner can then assist you in dealing with the situation.

## Journaling

Journaling offers a way to track your personal transformation, similar to keeping a travel diary. This practice is merely recording your journeys, dreams, experiences, and the teachings that resonate with you along the way. The act of writing offers a form to your experience and connects you to the information you received in a deeper way. Writing is therapeutic and helps you absorb or release ideas, energy, and negativities. This practice helps clarify issues and highlight insights and understandings, as well as remind you of teachings and experiences in your transformation process that may only make sense months later.

For those who find resistance to writing, we encourage you to consider why that might be so. Some potential reasons may be:

- Privacy: are you afraid someone else won't respect your journal?

- Writing time: what is your level of commitment to this work?

- Takes too long: can you use your computer or your tablet for your journal? Perhaps you could use your own form of shorthand.

- Writing block: do you feel you aren't a good writer? Perhaps recording your thoughts and impressions would work for you, then try writing at some later point.

- What's the point? Do you feel writing is not effective? We invite you to be open to trying new methods as a part of the learning process.

Change is good, and a healthy sense of adventure can transform your life!

If you still find yourself struggling to journal, try drawing a picture of your process. You can use the Medicine Wheel.

1. Draw a circle with four quadrants, with yourself in the east, your partner relationships in the south, your work and community relations in the west, and your contributions to the world in the north.

2. Stay in the present moment as you draw what's going on for you NOW, as simply or elaborately as you wish.

3. If this doesn't work, try dancing or singing your experience and feelings.

Remember, your process is only as effective as your ability to absorb and understand the teachings. Most of us in Western culture learned to do this via notetaking, not memorization as in an oral culture, which is why we recommend journaling to record your journeys and respond to the exercises for this set of teachings. You may find other teachers in other forums that stick to an experiential process with everyone fully present at all times, not madly scribbling notes.

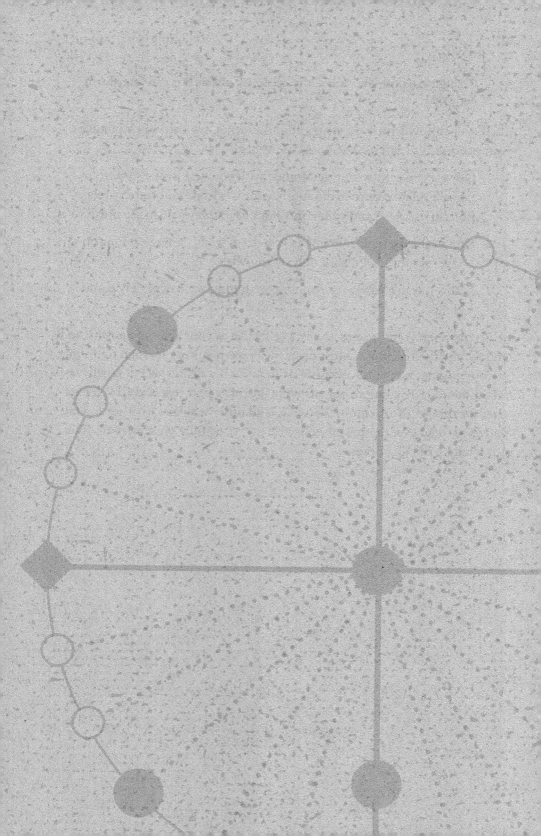

## Chapter 2

# JOURNEYING WITH BEAR

Bear medicine is that of the dreamer, the healer, the protector. She embodies the power of introspection found in the west on the Medicine Wheel. As a dreamer, she hibernates in silence to reflect on her experiences and nurture her dreams. Within her, Bear Dreaming holds the ability to travel beyond to commune with other dreamers and councils to seek answers. This technique of journeying to other worlds beyond our three-dimensional reality brings greater insight to inform our actions and our healing. As a fierce healer and protector, Bear does not apologize for who she is or what she does, because she acts from a place of deep truth, deep knowing.

## Getting to Know Bear

Bear's introspective and receptive qualities allow those who walk with bear medicine to weigh alternatives to determine right action for All Our Relations *before* initiating, before doing. Bear's medicine of introspection is key to healing, to developing goals that resonate with our soul's purpose, and to supporting others.

For thousands of years White Bear has guided people of wisdom. Okanagan chiefs who inhabited the Columbia Plateau of British Columbia and central Washington claimed her as totem; the Cherokee Nation of the eastern United States considered White Bear to be their teacher and guide. Stories tell of how the Cherokee Bear Clan is said to have all decided to become bears one summer and vanished in a great migration north; their descendants may yet roam the Great Smoky Mountains.

Fossil records show there may have been hundreds of bear species on all continents worldwide except Antarctica and Australia. Many peoples lived with Bear as their neighbor. Today there remain eight bear species:

- Black (North American) bear—color ranges from black to browns, to cinnamon or tan, to white or cream (Kermode, the white spirit bear)

- Brown bear (includes grizzly)—Northern Hemisphere, through Russia and parts of Europe

- Polar bear (white like snow)—the Arctic

- Asiatic black bear—often has a white patch on the chest—eastern Asia, including Afghanistan, China, Japan, Russia, Cambodia, and bordering nations

- Spectacled (Andean) bear—South America

- Giant panda—south-central China (previously thought a member of the raccoon family, as the red panda, but revised after DNA analysis)

- Sloth bear—India, Sri Lanka, and bordering countries

- Malayan sun bear—yellow crescent on the chest—Southeast Asia, Indonesia

As we introduce White Spirit Bear in these pages, you'll get to know her medicine better and appreciate her powerful gifts. Those who follow Bear are dreamers, journeyers, and healers who understand the heart of service and wield their wisdom wisely. They are willing to walk through their fear, make a commitment to a cause, and take action to manifest their soul's purpose, as well as work to improve things for those around them.

White Bear's path is for those who see the need to heal the Sacred Hoop (the energy that encompasses all beings and the earth) and want to walk in balance with All Our Relations with harm to none: two-legged, four-legged, winged ones, swimming ones, creepy-crawlers, standing people, stone people, the elementals (earth, air, fire, and water), star beings, and our own Earth Mother.

The Hopi tell us: *We are the ones we've been waiting for.* And so we pass these practices and this wisdom on to you as part of your journey with White Spirit Bear.

## Embodying the Shaman's Heart

*Journey of the White Bear* reflects a set of teachings we call the next round, the next cycle in the spiraling helix of our personal and collective evolution, all the more needed in this twenty-first century of persistent transformation. This next round asks us to develop spiritual maturity, personal mastery, and the Shaman's Heart—a heart of service for All Our Relations. The order and relationship of those three key attributes are important and, quite honestly, an ongoing set of lifelong lessons; spiritual maturity helps us embody ever-increasing levels of personal mastery and allows us to embrace an authentic and clear heart of service. This heart of service, the shaman or holy person's heart, holds unconditional love and respect for all who walk on the planet and beyond, unattached to outcome.

Every choice you've made, every step you've taken has brought you to this moment, this threshold of endings and beginnings, this powerful NOW that asks us to move to another level. All of us were brought to this NOW for a reason; we are all needed to blaze the trail to a new way of being on this Mother Earth, to bring our world out of adolescence and into interdependent harmony with all who walk, fly, swim, crawl, and grow on this planet.

In this chapter, we'll outline what spiritual maturity means and review the Wheel of Mastery. In the next chapter, we'll discuss the different roles shamans perform for and within their communities, some of which may resonate with your innate personal strengths and interests. This introductory material is intended to familiarize you with these concepts, which will be explored in greater detail in the coming chapters and can be researched through other sources as well.

## Becoming a Spiritual Adult

In a nutshell, spiritual maturity is knowing oneself—all parts of the self—our physical, mental, and emotional bodies, as well as the spiritual, intuitive, connected, soul-centered, authentic, and empathetic qualities that are part of our experience as spirit in body. These attributes make us complete and evolved human beings.

Spiritually mature human beings are, by definition, not busily do-ing, but totally be-ing. They are introspective and attentive to both themselves and their environment. They are curious and compassionate. They are willing to peel the layers of their own personal onion to discover the source of their wounds to heal and forgive, and to bring themselves into harmony in order to love themselves and others unconditionally. This level of personal work provides the experience of facing the self with all its light and shadow, hearing the soul's true desire, healing past trauma, and embracing our authenticity and sacred purpose. Spiritual maturity gives us permission to cast away the attitudes and judgments and patterns we may have learned in our families or experienced in society that no longer serve us, and to detach from those practices that do not support our highest truth. We get to dissemble the lies that limit us, disengage from the effects of the oppressive experiences that made us lose heart and perhaps soul, and revise our personal stories to embrace a perspective that supports our future endeavors, to walk with Spirit.

Because when we change, the mirror changes. And the world around us changes.

This is a process many of you may already have some familiarity with, an understanding to build upon. Furthering this work toward spiritual maturity allows us to return to right relationship with ourselves, which becomes the foundation for all future endeavors. Peace always starts at home, in the heart. And, in returning to right relationship with the self, spiritual adults are more able to mend and blend contrasting dualities—masculine and feminine, elder and youth, individual and collective—seeing these as not so different, but intrinsically interconnected, even complementary. They see that things are not so black and white; that harmony and consensus mean everybody wins. This is the perspective transition from the "me" to the "we"—a "we" that includes all life.

With this maturity, we are also able to return to right relationship with the mystical sacred wildness inside ourselves and in nature, a sacredness that is around us, above us, below us. All the time. This connection, this unity—with Mother Earth and all who live on her—helps ground, support, and inspire us into right action.

Becoming a spiritual adult means we are no longer adolescents; it means we take responsibility for our actions in the world. This maturity prepares us for embracing a true and powerful heart of service, where we can contribute to healing divisiveness, participate in innovating lifeways that work in harmony with our beautiful planet, teach the next generations, and so much more. With a strong and healthy personal foundation, we can more easily choose love over fear, bring harmony to those we can in our immediate world, and help graduate mankind to a more holistic way of life.

## The Wheel of Mastery

The Wheel of Mastery depicts some of the key core qualities of the spiritually mature: someone able to look into their own darkness and choose healing over numbness, commit to their soul's sacred purpose, and connect to the earth and the interdependent sacredness of her ecosystems as well as the Divine within and without—someone willing to embrace their personal power and wield their intent with love as an agent for change. We place these qualities into the Seven Sacred Directions, as we do for the other teachings in this book, and yet they are all related, a part of the whole, a roadmap of sorts.

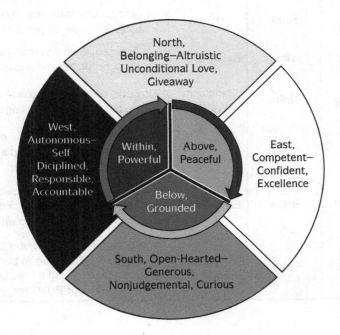

## Prayer of St. Francis of Assisi

Great Mystery, make me an instrument of peace.

Where there is hatred, let me sow love,

Where there is injury, pardon;

Where there is doubt, faith;

Where there is despair, hope;

Where there is darkness, light;

And where there is sadness, joy.

Grant that I may not so much seek

to be consoled as to console,

to be understood as to understand,

to be loved, as to love.

For it is in giving that we receive ...

| Attribute | Direction | Relationship | Example |
|-----------|-----------|--------------|---------|
| Competent | East | Self | Mastery in many areas, confident, striving for excellence, but not superiority; accepting responsibility with humility |
| Open-Hearted | South | Others | Caring, compassionate, generous, nonjudgmental, engaged, curious |
| Autonomous | West | Family/Group | Self-disciplined and responsible, accountable and present |
| Belonging | North | Community/World | Altruistic, connected, unconditional love even in the face of hate, willing Giveaway |
| Peaceful | Above | Divine/Creator | Connected to the Divine, the mystical, and other worlds. Every step a prayer, every breath a prayer. |
| Grounded | Below | Earth/Nature | Healthy grounding and maturity in the physical, emotional, mental, and spiritual bodies, in close relationship with nature |
| Powerful | Center | Within/Between | Integration of all attributes brings powerful intent and sacred purpose to Bear in service to and for the benefit of All Our Relations |

The teachings and exercises in this book are designed to outline personal work along the path of spiritual maturity, working toward the Wheel of Mastery. Perhaps you have done some of this work before and it is familiar to you. Perhaps taking the time to do it again will bring you greater understanding and insight and reveal new capabilities and interests. This is work you can learn, master, and share with your spiritual circles, and in the sharing weave your community closer. These teachings include:

- Co-creating with collaboration and consensus—east

- Balancing sacred masculine/feminine and embracing shadow—south

- Healing ceremonies and rites of passage for life transitions—west

- Committing to use the gifts of all our ancestral lineages—north

- Expanding our connection with the Divine across time and space —above

- Deepening our connection to Mother Earth and becoming an Earth Keeper—below

- Embodying the powerful grace that reflects your soul's sacred purpose and embracing a heart of service—center

The heart of service is the Shaman's Heart, a heart that beats for the people, with the people, and with all of creation. You don't need to be a shaman to hold a heart of service, but you may be surprised to discover what shamanic skills you might already have, as well as how shamanic practices can enrich your spiritual work. The next chapter discusses shamanic roles and introduces the core shamanic journey skill we'll be using in this book.

## *Chapter 3*

# EXPLORING SHAMANIC ROLES AND TECHNIQUES

Shamanism and shamanic journeying are ancient healing arts originally ascribed to the Siberian *sha-ma,* or seer. Every tribal society throughout history has practiced some form of what we call shamanism. Even certain modern Christian denominations (for instance, the Pentecostals and Charismatics) practice a form of connection to the spirit world, through which they bring back information and guidance from the spiritual, invisible realms.

Michael Harner, author of *The Way of the Shaman,* reminds us, "You are human, whether your ancestors come from Europe, Asia, Africa, or wherever, shamanism once existed there. We are just attempting to go home to our spiritual roots before the state religions, the agrarian centralized religions rose up with autocratic governments and said, 'This is what you're going to believe, these are the official revelations, take it from us, you can trust us, we got it.'" If you go back far enough in your lineage (see the North chapter), you'll undoubtedly find ancestors who lived by a core shamanic belief system: the knowledge and understanding that everything is alive and everything is sacred. This truth lives in your blood, your DNA, should you choose to embrace it.

Certain traditions in parts of the world managed to hold on to some of their shamanic practices into these modern times. Although we do not advocate or condone cultural appropriation, we acknowledge the challenge of trying to reconstruct some of those spiritual practices eradicated by the very state religions Harner references. So, we credit wisdom and the Wisdom Keepers wherever we find them—as should we all—be they in our blood heritage or passed on by our teachers. There is a growing acceptance in some indigenous traditions to instruct those with pure intention, those whose hearts want to respectfully learn, regardless of the color of their skin or nationality. This was foretold in the Hopi prophesies, and this we see happening now across the globe.

The ancient shamans were the forerunners of modern doctors and medicine people. They healed mind, body, and soul as they journeyed on behalf of the patient to the invisible realms, to non-ordinary reality, to retrieve lost parts of the patient's essence (soul or spirit retrieval). During these expeditions, they acquired information about herbs and other medicines with which to treat a particular ailment, and they sometimes fought spiritual battles with outside influences affecting the patient's spiritual, mental, emotional, or physical balance. As modern shamanic practitioners, we can obtain training to use these same techniques to assist our own and other's healing.

There are many different types of shaman: Seer (Visionary or Hollow Bone), Teacher, Healer (Ceremonialist), Spiritual Warrior, Traveler, Earth Keeper, and Sage. As we deepen our discoveries, learn, grow, and accept the gifts of our calling, we may find more than the original talent we were blessed with appears. A shamanic practitioner who helps people heal may find that they are called to be a Shamanic Warrior who has the ability to find and release a family curse or an entity that has attached to a person. A Shamanic Warrior might find that they receive the gift of sight, in order to help them protect those they are working with. There are many gifts, choices, and combinations. The result of learning to be adept is that one eventually becomes a shamanic Sage, able to grasp exactly what modality, or combination thereof, is needed at any moment, and eventually a master of the elements: earth, wind, fire, and water.

The shaman's tasks are many and varied. For example, shaman as Hollow Bone serves as a communicator between seen and unseen worlds. Shaman as Traveler is a messenger across time and space, a bridge between ancient and modern times. A shaman can be a Wisdom Keeper, a warrior for lost and troubled souls, a finder of lost things, a ceremony facilitator, a plant medicine healer, a bodyworker, and more. We'll explore specific shamanic roles, summarized below, in greater detail in the chapters that follow.

- Seer—East—Hollow Bone or Visionary who straddles the seen and unseen worlds, bringing information to light

- Teacher—South—Wisdom Keeper willing to share knowledge and techniques with apprentices or students

- Healer and Ceremonialist—West—Practitioner who helps heal dis-eases of body, mind, emotions, and spirit to bring individuals, families, and communities back into balance

- Spiritual Warrior—North—Protector of humanity, nature, and those who cannot speak for themselves

- Traveler—Above/Sky—Messenger across time and space; a bridge between ancient and modern times and other worlds

- Earth Keeper—Below/Earth—Caretaker of the earth and all that walks, swims, flies, and grows upon her

- Sage—Center/Within—Weaver of modalities, one who is the medicine, lives the medicine; adept whose work can defy time/space agreements

Shamans can facilitate many different types of ceremonies: honoring the elements of earth, air, fire and water; celebrating the four seasons of spring, summer, fall and winter (and sometimes the betweens); rites of passage for children becoming adults and life transitions such as marriage, maturity, and elderhood; quests for seeking visions and understanding one's life events and purpose; sweat lodges and ceremonial cleansing rites for purification and rebirth; prayer ceremonies for the people; and other rituals for personal and group needs, ministering to their community. (See Community appendix B in the Resources section at the back of the book for ceremony definitions.)

When we journey with White Spirit Bear around the Medicine Wheel, and the wheels within wheels, we become initiated into new perceptions, understandings, gifts, techniques, tools, and the wisdom and guidance to use them effectively. But most important, every would-be shamanic practitioner is taught from the very first that we are here to serve all life, and that everything is alive with the breath of Spirit, even the land and the very stones. Once we receive a new gift/talent, tool, or technology, it is up to us to practice and refine until we know it so well it comes naturally when needed. Some shamanic skills take years of practice, and we continue learning and increasing our skill throughout the course of our lives.

One of the core shamanic skills we discuss in this chapter is what Eliade termed the shaman's "magical flight," the technique of "journeying" to non-ordinary reality or the dreamtime, the upper and lower worlds that exist side by side with our three-dimensional reality (sometimes called the middle world). Yet, even if a shaman doesn't journey with or for you, they remain the Wisdom Keepers who hold the Original Instructions and remind us all that we are children of creation, and that natural law supersedes all man-made laws.

There are other simple, but powerful, skills—such as the exercise to follow—that anyone can master to apply to situations encountered in daily life.

One way to be able to access what's needed in any situation, any time, any place (even in the middle of the supermarket, and yes, public places are sometimes where we're most needed!) is to visualize, conceptualize, and "build" a sacred place inside yourself, your mind's eye if you will: a place where you can access your tools, teachings, talents, and techniques instantly; a place connected with both your heart and mind. It's your sacred place, so visualize a setting that is beautiful, comfortable, and relaxing. A place where you can immediately remember the best song or dance for the situation, play a flute or drum, shake a rattle, or light sage or cedar to cleanse a space and people. Get so comfortable there that when an argument or altercation starts in the grocery store line or in traffic, you can go to your inner sacred place, pick up the tool that will quiet and calm the situation, and secretly take care of it in the spirit world. This really does work, *if you practice it.*

We've found it helpful to ask ourselves three questions every time we start something new—whether a new day, a new endeavor, or a new skill set:

- How do we envision ourselves working with this from the heart in daily life?

- How does any of this apply in the world and with our community members?

- How is this a bridge between ceremonial and daily life for ourselves and others?

Whenever we incorporate a new belief, practice, or another method or technique into our personal ceremonial routines or into the ways we work with others, we ask the above questions. This helps us to hone our intentions, and to become Hollow Bones in each experience.

Can you become a shaman by reading a few books, attending a few ceremonies? Not really. You can certainly study how to use shamanic gifts and techniques for yourself, and listen and learn from the spirits, which is a manner of teaching and learning that is key to the shamanic path. But becoming a shaman is a life path. We have observed a few people who came to a couple of sweat lodges, did a vision quest, perhaps attended a Sun Dance, then decided they knew enough to name themselves a shaman and advertise their services. This is dangerous—for them and their clients. Please use the information in this book to transform yourself in whatever ways you see fit, and to help your family and community by offering the kinds of co-created ceremonies we suggest.

If you want to go farther and deeper along the shaman's path, find a teacher you can apprentice with. We have both done this work, mentoring and teaching others, and Robin is still actively training practitioners. There are many other medicine teachers as well. Question any potential teacher to find out who taught them, what they're authorized to pass on, and get recommendations from others before you make a decision.

## Experiencing the Journey World

Visualization and journeying are key techniques that allow us to obtain information from the astral plane, otherworld, or dreamtime. You'll use visionary practices often in the work you do in *Journey of the White Bear*.

Visualizations, or guided meditations, teach you how to move through inner space to other realities. With these visualizations—usually done while listening to another's voice—you are guided to a particular place with a specific goal in mind. You probably noticed the colors and shapes of trees, animals, mountains, seas, and rivers you saw in those guided meditations might have been quite different from your waking world. In this alternate reality landscape, your animal guides, or spirit guides in human, angelic, or other forms, led you to information. Each journey took you through a part of the labyrinth of the invisible, until you reached a source that imparted knowledge and gifts designed to aid you in the physical, day-to-day world, your personal evolution. As you gained more experience, you undoubtedly developed your own format for setting out on your inner voyage.

Journeying is similar to visualization, but it is usually directed by the inner guidance of the journeyer and their spirit helpers, with little instruction from an outside source. Journeyers enter a dreamtime state, often through drumming, rattling, chant, and/or dance. The beat of the drum, the shaking of the rattle, or the cadence of the chant or dance is the vehicle used by the journeyer to travel into other worlds—what Eliade called the shaman's "magical flight"—according to the cosmology of their culture, beliefs, traditions, personal visions or experiences, and dreams.

Typically, the sound of the drum or rattle holds the journeyer to the earthly plane and assists him or her in reaching and maintaining an alpha state in which altered realities become apparent. A change in tempo signals the time to return to normal consciousness. The drum rhythms used in shamanic practices vary from tribe to tribe and purpose to purpose. A fast beat accesses beta waves and carries you into a trance state. According to your journey's purpose, different beats will facilitate the objective. There are many drumming and rhythmic sound tracks available to help you with personal journeying.

Non-ordinary reality is typically described as comprising three distinct worlds:

- The overworld or upper world, which is the realm of the super-conscious, the angelic, the extraterrestrials, Father Sky, creature beings, often ancestors and spirit teachers. You may or may not recognize them, as many of them come from other star systems or have never manifested on Earth in physical form. Entrance to the upper world is often via flight, on a rainbow, up a tree, through the clouds, or rising into space through the earthly atmosphere, with a sensation of moving upward before onward.

- The underworld or lower world is the abode of the subconscious and of the Earth Mother, and is inhabited by subterraneans, such as the insects and mushroom people, our personal power animals, elementals, devas, fairies, elves, gnomes and other wisdom sources, and, sometimes, our ancestors. Entrance to the lower world is often via a cave or tunnel, a flowing stream or deep pool, or the trunk of a tree, with a sensation of moving downward before onward.

- The middle world is not commonly used for personal journeying. It is a world most closely akin to the world we see around us, more or less a parallel dimension to our three-dimensional, physical reality. Typically, this world is visited for specific healings or for informational purpose by experienced practitioners. It requires more accumulated wisdom and experience to venture into the middle world, as this is also the place of discarnate spirits, often of people who have died violently or instantly. There's a special designation called Psychopomp for those who can assist these beings to complete their passage and be welcomed into the arms of the ancestors. Please consult someone who specializes in this type of shamanic healing work if you have questions or think this may be one of your gifts.

Your spirit guides and animal protectors may lead you through any or all of these worlds, according to your intention and what you need to experience on any given journey. In certain realms you may find help and assistance, but you may also find archetypal creatures whose purpose is to challenge or obstruct your journey. As in aikido or any other martial art, often the way to fight such creations is by flowing around them, rather than engaging in attack. Sometimes, your guides may suggest you ask what these creatures need. See if you can find a way to help them rather than fight them.

In the way that we've been taught, we do not journey alone. Ever. We always have our power animal or guide with us—sometimes more than one. Sometimes another joins us in the journey world; other times, your power animal may shapeshift as needed to navigate a particular situation. Your journey companions are resourceful, wise in the ways of non-ordinary reality, the otherworld. At any point, feel free to ask them for assistance, intervention, clarification, or to lead you out and away, back to full consciousness. In alternate reality landscapes, these animal guides, or spirit guides in various human(ish), angelic, or other forms, lead you to the information you need. Each journey takes you through the otherworld—typically the lower world or upper world—until you reach the source that possesses the knowledge you seek. In some practices, you will leave a gift in return for their assistance. Returning from your journey follows the trail you traveled in, thanking all who helped you along the way, until your consciousness is fully present in your body.

For your first journey assignment in this book, we suggest you journey to see if a different totem or guide may be the one to accompany you for this new cycle of learning. Although we know of some practitioners who maintain an entire baseball team of guides, many practitioners hold only a close few who have been with them for many years. This is a personal relationship between you and your guides, so we encourage you to do what feels right for you. As well, it's important to ask any being you haven't worked with before if they have joined you for a reason, a season, or a lifetime. This will help you understand their place in your retinue of helpers.

If you are unfamiliar with journeying, we encourage you to seek out a teacher in your area to learn this key foundational practice. To journey into non-ordinary reality in a more freeform way, it is important to seek direction and assistance from someone familiar with those landscapes and the worlds within. This teacher/mentor will be able to teach you how to set protection for your journey and can help you understand and interpret what you are seeing—as well as assist you in moving through each dimension with ease. See the Preparing for Study chapter, as well as the Resources section at the back of this book for the Tools for Visualization and Journeying checklist with setup instructions and additional information.

As with many beginning journeyers, when you first start practicing this technique you may find you don't seem to "go" anywhere, or you simply fall asleep. Stay with it, and as you practice, you will go deeper, further. Prepare for journeying using the methods we describe, remembering to set protection for yourself and to give yourself permission to end any journey you don't feel ready to experience.

Over many years of journeying and training journeyers, we have come to understand that people receive information in four predominant ways: visual, audio, sensing/feeling, and kinesthetic. Some people never "see" anything when they journey. Don't worry about it. Just journey and trust. You may hear something, feel or sense what wants to reveal itself, or you may have a huge insight while doing the dishes later! Or you might meet a perfect stranger two days later who tells you exactly what you need to know. Remember, Spirit and your ancestors, guides, and helpers already know who you are and what you need. Trust that the entire universe is supporting you.

On a final note, we encourage you to be as clear as possible when you frame a question for journeying. A clear question does not mean a limiting question, but one with a specific intention and focus, usually for healing, guidance, or information. Lack of focus can lead to murky journeys that can seem unfulfilling or confusing. As you gain experience and develop relationships with your allies, this gets easier over time.

## The Shaman's Sacred Imagery and Symbols

Throughout this book you will work with many symbols and images. Most shamanic cultures include the same basic cosmology of upper, middle, and lower worlds. Some cultures explore other worlds as rooms or dimensions, sometimes portals, added to the basic cosmology.

As well, almost every shamanic culture we've studied includes the Sacred Tree, the Tree of Life, often referred to as the *axis mundi*. The movie *Avatar* (a film essentially about shamanic beliefs and practices) showed two examples: the Home Tree and the World Tree. The Sacred Tree represents the lower, middle, and upper worlds. Often, as in the poetic descriptions of Yggdrasil (the Norse sacred tree), there's a creature like Ratatosk, the squirrel, who carries messages from the underworld—the Sacred Tree's roots — to the many branches of the upper world and back again. In daily practice, the shaman is the squirrel. And for our purposes, each of us is the squirrel: listening, learning, seeking, praying, and visioning intentions between the lower and upper worlds through our core intentions in the middle world. The middle world is the trunk of the tree, including its stabilizing core, its receiving and giving heart, branches always reaching towards Father Sky, roots grounded in the earth. The axis mundi, the center of the world, is also represented by the Sacred Tree, a connection between heaven and Earth. In astronomy, *axis mundi* is the Latin term describing the axis of Earth between the celestial poles.

When viewed this way, we can see how we are both like the tree and like Ratatosk, ever scurrying back and forth among the many realms and dimensions encompassed in our personal and collective understanding of the universe in which we live. We are the message, and we are the messenger.

Years ago, Robin learned a simple circular song titled "Dancing Like a Tree" (various versions are accessible on YouTube) to help us ground with our roots, reach high with our arms/branches to seek our visions, understand the messages we receive down into our core, and share our open hearts in connection with all that is: sun, rain, sky, wind, and earth. This type of connection song is intended to be sung multiple times as we touch the world around us and experience the moment. There is significance in the repetition as well. Our ancestors devised the construct of linear time to assist us in getting from point A to point B; however, they also knew that in universal time, everything is NOW. Songs like these help us to experience that all things are coexisting in this moment. Therefore, we are rooted, connected and aligned with all of creation: dreaming, visioning, enacting, and serving all at the same time, in this and every lifetime in all of our lineages at once. In parallel dimensions, we may even be acting out our different choices in every moment.

Before this discussion becomes too cerebral, take a deep breath and simply trust that all is exactly as it needs to be for you right now. Whatever you need to understand will be … is being … given to you at exactly the moment you can best receive it.

Also, as you become familiar with your guides and helpers, you will realize they, too, offer us much, as symbols pertaining to who we authentically are. By observing who they are, we can determine our best ways of responding to certain situations or to receiving information. You might even ask yourself a question, for example: What would Bear say? What would Eagle do? What would Whale think?

Shamans follow energy. Serge Kahili King, author of *Urban Shaman* and other works on Hawaiian shamanism, taught "energy flows where attention goes." We've observed traditional shamans who can change the energy in a room full of discord simply by starting a chant. Within minutes, the discord has dissipated, and all the people there are flowing with the energy of harmony within the chant.

The universe is composed of energy. What appears as dissonance can be brought into balance by its equal and opposite energetic pattern. The great "secrets" of shamanism are in the observation and study of the energetic patterns in the upper, middle, and lower worlds, learning how to move energies to create what is necessary in the NOW. We will be working with these dynamics throughout this book, and you can continue to explore this for the rest of your life, if you so choose.

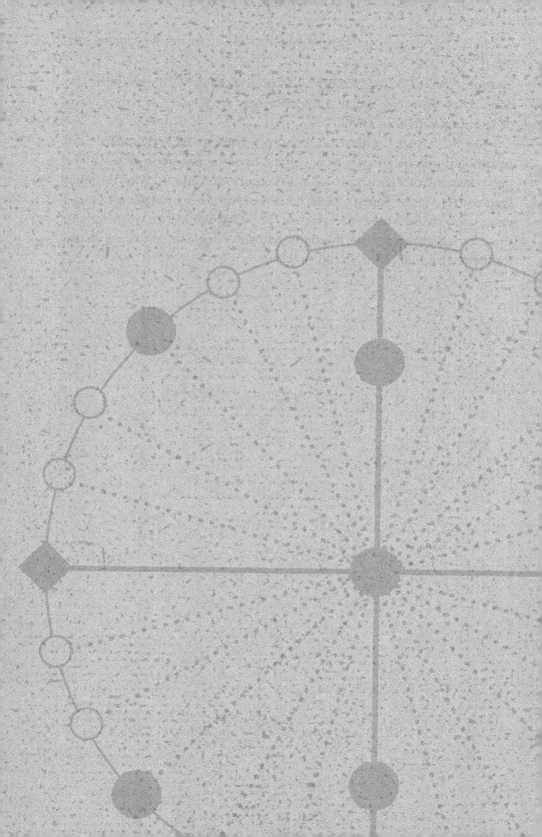

# Chapter 4

---

# CO-CREATING IN THE EAST

In the east, we encounter and embrace the aspects that reflect and support our journey as a Visionary/Seer. You may find other traditions place the aspects in a slightly different manner, or that certain aspects may come to your attention strongly in a direction other than the one expected. This is all a part of the mystery of the wheel and the timeless medicine of these teachings.

## ASPECTS OF THE EAST

| | |
|---:|:---|
| Element: | Air |
| Embodiment: | Spiritual |
| Emotions: | Awareness/Excitement |
| Season: | Spring |
| Day Cycle: | Dawn, Morning |
| Moon Cycle: | Waxing |
| Phase of Life: | Being without Form |
| Color: | Yellow |
| Creatures: | Winged Ones |
| Expression: | Voice, Flute, Instruments using Breath |
| Way: | Seeker of Vision, Seer/Visionary |

| | |
|---:|:---|
| Place on the Wheel: | New Beginnings and Inspiration |
| Lesson: | Awareness and Illumination |
| Relationship: | Solo, Self |
| Wheel within Wheel: | Co-Creation |
| Ceremony: | Calling |

. . . . . . . . . . . . . . . . . . . . . . . .

East is where we enter the Medicine Wheel as Spirit, the place before birth, where we begin each life, each cycle of learning, again and again. We each decided to incarnate at this time, in these bodies. Before we materialized, we made agreements with the Divine Source, our guides, and our helpers. We chose the kinds of lessons we wanted to learn here. We chose the mission(s) we wanted to accomplish. We may have even chosen the parents and siblings we wanted to experience. And then, most of us forgot the choices we made as we entered this world through the birth canal.

Now we're adults, making our way in the world. East is the place of vision and deep listening... of allowing what's authentic in us to rise as a new dream or vision. It's our solo journey through life. We may have different dreams for different areas of our lives. A personal dream is something we cherish and want to accomplish or receive in this life. We may also have an aspiration for a career, or a desire for a family life or partner. In the east, we examine our ideals, dreams, and goals. Some may have already been fulfilled. Some may have changed, or need changing to reflect our current growth and beliefs.

We hope you all live in the Source of Love. Wherever we see fear in ourselves, it is love's job to shine light into the fear to dispel it. That doesn't mean we don't stand up when necessary. White Bear does not ignore what is important. But it does mean we stand in a different way. When we live from the Source, we can create a protected sacred space around ourselves. We have arms for a reason. Your sacred personal space is both arms' length all the way around your body, and you can envision yourself inside a protected bubble of light as you walk with White Bear or your personal guide beside you.

### Navajo Beauty Way Prayer

In Beauty may I walk.
All day long may I walk.
Through the returning seasons may I walk.
On the trail marked with pollen may I walk.
With grasshoppers about my feet may I walk.
With dew about my feet may I walk.
With Beauty may I walk.
With Beauty before me, may I walk.
With Beauty behind me, may I walk.
With Beauty above me, may I walk.
With Beauty below me, may I walk.
With Beauty all around me, may I walk.
In old age wandering on a trail of Beauty,
lively, may I walk.
In old age wandering on a trail of Beauty,
living again, may I walk.
It is finished in Beauty.
It is finished in Beauty.

Every human has dreams, inspirations, and aspirations. Our dreams and passions are inspired and informed by our life purpose. Now and then we receive new information that challenges or changes our vision in some way, new perspectives that change our awareness and illuminate things we've never seen before. Sometimes this can feel as if we are being challenged on almost every level, and for many of us something new may well up in our hearts and move us in new ways and directions. This is what the east is all about.

In the east we find the winged ones soaring through the air, Eagle and Hawk with their keen eyesight and high-spiraling flight, who teach us about perspective, seeing things from a great height. We find gentle Deer, shape-shifter Weasel, and other animals here in the east as well.

East represents spring, morning, dawn, dawning understanding, and awakening. Signified by the color yellow and the element air, east is about breathing newness deep into our lungs, down into our solar plexus, then exhaling the old. It is connecting one's heart and mind to know what's most authentic for us so that we can move forward, congruent with ourselves and all life.

In modern Western culture, we've been taught all decisions should be logical and intellectual. But perhaps that is slowly changing. Hawaiians, some other indigenous tribes, and even Western doctors, are recognizing that humans have three kinds of intelligence. We have the brain (logical) mind, the heart (feeling) mind, and the gut (instinctual) mind. Before some of our Hawaiian teachers made any decision, they would rub their bellies. Remember the saying about butterflies in your tummy? Well, while linking the heart mind to the brain mind, they would consider all options, rubbing their bellies all the while. When the belly settled down, the butterflies landed, they knew that choice was the right decision.

There are many other ways: deep breathing, playing a flute, meditating, sounding with our voices—all east expressions. If you experiment, you will find the way that works best for you. The important thing to remember is that your logical mind is only a tool of your heart, which KNOWS what's correct for you through an instinctual rightness that reverberates in your very bones.

East is the start of a new cycle of learning, and although change can often be painful, we're encouraged by what's happening with the demonstrations around the world. Most protestors seem to be coming from love, wanting to resolve age-old issues, especially for the dark-skinned and marginalized people of the world. Like Jesus throwing the money changers out of the temple, anger is sometimes a necessary form of love that impels change.

Yet, there are other forums. We've participated and shared in many gatherings and online presentations. The Recommended Reading section at the back of this book includes a few websites that present videos and key information that may help each of us determine our path forward—and there are many others. We've all been talking about what needs to change, with discussions such as Honoring the Sacred; Healing Global Multigenerational Trauma; Towards Healing Systemic Racism; Indigenous Social and Restorative Justice; the Circle of Courage; and the Medicine Wheel of Mastery. There are other people and organizations coming together to investigate and heal cultural fragility, privilege and entitlement, economic disparity, racial injustice, etc.

As well, many employees are choosing to work from home (lessening pollution and reducing the impact of climate change). Some of those huge, now-empty office buildings are being renovated to provide communities and housing for our homeless. Mother Earth is healing, even though there may be a great cost to humanity and the tree, plant, and animal nations. Some of our animal relatives are reclaiming their space, coming home to a few of their natural habitats, and laying eggs to birth their young in places where for decades there have been too many humans and too much trash for them to do so. Others are dying as they flee the flames of the unprecedented, ever-increasing wildfires in America's West, as well as Siberia, Asia, Australia, and Africa. Climate change is inevitable, but there are opportunities for us to curb and slow its effects if we choose.

Between pandemics, fires, floods, earthquakes, superstorms, and the demonstrations, we've been given the opportunity to co-create a whole new world—the world we all really want. So let's do that, rather than focusing all our attention on what's wrong with everything. That doesn't mean we should ignore our current reality. No spiritual bypassing, please! Just recognize it and begin to ask yourself what YOU want to do about it that will create more harmony, happiness, and balance. What do you bring to the table for All Our Relations?

As Serge Kahili King taught: energy flows where attention goes. We want to set our intentions and focus our—and your—attention to help to birth a new Earth. Our prayer is that everything you read here, and everything you do, will assist you to discover, hone, refine, and focus your purpose, mission, passions, gifts, and abilities, so that you can better serve yourself, your family, your nation, and your world. The Cherokee have a blessing for new endeavors:

Yigaquu osaniyu adanvto adadoligi nigohilvi nasquv utloyasdi nihi
*(May the Great Spirit's blessings always be with you)*
Ea Nigada Qusdi Idadadvhn
*(All My Relatives in Creation)*

Shaman as Visionary lives in the east, those seers and psychics who can push aside the veil and peer between the worlds. These shamans become the "Hollow Bone," channeling information from beyond. The great medicine people and traditional shamans all use the term Hollow Bone or something very close to it. Robin tells people she's capable of being a true Hollow Bone between 5 and 10 percent of the time. Being a Hollow Bone means being a conduit between unseen realms and dimensions and this one; it means clearing yourself of all your opinions, and allowing messages and information that does not belong to you to come through you, unfiltered by your own perceptions.

The Oglala Lakota (Sioux), Black Elk (December 1, 1863–August 19, 1950), was a famous visionary, shaman, and holy man. His vision at nine years old held a powerful message that he lived with his entire life in service to his people, a vision of the Sacred Tree and the Sacred Hoop of the world that yet holds meaning for many. The Sacred Tree, the Tree of Life, nourishes all life. In his vision, Black Elk saw people of all nations gathering to dance in a sacred way around the tree of life. This represented a time of recovery and peace among all nations.

> *Then a Voice said: "Behold this day, for it is yours to make. Now you shall stand upon the center of the earth to see, for there they are taking you." I was still on my bay horse, and once more I felt the riders of the west, the north, the east, the south, behind me in formation, as before, and we were going east. I looked ahead and saw the mountains there with rocks and forests on them, and from the mountains flashed all colors upward to the heavens. Then I was standing on the highest mountain of them all, and round about beneath me was the whole hoop of the world. And while I stood there I saw more than I can tell and I understood more than I saw; for I was seeing in a sacred manner the shapes of all things in the Spirit, and the shape of all shapes as they must live together like one being. And I saw that the sacred hoop of my people was one of many hoops that made one circle, wide as daylight and as starlight, and in the center grew one mighty flowering tree to*

*shelter all the children of one mother and one father. And I saw*
*that it was holy.*

—Excerpt from Black Elk's Vision, *Black Elk Speaks*,
by John G. Neihardt

Black Elk's vision was, in part, a prophecy about the rough road ahead for the Lakota Nation, as well as for his life as a medicine man. When a shaman Seer becomes a Hollow Vessel as Black Elk did, messages emerge across time and space, from human ancestors, star beings, the collective conscious, and the Great Mysterious One. This ancient form of communication to our modern world may help us perceive and understand what's happening in our own lives, in our communities, nations, and world in a different way. The shaman may share ancient ways to resolve our current situation or help someone find and integrate a lost part of themselves. Sometimes a shaman can locate articles lost for centuries, or were lost yesterday, if the articles are pertinent to the current situation.

Shaman as Visionary or Seer has the great responsibility of both honoring and communicating his vision, deciding who, how, and when to share it, and how to hold it and manifest it in the world. There are many famous visionaries across history, including those in business, science, technology, medicine, engineering, and art. We are all visionaries in some way, both for ourselves, and in service to All Our Relations.

## Wheel of Co-creation

In 2011, Robin graduated from Barbara Marx Hubbard's Agents of Conscious Evolution course, with permission to share the Wheel of Co-creation as she teaches around the world. Barbara was a futurist who saw possibilities for a new and bright future emerging. After WWII, at the tender age of seventeen, she acquired an appointment with President Eisenhower. The atomic bomb had been dropped on Hiroshima, and her only question to the president was: "How are you going to use this immense power for good?" Barbara is gone now, but her legacy lives on through her books and her foundation.

When Robin saw the Wheel of Co-creation, she thought *this is the next iteration of the Medicine Wheel, meant for the changes we must begin making to support all life.*

Yet, many who took that course in 2011 believe they only truly understood it and could help others to fully understand HOW it works, in 2018. Why? Because it requires such a radically different perspective than all of us have embedded in our DNA over the last millennia that we have to deconstruct—shamanically *dis-member*—everything we've ever been taught about project management, coordination, and control. Robin includes herself here, because as a mixed-blood woman who worked in the corporate world for many years, she'd been just as enculturated as anyone.

We can hear some of your—and our—modern impatience right now. *"Oh, boy! Could she just get on with it? I don't have time for all this!"*

Here's how the Wheel of Co-creation works:

- The vision goes in the center of the circle. It never moves; it's never replaced.

- The next ring of the wheel is for all those whose dream matches and is congruent with the vision. Those who hold the vision as sacred

are vision holders, space holders, and advisors, and those who take leadership for select areas would be considered the Team Leads.

- The segments of the wheel represent the things that will support the vision, e.g., funding, infrastructure, etc. Each vision will have its own needs and functions, thus these attributes will change.

- The outer circle includes our tribe of affinity—all those who want to contribute time, energy, and resources to whichever segment of the wheel they choose.

- Each person chooses the segment they belong to by desire rather than the needs of the vision.

- The wheel is nonhierarchical and egalitarian; therefore all can contribute ideas, suggestions, methods and techniques equally.

- All decisions are made via consensus in talking circles, etc. (See Talking Circle discussion below).

## Talking Circle—A Lesson in Perspectives

*by Robin Youngblood*

Have you ever noticed that people today interrupt each other, often answering questions that haven't yet been asked—and possibly weren't the questions that were going to be asked? Native peoples have a remedy for that. Whenever indigenous people gather to discuss important issues, changes that need to be considered, even family challenges, we use a method called talking circles. There are strict protocols for talking circles, and they're very valuable because they *work!*

The Medicine Wheel teaches us that there are many points on the wheel, from four to infinity. Each directional shift offers us the opportunity to view the central question from a slightly different perspective. In the Circle of Life, every point of view is equally valuable, and the circle isn't whole until all viewpoints have been expressed.

To work together in a circle, a facilitator is chosen whose role is to open the circle, acknowledge speakers without either approval or judgment, and pass the talking stick to the next person, until all have been heard. Cross talk is not allowed, as all respect the need of each person to be truly heard. The first round of a talking circle is about hearing every perspective without making decisions. For some people in our modern, hurry-along culture, it may be the first time they've ever felt accepted, received, valued, and heard. This can be a huge healing in itself.

For indigenous people, decisions are made with consideration as to how our actions today will affect the next seven generations and beyond. This is a process, and may take several talking circles, consultation circles, perhaps a healing and forgiveness circle, until all involved reach clarity and the best course of action for the good of the whole emerges. It can be a difficult process for modern people, who always seem to be in such a hurry! Yet, as those with a foot in both worlds, we see far more mistakes with devastating consequences come from making decisions too quickly without enough information.

May your past, present, and future exploration of talking circles and the Wheel of Co-creation bring you healing, confidence, peace, and wisdom.

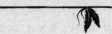

## Journey of the East

Journey with your current totem or power animal to locate the totem or guide who will accompany you for this new cycle of learning with White Spirit Bear. Totem animals appear at different times for different reasons. The guide you find in this meditation may be one with which you already have, or will have, a long history; or it may be in your life for a short time for a specific reason. You can always ask the animal why they've come—for a reason, a season, or a lifetime? Do listen, and don't overanalyze this in your journey. Just be open to what comes.

If you see many animals or beings and are uncertain which is yours, the rule we go by is the one who shows itself to you multiple times is the one for you. If you find yourself uncomfortable at any point in your journey, as always, ask your current totem or power animal to intervene, assist, or guide you back. If you find yourself unable to get too far in this journey or are not entirely certain which new ally is for you, come out and try again another time.

Once you are introduced to your new helper, ask them to guide you toward—or help you access or clarify—any new dreams, visions, or beginnings that want to emerge in your life.

Prior to beginning the journey, consult the setup instructions described in Tools for Journeying in the Resources section at the end of the book. You may wish to also review the Journey World discussion in the chapter entitled Journeying with Bear.

Remember, we do not journey alone, so always call in your current totem or guide before beginning. We recommend a fifteen-minute journey.

### Journal

1. After you complete your journey, use your journal to record the events and your impressions. Is this new ally or guide someone or something familiar?

2. Describe this ally, nose to tail. If an animal or animallike, research: what are its habits, habitats, strengths, patterns? What does this animal mean to you? Is it predator or prey? If a different type of being, what characteristics and traits do they possess and where might those have originated? If possible, acquire or create a representation of this new helper.

3. If you were to classify what role best fits this ally—Seer, Teacher, Healer, Warrior, or something else—what might it be? How does this ally's role mirror or augment the role you feel most resonance with at this time? How does this ally's role mirror or augment the role you are currently best suited for or trained to perform (these roles may be different)?

4. Where would this new ally sit on the Medicine Wheel? What does that tell you about them?

5. What is the new dream or vision that has come forward in your journey? Are there other dreams or visions that are calling you? Does one in particular stand out?

6. If you feel called to, return to the journey world with your current totem and have a conversation with your new ally. How might your new ally help you manifest your new dream or vision? What can you bring them in appreciation for their assistance? What and how does this ally like to be called?

7. Use your journal to record dreams and other visions experienced during this time. Identify how these supplement or clarify your co-creation work in the east.

### Assignment

1. Think of a project you need help with. What components do you need?

2. Draw a Wheel of Co-creation, always remembering that your vision goes in the center. Place the components you will need in the segments of the wheel.

3. Now pray...who are the people you already know who would love to act in one of those positions? Write their names in the corresponding section. Do you have empty sections? Ask Spirit, your guides, and helpers to bring those people into your life. Let go and trust.

4. Are there opportunities in your vision for you to learn something new? What steps are you willing to take to make that happen?

5. If you feel called to, return to the journey world to have a conversation with your new ally about your vision. Note any new directions you might receive.

6. Pay attention to what happens in your three-dimensional reality. What comes across your radar that might be the universe supporting your vision? Who finds their way into your life with skills to contribute?

## Calling Ceremony

This is a Calling Ceremony. For a list of tools and general setup instructions, see the Tools for Ceremony discussion in the Resources section at the end of the book. To prepare for this ceremony:

- Locate a medium-sized clear quartz crystal that fits easily into your hand. Cleanse the crystal by soaking overnight in salt water.

- Choose a private indoor or outdoor site for your ceremony.

- Build a simple four-directions Medicine Wheel circle, with one stone in each cardinal direction.

- Bring your drum or rattle.

- Put the environment in order and have your journal at hand.

- Set sacred space.

- Use smoke or other items for clearing and cleansing.

- Ground yourself, establishing your connection to the earth.

- Review your intention.

- Say a prayer for protection.

- Request the presence of guides and other helpers, particularly the new ally who came to you during this work in the east.

- Place your Wheel of Co-creation in the center of the circle.

Stand facing the east at the east point of the wheel. Call in the Great Eagle and all the Powers of Good in the east to the stone circle and ask them to help you manifest what you wish to co-create. Begin to sing to the spirits of the east using your drum or rattle as accompaniment. You can sing songs that you know, or just allow your voice to create melodies with sounds or vocables like *oh* or *heya*. It doesn't matter if you think you sing well or not. Just allow yourself to express through your voice what you feel and experience. Experiment with singing, in words, a prayer to the spirits of the east or Eagle. Let it rhyme if it wants to and allow your music and song to flow naturally. Ask Spirit to give you words and phrases. Open to the *feeling* of Spirit within.

When you have finished in the east, move to the south and call or sing in the medicine of the south: trust, innocence, love, and joy. Repeat this in the west (introspection, dreaming, and balance) and north (ancestral wisdom, integrity and authenticity, leadership). Then ask Father Sky and Mother Earth to bless you abundantly in your co-creation project.

Now, at the point where you call in the center of the wheel, take out the crystal. Remember, this is where your dream, project, heart's deepest desire is embodied. Sit near the center of the circle next to your Wheel of Co-creation, and hold the crystal in your left hand, your receiving hand. Relax and ground, feeling yourself and the crystal to be the center of the Medicine Wheel circle.

Focusing on the crystal, send it the energy of your love. Do you feel a response? Crystals are record keepers and holders of wisdom. This crystal will work with you to hold the vision of your co-creation. Ask the crystal to help hold this vision for you.

Now visualize what you wish to manifest. Close your eyes and send the images and pictures from your mind, your Wheel of Co-creation, into the crystal. As you see this vision in your mind's eye, remember to add the thought/words: *this or something better suited for All My Relations.* Take as long as you need to do this.

From now on, when you need this vision with you or wish to connect with this image, you can tap into the information/image stored in your crystal. If it is difficult to see your vision coming to be in the world, use the crystal in meditation—hold it in your hand or place it in your lap—to connect with your vision, with your work in service to all.

Now hold the crystal to your heart and sit for a while in the center of the Medicine Wheel. Let go of your thoughts and let them flow through your mind without paying attention to any of them. Visualize Grandfather Eagle. Feel his eyes upon you and sense his keen awareness. Imagine the clarity and illumination he possesses and ask if he has any messages for you as you complete the lessons of the east. Listen for his answer. When you are finished, open your eyes.

Consider this deepest desire, your soul's purpose, and remember you are meant to be here. You are meant to stand in the circle with All Your

Relations and share your medicine. This is both your birth right as a human be-ing and your responsibility this lifetime. As Sherri Mitchell writes: "It is no coincidence that we find ourselves here, at this place and this time. We have all agreed to be here. In fact we were born into this time purposely. We have all followed an evolution of awareness that has led us to this moment, where we possess this exact understanding of light and darkness, connectivity and interrelatedness, and our co-creative abilities. Thus the question is not why we are here, but how we show up most powerfully to meet the times that we are part of." You are exactly where you are supposed to be.

Close the circle by releasing each direction in the reverse order that you called it in. Thank the spirits and guides for their support, including the spirits of the land where you spent this time. Leave the site more beautiful than when you found it by placing a small offering, a bundle of herbs, a flower, or a pinch of tobacco.

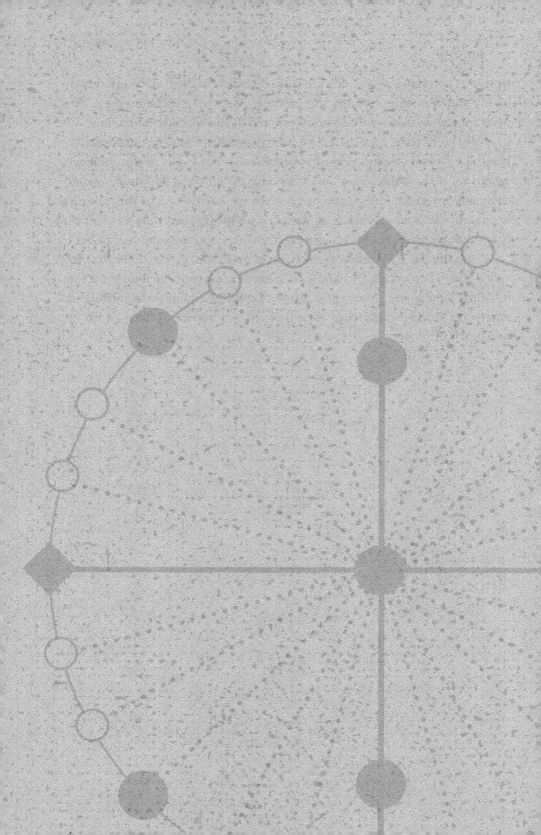

# Chapter 5

---

# BALANCING IN THE SOUTH

In the south, we encounter and embrace the aspects that reflect and support our Shaman as Teacher journey. You may find other traditions place the aspects in a slightly different manner, or that certain aspects may come to your attention strongly in a direction other than the one expected. This is all a part of the mystery of the wheel and the timeless medicine of these teachings.

## ASPECTS OF THE SOUTH

. . . . . . . . . . . . . . . . . . . . . . . . . .

|  |  |
| ---: | :--- |
| Element: | Fire |
| Embodiment: | Physical |
| Emotions: | Anger/Passion/Elation |
| Season: | Summer |
| Day Cycle: | Noonday |
| Moon Cycle: | Full |
| Phase of Life: | Young Adult |
| Color: | Red |
| Creatures: | Four-Leggeds |
| Expression: | Drum and Dance |
| Way: | Creator of Movement, Teacher |

Place on the Wheel:   Growth, Learning, Work with Joy

Lesson:   Trust and Innocence

Relationship:   Partnership

Wheel within Wheel:   Relationships

Ceremony:   Making Right Ceremony
(Ho'oponopono)

. . . . . . . . . . . . . . . . . . . . . . .

The south on the Medicine Wheel is the place where we are rapidly growing and learning in our physical embodiment, the three-dimensional world. The energetic fullness of the moon cycle, the fire of our emotions, and the dancer within all emerge. South is a place of possibility and truth, and learning to see through the eyes of a child allows us to interpret the world in a different light, a light that allows us to be free from the shackles of "shoulds," a light that encourages us to balance who we've become (sometimes an uncomfortable assessment) with who we wish to be. Who we know we can be. Who we are as a spark of the Divine when we stand before the Creator's mirror—not who others expect us to be or who we have been in the past.

White Bear does not apologize for who and what she is; she simply is. She lives fully in her skin, feet on the ground, nose scenting and sensing the world around her—as do most wild creatures and small children in their own way (before they become domesticated). As a parent, White Bear balances her cubs' needs with her own. She shows them the way of the world, then encourages them to explore it, to make their own mistakes. Bear also fiercely defends her young from predators, including other bears, and shelters cubs for two seasons, at which point she insists they go. Without question. Her boundaries are crystal clear.

South is the place of the young adult, pursuing their heart's desire with full expression, dancing and drumming around the fires of creativity. It is also a place of choice and transformation, and with that choice, you create movement and transformation, learning as you go, becoming more than the sum of your parts as you work in partnership with all of who you are, the twin male and the female within, the light and the shadow.

Represented by the color red—blood, birth, and fire—this is a place where the work required as a result of co-creation happens. Chopping wood and carrying water, weighted with your choices, your duty *and* desire. In this way we find a balance, fulfilling our responsibilities, showing up for our relationships, sharing our wisdom when and where appropriate, as well as pursuing our vision.

In this chapter, we explore the teachings of the south with the story of a child who, like many others, finds himself learning from his grandfather. In this well-known Cherokee story, the white wolf symbolizes our light, the black wolf our shadow.

> *An old Cherokee man is teaching his grandson about life:*
> *"A fight is going on inside me," he said to the boy. "It is a*
> *terrible fight and it is between two wolves. One is evil—he*
> *is anger, envy, sorrow, regret, greed, arrogance, self-pity,*
> *guilt, resentment, inferiority, lies, false pride, superiority,*
> *and ego." He continued, "The other is good—he is joy, peace,*
> *love, hope, serenity, humility, kindness, benevolence, empathy,*
> *generosity, truth, compassion, and faith. The same fight is*
> *going on inside you—and inside every other person, too."*
>
> *The grandson thought about it for a minute and then asked his*
> *grandfather: "Which wolf will win?"*

You might have heard the story ends: *The old Cherokee replied, "The one you feed."* In the Cherokee world, however, Robin learned the story ends with a bit more unfolding: *"Some people only feed the white wolf, which leaves the black wolf ready to jump out and bite at the least provocation. So it's best to honor and feed both the black and white wolves inside us. The black wolf, our shadow side, is our teacher and early warning system that tells us we're out of balance and something is asking for healing. The black wolf is a key."* If we use that key and open the door to discover the treasure inside, it will help us heal ourselves, our multigenerational trauma, and the trauma from this and past lives.

How you choose to interact with the opposing forces within you will determine your life. Starve one or the other? Or guide them both? Unless you feed them both, the dark wolf will eventually become ravenous and eat everything in its path. This is part of the dance of balance, a dance of relationships—within yourself, as well as in partnership. In community, as well as with the Divine. Honoring the earth, as well as all who live on the Sacred Hoop of All Our Relations.

In the south we find the four-leggeds: Coyote, the trickster, who travels the crooked trails and teaches you how to laugh at yourself (particularly if you forget how) so you do not take life too seriously; Mouse, who lives close to the ground, energetically examining everything, busy and focused, categorizing details. Often, we'll see Beaver, the builder; Snake, the transmuter; Rabbit, the fear-caller, and other creatures who become our teachers in the south. All are reflections of whatever you most need to know, so it is important to sit with whatever medicine puts itself in your path as you do this work.

Shaman as Teacher steps forth in the south. There are many kinds of teachers, some out in the world setting or squelching fires, while others are more subtle like a glowing candle, but no less important. Shaman as Teacher knows in her bones that we are all teachers and students in any given moment. Sharing wisdom does not preclude the opportunity and the privilege of learning something new. Cycles of learning are continuous, otherwise you become stagnant. With every turn around the Medicine Wheel, we continue to work on ourselves—all parts of ourselves—peeling the onion layers away to find out who we are and what we stand for, humbly dissembling the lie of separation and healing the wounds from our past, so we can better serve humanity and reflect an authentic, honorable example for our children and students.

As teachers, we often tell our students to please not put us on pedestals, because in our humanness we *will* fall off. Students should not give away their power to teachers in that way. Honor, respect, and gratitude, yes; but do not place your teacher high in the sky. Most teachers have not yet earned their bodhisattva wings.

To embody shaman as Teacher requires not only that you do the work (and play) of teaching, but that you also examine the concepts of ethics, integrity, and right action. That you release your attachment to outcome and simply do the work with as much humility and grace as you can muster. That you stay objective and curious, and detach from your own sense of importance so that you can honor the divine wisdom in all of creation. That you give credit where credit is due, including to your own teachers. And do not take things personally. That you *know* you do not always have THE answer, but somebody somewhere does, and a little bit of silence can work wonders. Sounds almost impossible, doesn't it? Some say it gets easier with time, but that doesn't always hold true because every situation differs.

What is true is knowing yourself at ever deeper levels. Doing your own personal work helps you stay grounded with the teachings, as well as those you are instructing, and those from whom you are learning.

## Wheel of Relationships

The wheel we are exploring in the south is the Wheel of Relationships. This wheel illustrates the ways in which we interact in and with the world, our many roles, and the responsibilities we hold within those roles. At any one time, we may be wearing many hats, but in our busyness working and playing, creating and destroying, we may forget these hats. Shaman as Teacher reminds us of all these different relationships, along with the attributes

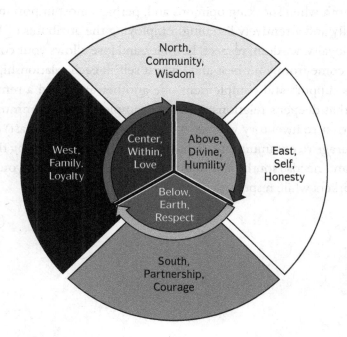

needed to facilitate cooperative living in good relationship to all creation and the holographic universe. These attributes, sometimes called cornerstones, are often placed on staffs positioned in the different directions on the Medicine Wheel.

## Attributes
### Cardinal Points
East, Self—Honesty

South, Partnership—Courage

West, Family—Loyalty

North, Community—Wisdom

### Center Directions
Below, Earth—Respect

Above, Divine—Humility

Center, Within—Love

With each relationship on the wheel, not only do we find an important attribute, but in some fashion all attributes on the wheel apply to all relationships. They are all linked, all parts of the whole, leaning on each other. Relationships work best when we are committed to transparent communication—both when speaking opinions and, perhaps most important, when respectfully and attentively listening. Employing the attributes of honesty, courage, loyalty, wisdom, respect, humility, and love allows your communication to come from your best and highest self in each relationship. These attributes support and complement one another and build a remarkable synergy that deepens relationships. For example, honest communication with yourself to inventory your own thoughts and behavior (east) can lead to the courage to communicate with your partner while honoring their perspective and needs (south) and help maintain your loyalty to your family and coworkers while respecting differences (west), etc.

| Direction | Relationship | Example | Attribute |
|-----------|--------------|---------|-----------|
| East | Self | Sacred Masculine/Feminine Dance of Light/Shadow | Honesty |
| South | Partnerships | Spouse, Friend, Business Partnerships | Courage |
| West | Family/Group | Family of Origin and Family of Choice, including Workplace | Loyalty |
| North | Community/World | Town, State, Country, Global Communities, Ancestors | Wisdom |
| Above | Divine/Creator | Great Mystery, a Power Greater than Ourselves | Humility |
| Below | Earth/Nature | Planet, Elements, All Living Beings | Respect |
| Center | Within/Between | All We Are, All We've Been, and All We Will Be, across All Dimensions | Love |

The Wheel of Relationships is a substantial teaching in itself. We are brushing the surface on these concepts to present them in total, but we will focus on two primary relationships here in this chapter. Peace starts at home, in your own heart, so we come back to the core of working on your relationship with yourself.

## Embracing and Balancing the Sacred Feminine with the Sacred Masculine

The Sacred Feminine and the Sacred Masculine are complementary energetic essences that reside within each of us and within all natural systems. Optimally, the receptive, reflective internal (feminine) and creative, active external (masculine) work in harmony, creating a synergy that ensures balanced well-being.

For those unfamiliar with these terms, it can also be described as the marriage of yin/yang. In this section, we include a nutshell definition, but this is a wide and heavily debated topic and the subject of many books and teachings.

- The Sacred Masculine represents rational thought and expression, the drive to design and build. This is the active, doing principle. Without the Sacred Feminine, the Sacred Masculine can be scientific and mechanistic.

- The Sacred Feminine represents the nurturing intuitive expression, the pause to consider and weigh before action. This is the internal, reflective, dreaming principle we see in Bear. Yet without the Sacred Masculine, the Sacred Feminine can be depressive and manipulative.

The imbalance we see between the Sacred Masculine and Sacred Feminine in Western culture is the outgrowth of an oppressive and judgmental patriarchal hierarchy that values men over women and endorses dominion over the earth and all her creatures for immediate gain without consideration for future generations. This has been a cultural pattern for millennia; when men began ignoring and condemning feminine wisdom, women's opinions were silenced and trivialized, and women, the earth, and earth-based societies became subjected to increasing violence. This imbalance has been a prevailing condition of Western government, culture, religion, economics, politics, and society, creating structures and strictures intended to maintain control for the benefit of kings and popes and colonizers. Institutional hierarchies unfold in a linear, masculine way where a chosen few occupy positions greater than others and their agendas rule the day, rather than a circle where we meet as equals to develop consensus, a feminine way where all perspectives are honored.

As above, so below; as within, so without. Embracing and balancing the Sacred Feminine and the Sacred Masculine within yourself unites intuitive wisdom with active wisdom, allowing outward creative expression to be balanced and nurtured with inward reflection and dreaming. This ensures whatever creation comes next is sufficiently informed by what already is, and considers All Our Relations, including the Earth Mother, as we move forward into the future.

White Bear represents this balance: power in action balanced with dreaming. Below we detail some slightly different challenges sisters and brothers face when balancing the Sacred Feminine and Sacred Masculine—yet because so much of this crosses boundaries, we recommend you review both and use what best applies to you.

For many sisters, balancing the Sacred Feminine and the Sacred Masculine may mean dissembling the shadow feminine that can keep you invisible, empty, appearance- and youth-focused, powerless, and co-dependent. This also means inventorying your competitiveness with other sisters and how you use femininity (or suppression of femininity) to "win," as well as how you enforce patriarchal values (the shadow masculine) to keep your sisters in line. Examine the cultural and personal beliefs you hold around women, including women's roles, women's wisdom, and women's equality, as well as the earth. You may want to make a list. Are these beliefs colored by patriarchal values or your own experiences at the mercy of the shadow feminine? This also means assessing your own nurturing intuitive nature—where that lives in you, as well as how and why you value or suppress this nature. In this examination, ask yourself: When did you learn this? Was nurturing intuition represented with love or dismissed as something without value? Conversely, examine the cultural and personal beliefs you hold around your brothers, including men's roles, men's wisdom, and the cultural expectation that men are stoic protectors and providers. Are these "old" pictures that are outdated and no longer applicable, yet seem to linger?

For many brothers, balancing the Sacred Feminine and the Sacred Masculine may mean examining cultural and personal beliefs around men, men's roles, men's wisdom, and the same cultural expectation that men are stoic protectors and providers. This may also mean inventorying your competitiveness with other brothers and how you use masculinity (or exploit others' lack of masculinity) to "win" and how you enforce patriarchal values (the shadow masculine) to keep your brothers in line. For brothers, this also means assessing your own nurturing intuitive nature—where that lives in you, as well as how and why you value or suppress this nature. You'll also want to examine the cultural and personal beliefs you hold around your sisters, including women's roles, women's wisdom, and women's equality, as well as the earth. You may want to make a list. In this examination, ask yourself: When did you learn this? Was it taught with love or with cruelty? Are these beliefs colored by patriarchal values or your own experiences at the hands of the shadow feminine (details above)? Do you hold a persistent picture of the shadow feminine and are therefore unable to see the beauty and power of the Sacred Feminine? Are these "old" pictures that are outdated and no longer applicable, yet seem to linger?

For sisters and brothers, activating the Sacred Feminine brings you into connection with the Earth Mother and connects your own nurturing intuitive expression. This allows you to better employ the sacred art of reflection and dreaming, the pause needed to consider and weigh all sides of an issue or idea before taking action for the good of All Our Relations. Embracing the Sacred Masculine in partnership with the Sacred Feminine provides you with the data to initiate a clear active principle: if you can dream it, you can think it, and you can learn how to build it, using your creative imagination and the principles of co-creation.

The journey we include in this chapter and the linked journaling questions are intended to help you get in touch with your Sacred Feminine and Sacred Masculine energies at a deeper level. The Making Right Ceremony at the end of the chapter provides an opportunity to meld these sacred aspects into a better internal working partnership.

### Embracing Shadow

We've already talked about shadow in this chapter: the story of the white/black wolf within and the shadow aspects of the Sacred Feminine and Sacred Masculine. There is, of course, much more to this teaching, and shadow work is a significant study on its own. But one of the troubling characteristics we frequently see in personal evolution and spirituality movements that we want to address here is the tendency to ignore shadow, to "love and light" our shadow away, as if by not talking about it or acknowledging its existence, it will simply disappear.

Some forget the law of equilibrium that makes a case for the brighter the light, the darker the shadow. Shadow can be defined as those parts of us, beautiful *and* challenging, that are not yet accepted. These parts will persist, and perhaps even control your life, until they are acknowledged. Acknowledging our shadow—feeding the black wolf—allows us to bring what might be unknown into consciousness, so that we can heal it to continue on our Medicine Road and become the Visionaries, Teachers, Healers, and Warriors we were born to be.

Lest we forget, each of these formidable and powerful shamanic roles has a formidable and powerful shadow. We describe some of these shadow characteristics below. You will undoubtedly find others in the course of your experience.

- The shadow of the Visionary/Seer is the Fortune Teller, one who becomes a false prophet, pretending expertise and manipulating a "message" for an alternative agenda, sometimes money or prestige. This individual is smoke and mirrors, using artful and insightful projections to paint an inauthentic picture of themselves and suck in followers.

- The shadow of the Teacher/Wise One is the Judge, one who makes it their business to criticize under the guise of teaching (or quasi-caring), and tear down and destroy without building up and encouraging. This person uses wisdom as a way to cement their own superior position and creates confusion in order to control outcomes and people to their advantage.

- The shadow of the Healer/Medicine Person is the Martyr, one who ministers without being in personal balance, sometimes due to their own self-absorption or unhealed woundedness. This person rides the high of accomplishment and recognition as an addiction of sorts, and may indeed be an addict or exhibit borderline personality traits.

- The shadow of the Warrior/Protector is the Berserker or Gladiator, one who fights for the sake of fighting, angry bloodlust fueling the killing rage that consumes them. This person fights for recognition and power, not to protect those unable to protect themselves, but to feel the rush of the conflict and feed their own ego.

As we explore each role in this book, you will have an opportunity to see how these shadows might manifest, but one of the common ways to create imbalance is to forget the Wheel of Relationships and your various interactions with—and commitments to—all that is. How to be in relationships in a good way, in a balanced way, and the humility, respect, and love that occupy the center directions. This means that, regardless of your shamanic role, you are honoring your partnerships, respecting your family and ancestors, and showing gratitude while humbly doing the work.

## Law of Complementary Opposites

The Cherokee believe in the Law of Opposites. If we are the center of our own Medicine Wheel, we're full of opposites—up/down, left/right, in/out, masculine/feminine. Our world is full of opposites, too—day/night, black/white, earth/wind, fire/water, etc.

Many of us were taught that opposite connotes enemy, an opposition that creates conflict. Is that really true? Does it have to be true? What if it isn't? When we talk about embracing our shadow, the black wolf/white wolf story in this chapter, you get a hint there could be something different.

What is the complementary element for the wildfires raging in America's West? Many in the United States have been praying for it: rain! Water, in the right proportion, is a complement to fire. Vice versa, if we need to melt ice, what do we use? Why, fire.

So, if our shadows are our best early warning system, telling us something is out of balance, how can we use our anger, pain, grief, sorrow, procrastination, and all the other emotions we consider to be negative as helpers instead of enemies? If you're angry, you've probably been "triggered" by something. Your triggers are keys ... what's behind that door? It might be treasure. So perhaps you can use anger's opposite, for example deep breaths until you feel peaceful, and in peace, you can open that door to reveal your old wound and heal it. Can you see the possibilities this opens up?

There's more to this concept, though. Complementary opposites in society can learn to work together through honest, needs-based communication. Sandy has been married to her opposite for decades. Robin has admired their relationship for years. While Sandy's husband has a different spirituality, he supports hers. He's the guy who chops wood for her sweat lodge. She's the one who remains calm when there's a crisis. It works remarkably well.

The only way to co-create a better, more harmonious world that starts to meet the needs of all our relatives, human and other, is by working together and truly listening to our common needs. Then, those we see as our opposition receive the respect of being heard. Once they've been heard, they become more receptive to hearing us. Once all perspectives have been acknowledged and understood, we have opportunities to create change that benefits all. In today's divided world, this is absolutely necessary if we are ever to find balance, center and create a unified resonant field.

Everything in our world is vibration. The formula for creation is Sound + Light (Color) + Movement = Manifestation.

Talking is a vibration, a part of the sound current. Moving our hands, creating a physical model of our ideas, is movement. Letting our light and love shine, wearing particular colors, using color in a presentation, creates a vibration that either resonates (vibrates) with others or sets off negative emotions. We can learn to use sound, light, and movement to effectively communicate and create harmony and balance as we work together to transform outmoded systems into new methods, organizations, and infrastructure that supports life instead of destroying it.

We invite you to draw a line down a piece of paper and write your positive emotions and behaviors on the left, then think about their complementary opposite and write those on the right side of the paper. You may actually find that some of the things you've always thought were negative have some very positive applications.

## Talking Circle—Dispelling the Lie of Separation

### by Sandy D'Entremont

I was six years old when I began questioning the Catholic Church's teachings. Six. I'd just received my first Holy Communion and had been hearing a lot of catechism that insisted there was only one true God and that the Catholic Church was the one true church, and you'd *never* get to heaven if you weren't baptized into the church or "converted." That stopped me in my tracks (yes, even at six). I couldn't believe it. I couldn't believe that my best friend (a Presbyterian) who lived across the street would not go to heaven with me if we were one day hit by a bus because we rode our bikes too far out into the street (*we always did*). Or that her beloved cocker spaniel wouldn't go to heaven with us for that matter.

I drove my father crazy with questions. Why, I lamented ... *Why?* I never got a satisfactory answer.

My questioning persisted through childhood—I was a pain-in-the-rear kid, no bones about it—until I finally read enough about reincarnation by age twelve to declare myself a Buddhist. Bad timing on my part because it was right around my confirmation. But like a good Catholic girl, I obediently went through the ceremony along with all my friends. I even took the name my mother insisted I take (hers), rather than the name I wanted to take (Bernadette, as in the movie, *Song of Bernadette*, who was a dreamer and visionary, go figure).

When I finally got old enough to put some things into words and read some history, I cobbled together an opinion. Born sinners, the church told us we were inherently wrong from the beginning, and that they had the answers for us. Put your money in the collection plate, tell your secrets to the priest, live your one life according to their rules, attend their ceremonies so they could be your intermediaries with God, and you'll get your ticket to heaven. Religion seemed a masterful political, economic, and social institution that controlled the masses; made women, their sexuality, and their children property; expropriated land and resources and knowledge; and provided the government with an army of young men who were pre-absolved from any sin on their soul when killing in God's name.

Yet none of that would have been possible without prevalent monotheistic religions perpetuating the lie of separation. This lie is a belief in our separation from God, nature, other humans, other creatures; a separation from the Sacred Feminine who lives at the core of earth-based traditions; a separation from Gaia, the Earth Mother herself. Easier to exploit something not an integral part of you.

So, where might this lie live inside us? What does it mean? How do we unravel it?

We begin by digging deep into the bones of the stories we've been told, looking beneath the rubble to see how these tales and legends (and even holy texts) were slightly changed to support socio-political agendas. We look at our own stories and see the Western cultural overlays that may have kept our wildness and intuition jailed, kept us from communion with God. And we open the gates to our own innate wisdom, repair the relationships with the sacred inside and out.

Then, like our child selves, we ask questions: Why? Does this ring true for me? Is it an old story, an old picture, that has no place in my current life? Does this or that make sense and how does it impact future generations? How do I want to be in the world?

How do I dream myself whole? No longer separate.

And together we dream a new reality.

## Journey of the South

Ask your new totem or ally to guide you on a journey to meet the feminine and masculine within. This exercise can be done as a single journey or two individual journeys.

Trust that your guide will bring you to a place in the journey world where you'll be able to meet these distinct energies. They may take any form: an animal form, or a person, or a different type of being. In this journey, we ask that you approach this being with honor and respect and request to have a conversation with them. If you need assistance communicating with them, ask your ally to translate for you. You might ask these beings who they are, or what interests them. What are their ancestral, spiritual, or cultural lineages? What strengths do they bring and how can you adopt those strengths? How might these strengths manifest within you? How can you best honor them? What gift might you bring them when you visit again?

Prior to beginning the journey, consult the setup instructions described in Tools for Journeying in the Resources section at the end of the book. You may wish to also review the Journey World discussion in the chapter entitled Journeying with Bear.

Remember, we do not journey alone, so always call in your totem or guide before beginning. We recommend a fifteen-minute journey.

## Journal

1. After you complete your journey, use your journal to record the events and your impressions. Are either the feminine or masculine beings you encountered someone or something familiar?

2. Describe these feminine and masculine beings, their ancestral, spiritual, and cultural lineages, if they shared that information. If an animal or animallike, conduct research to discover: what are its habits, habitats, strengths, patterns? What does this animal mean to you? Is it predator or prey? If a different type of being, what characteristics and traits do they possess and where might those have originated? If possible, acquire or create a representation of these aspects for your altar.

3. If you were to classify what role best fits these aspects of yourself—Seer, Teacher, Healer, Warrior—what might it be? What does that reveal about yourself?

4. Where would these beings sit on the Medicine Wheel? What does that tell you about them?

5. If you feel called to, return to the journey world with your ally and ask the feminine and masculine representatives any additional questions. How might your new ally help you? What can you bring them in appreciation for their counsel? What and how does this ally like to be called?

6. Use your journal to record dreams and other visions experienced during this time. Identify how these supplement or clarify your work in the south.

## Assignment

For the next three weeks—twenty-one days—your task will be to write for approximately fifteen or twenty minutes per day. The effectiveness of this exercise depends on its being done every day, preferably at the same time each day. There are several parts to this assignment.

First, you'll begin by writing about "The Ultimate BE-ing." This person is the most balanced, inspired, and enlightened person you can imagine.

Begin each day's essay with the phrase "The Ultimate ..." Describe the details of this person's life: where they go, who they are in the community, where they live. Describe how they look: posture, manner of walking, sound of voice, style and color of clothes, etc. You've got lots of time to be descriptive. During the three weeks, explore every aspect of this ultimate person's life.

- Significant relationships and family
- Job or daily routine
- Living environment and location
- Recreational activities and interests
- Spiritual practices
- Important possessions
- Talents and abilities (such as artistic or culinary, business or organizational, physical or dexterous, people skills, etc.)

And then, second, turn the page and write about their shadow, the opposite of their light, things that trigger them, irritate them, get under their skin. Things that make them angry, sad, afraid, immobilized, impatient. Wounds they carry, external or internal. Shame, guilt, addictions, grief, and traumas, seen and unseen.

For the first half of your writing session each day, you'll write about a person who is the same sex as your birth sex, and their light/shadow. For the second half of the session, write about a person who is the opposite sex of your birth sex, and their light/shadow. If you find these distinctions blur a bit, that's totally fine. Go with it and explore that.

You'll find that your writing will go through stages, or a progression. Perhaps for a day or so you will write along the same thoughts or in the same form, and then another day it will seem radically different. Just keep going. This writing exercise is an important commitment and, in the end, you'll find it valuable.

Of course, the process may bring up issues for you. Remember: what comes up is on its way out. Use your journal (or an alternative method that works for you, such as a recorder or art or dance) to process your thoughts and feelings, and to gain clarity and understanding. The shadow pieces may be the most challenging, but it is important to keep these questions in mind: How have your "negative shadows" helped you survive? Can you embrace them with love, knowing that they have been your early warning system, telling you that something is wrong? Can you find empathy and compassion for the self?

At the end of the three weeks, you will begin to release what you no longer need in the manner that works best for you. Use your completed essays in the following ceremony.

Remember to also use your journal to record dreams, journeys, conversations, and other experiences that occur during this time. Identify how these support or clarify your relationship work.

### Making Right Ceremony

This is a Making Right Ceremony. For a list of tools and general setup instructions, see the Tools for Ceremony discussion in the Resources section at the end of the book. (See also the Calling Ceremony description in the previous chapter.)

Read the ceremony through before beginning. Note that for this ceremony, you'll want to also:

- Place a representation of the feminine and masculine representatives you met in your journey in the center

- Set something black and something white side by side in the south

- Request the presence of guides and other helpers, particularly the new ally who came to you during your recent work in the east

- Bring your last Ultimate essay to read aloud to yourself, including the shadow aspects

Circle the wheel once, calling in the powers of the Seven Sacred Directions with your drum or rattle, and pray, asking them to help you unite the masculine and feminine within, as well as the light and shadow. Enter at the gateway in the south, circle the wheel clockwise again, and sit in the place of the Teacher in the south.

Read a part of your Ultimate essay to read aloud to yourself, including the shadow aspects. Remember the story of the white and black wolf, perhaps even read it again, and consider the questions we mentioned earlier: How have your "negative shadows" helped you survive? Can you embrace them with love, knowing that they have been your early warning system, telling you that something is wrong? Can you find empathy and compassion for the self? Sit with these questions and thoughts, then rattle around yourself to "shake up" your energy field so you can adopt and embrace this new information, to see the black wolf that lives inside you and make friends with him.

Now, imagine the feminine and masculine representatives you met in your journey are sitting in the circle with you, the male representative in the east, the female in the west. To support your work going forward, it is important these two begin working more closely together as partners, each respecting the other's gifts and abilities. As a step toward future partnership, the next part of this exercise involves a Ho'oponopono ceremony, also called a forgiveness ceremony, based on Hawaiian teachings. In some traditions, this would be called a Making Right Relationship ceremony. You will be performing this ceremony on behalf of the Sacred Masculine/Feminine within yourself. Your challenge is to act as translator for them, as needed.

Ho'oponopono is a method of conflict resolution and problem-solving used to set relationships right. This process clears any wrongdoing, releasing the negative effects of past and present indiscretions by physically, mentally, and spiritually cleansing using prayer, confession, amends, forgiveness, restitution, and transmutation, via honest communication. In this way, you can cut the invisible cords that bind parties to the wrongdoing (both in current and past lives)—victim(s) *and* perpetrator(s)—then choose to make a renewed commitment to a relationship based on harmony. This is a simple, condensed explanation for a complex set of teachings handed one generation to the next in Hawaii for hundreds of years, a considerable study in itself.

Begin with the representative who shares the same sex as your birth sex. In this example we are starting with the Sacred Masculine.

Close your eyes and rattle softly. In a prayerful way, imagine you are speaking to the sacred masculine representative you met on your journey.

Ask him if he is willing to sit down with the Sacred Feminine representative and participate in the Making Right Relationship ceremony. This may or may not take some convincing. Listen and understand his resistance, then find a way to bring him to the meeting. Perhaps using some language that hints he would be meeting an ally or partner that could help him be more productive and effective in the world, and that to do that the two of them need to clear up any past misunderstandings.

Now repeat for the Sacred Feminine representative you met on your journey.

For purposes of this exercise to unite the Sacred Masculine and Sacred Feminine, we are outlining the "short form" of Ho'oponopono. Begin with the Sacred Masculine: four steps, four statements: *I'm sorry. Please forgive me. Thank you. I love you.* If, during the process, other details come forward, fill them in. The italics represent an *example*:

1. I'm sorry *for discounting your wisdom and ignoring your guidance...*

2. Please forgive me *for not trusting you...*

3. Thank you *for all that you've tried to do to keep me in balance...*

4. I love you, *and I vow to listen more. That is my promise to you.*

Now sit and listen inside to the Sacred Masculine. Is there more that needs to happen, such as a discussion? If so, let your creative imagination accommodate this. Does the Sacred Feminine have something to share at this point? Be present for yourself with this process.

Now repeat for the Sacred Feminine, four steps, four statements: *I'm sorry. Please forgive me. Thank you. I love you.* If, during the process, other details come forward, fill them in. The italics represent an *example*:

1. I'm sorry *for discounting your wisdom and ignoring your guidance...*

2. Please forgive me *for not trusting you...*

3. Thank you *for all that you've tried to do to keep me safe...*

4. I love you, *and I vow to listen more. That is my promise to you.*

Now sit and listen inside to the Sacred Feminine. Is there more that needs to happen, such as a discussion? If so, let your creative imagination accommodate this. Does the Sacred Masculine have something to share at this point? Be present for yourself with this process.

If you find that both representatives come willingly to the circle and participate in a different type of discussion, or if they choose to speak the four statements outlined together in some fashion, simply allow this to unfold as it will. When all seems complete, then rattle around yourself to "shake up" and reset your energy field so you can adopt and embrace this new information and forge this new partnership.

Before you leave the circle, bless and release the powers of the Seven Sacred Directions with your drum or rattle following the opposite order in which you called them. Thank them for their witnessing. Bless the Sacred Masculine and Sacred Feminine representatives who sat with you this day, as well as your totems and guides, your ancestors, and the spirit of the land on which you stand. Exit the circle counterclockwise. Return everything on your site to its natural order, leaving the space a little better than how you found it.

*Note: We give great thanks to our Hawaiian teachers who brought the Ho'oponopono tradition forward for the good of All Our Relations. We honor Aunty Nahi Guzman, Aunty Mahialani, and Morrnah Simeona for this work, as well as the other Hawaiian Wisdom Keepers who generously shared and continue to share their wisdom. Deep, deep Aloha.*

## *Chapter 6*

---

# HEALING IN THE WEST

In the west, we encounter and embrace the aspects that reflect and support our journey as a Healer. You may find other traditions place the aspects in a slightly different manner, or that certain aspects may come to your attention strongly in a direction other than the one expected. This is all a part of the mystery of the wheel and the timeless medicine of these teachings.

## ASPECTS OF THE WEST

|  |  |
|---:|:---|
| Element: | Water |
| Embodiment: | Fluidity/Emotion |
| Emotions: | Grief/Joy |
| Season: | Autumn |
| Day Cycle: | Dusk |
| Moon Cycle: | Waning |
| Phase of Life: | Mature Adult |
| Color: | Black |
| Creatures: | Swimming Ones |
| Expression: | Flowing Water, Waves against the Shore/Silence |
| Way: | Mirror, Dreamer, Healer |

| | |
|---:|:---|
| Place on the Wheel: | Fluid Balance |
| Lesson: | Introspection and Dreaming |
| Relationship: | Family / Small Groups |
| Wheel within Wheel: | Ceremonies |
| Ceremony: | All |

. . . . . . . . . . . . . . . . . . . . . . .

As you move into the west, you step into the cleansing waters, the dreamtime, the realm of emotion. In the west we find the element of water, fluidity and flexibility. Water always seeks its balance, and as we employ the skill of introspection, we too seek the balance dreaming and healing provide in our lives.

When you come to the west, you bring teachings from the east and south, vision and trust and innocence, to gaze openly and honestly into the mirror of introspection. White Bear stands behind you, asking you to go deeper, see clearer, dream into your choices, your desires, and dive under the surface in order to reveal patterns which no longer serve you or wounds that need healing. Remember, if you don't like what you see in the mirror, you can heal it and change it. And, when *you* change, the reflection in the mirror changes.

Represented by the color black, west invites us into the depths of our emotions, into the dusky night, into the murky waters, to bring whatever needs to be understood and healed to light. In the west, you are at the phase of mature adult, willing to take responsibility for all that brought you to this moment. In this way, you can mourn losses, process grief, release past indiscretions, employ forgiveness, and be reborn, renewed. And you can be there for others who wish to do the same.

West is associated with all forms of water: ocean, lake, stream, river, and the cool rain. Humans are, after all, mostly water, as is our lovely planet. Healing waters have been part of cultural myths throughout the world. The Cherokee have a legend of a healing lake located in the upper reaches of the Blue Ridge Mountains where animals go to be healed of their wounds. Legend says that when a bear is wounded by hunters or as a result of a conflict with another bear, they journey to this mountain lake, plunge into the waters, and swim to the opposite shore, where they emerge restored.

The expression in the west is the sound of flowing water, a calm and soothing balm to our mental and emotional bodies, our very souls. We find the swimming ones in the west: Salmon, Dolphin, Seal, Otter, along with Bear and her dreaming.

Bear Dreaming is the act of bringing information and wisdom from the dreamtime to inform our healing, allowing us to see with different eyes—compassionate, loving, and caring eyes—to transform and do the work that needs to be done for All Our Relations. Making time, taking pause, to dream, consider, weigh, and balance also informs your choices and the impacts downstream of those choices, the impact on others in the Sacred Hoop of life—not only other two-leggeds, but all nations, as well as Mother Earth and the environment. This is a step often missing in many decision-making cycles, both for individual and collective decisions, such as those made in businesses and by governments.

Shaman as Healer resides in the west. There are healers who help cure dis-ease in the physical body, those who focus on healing the mental or emotional body, as well as those who help address dis-eases of the spirit. Shaman as Healer works in partnership with not only the individual, but also the family, the spirits, and the ancestors. Healing is a collaborative pro-cess—healer or healers, healee, and often partners or families, all focused on what needs to be done for balance to be restored and health to return.

Bear is known as a healing totem. The Mi'kmaq, originally of Canada's eastern Maritime Provinces, tell how Muin (Bear) became keeper of the medicines.

> In the beginning, people lived in harmony with the land. They lived in harmony with their brothers and sisters, the plants and trees, the four-leggeds, insects, reptiles, the swimmers and the flyers, fish and birds. The people realized plants and animals were of Spirit, placed here on Mother Earth to help them. They were grateful for the help of the animals, the plants, and the trees, and for that they wanted to honor them. One day they heard a beautiful bird song, and realizing how this tiny creature made them feel, they wanted to sing in return, to make the spirit of the animals feel as they did when they heard the birds. So they prayed, asking for songs from the spirits to sing.

*And the songs came to the people: songs to be sung to the spirit of the eagle, the spirit of the tree, the spirit of the water—songs for all their relations.*

*One day Muin (Bear) was in the forest, and he heard one of these songs sung by the people. A song in his honor, many voices carried by the wind into the forest. When Muin heard this beautiful song, he felt honored and respected. He traveled to the edge of a clearing in the forest and saw the people in ceremony. As he watched and listened, he saw the offerings being made to his spirit, and he heard the kind words the people spoke of him. They referred to him as Brother. Then he heard the people ask him for medicines to help them.*

*At that moment, Muin realized he must make a journey for the people and bring back medicines. All summer long he ate … and he ate … preparing for his task. Finally, when fall came, he knew it was time. He sought a lodge where his physical form would be safe while his spirit traveled. Knowing he would be gone for several moons, as he approached his lodge, he looked back on the world one last time. Finally, with the words "All My Relations," he entered.*

*And so the spirit of Muin began its quest into the spirit world. As he journeyed, he collected the medicines the people humbly requested. He sat in council with the spirits of the plant people and sought their wisdom. The plants agreed to give their medicines, so long as Muin would cultivate and fertilize the land for them, so they could continue to return year after year. Muin agreed.*

*Finally, after many moons, Muin's journey was nearing its end. He wanted to let the people know he would be returning soon, so his spirit found a woman of the Bear Clan, praying in the sweat lodge. Muin spoke to her: "From this day, you shall be known as Muiniskw, the Bear Woman. I have a request: I am soon completing my spirit journey and returning to my physical*

*form. Would you be so kind as to prepare a Feast for me, as I
am weak?"*

*The woman knew that when a spirit made a request of a human,
it was to be done. Muiniskw listened to Muin's request—how the
Feast would be prepared and what ceremonies to be performed—
then she brought the request to the people. She told them of her
vision in the lodge, and Muin's request. The people immediately
began preparations for the Feast. Muiniskw told of the berries
Muin requested, the berries he feasted on through the year. He
wanted to honor the spirit of the plants that provided him this
food, as they also provided food for the people.*

*And so it was. People brought berries dried and stored over the
winter. Strawberries, first berry in the spring; blueberries, fruit
of summer; blackberries from fall; and cranberries gathered
in early winter. Then, the men went out to their weirs and
gathered fish to include in the Feast.*

*Four days after the Bear Spirit spoke to Muiniskw the Feast Day
arrived. The berries and fish were prepared by Muiniskw, and
more food was prepared by other women. As the people sat in
a Sacred Circle, the ceremony began with the Sacred Pipe, and
as the pipe was shared a story was told: the story of why we
must always honor the Bear Spirit. In the fall we honor him for
his long fast, and the journey he is about to make into the spirit
world for medicines for the people. In the spring we honor Bear
for the medicines he brings back from his long journey. In both
ceremonies a woman of the Bear Clan prepares the Feast for the
Bear, and in both ceremonies a song is sung to honor Muin.*

*And so it continues to this day. Muin tills and fertilizes the
ground to help plants grow, and during the long cold winter
he journeys to the spirit realm to seek medicines for the people.
And each year, fall and spring, native people gather together for
a feast in his honor.*

(As told to Sandy D'Entremont)

In this story, it is not only Muin's dreaming that brings healing medicines to the people, but the listening of Muiniskw, the Bear Woman, who honors and helps him return from the spirit world, and the collaborative efforts of the people who prepare a feast in gratitude. Shaman as Healer reminds us that we do not heal alone, for even in the most solitary healing journey, we are often walking the same trails as those who have gone before us. And we always have the spirits by our side.

Shaman as Healer caretakes the people, including him- or herself. Even Muin knew that to continue his work for the people, he needed sustenance, for he was weak, so he asked for help. Without care for the self, you may not be able to be in service to others the way you would like to be. Martyr is the shadow side of the healer. Knowing yourself and your limitations—as well as using the pause of prayer, introspection, and dreaming—allows you to evaluate what work is yours to do and what work is appropriate for you to do at any given time. And remember, when living and working in community, asking for help gives others a chance to learn, contribute, and participate, the synergy often expanded by the additional energy.

## Wheel of Ceremonies

The wheel we are exploring in the west is the Wheel of Ceremonies. This wheel illustrates the way different ceremonies, rituals, and healing practices, including initiations, fit together on the Medicine Wheel. Ceremonies can range from private and personal to global in scope.

As we discuss in the section titled Ceremony Design in the Resources section at the end of this book, ceremony is defined as an activity prescribed by custom, ritual, or religious belief that unites group members and celebrates accomplishments or milestones. There are a few differences between ritual and ceremony as practiced by native peoples: generally, rituals are contained within ceremony, and there may be several ritual components in a complete ceremony. The section entitled Honoring Sacred Ceremonies provides expanded descriptions on the ceremonies we list on the following page. These ceremonies follow a common pattern adjusted and expanded by facilitators in accordance with the way they were taught.

The Wheel of Ceremonies reflects the different focus certain types of ceremonies typically hold. Placing the ceremonies on the Medicine Wheel provides a different lens for understanding the intention, participants, and range of influence. Yet there are overlaps in all of these areas, within and without. Threads woven in one ceremony impact other people and other ceremonies, ripples that touch us personally and collectively.

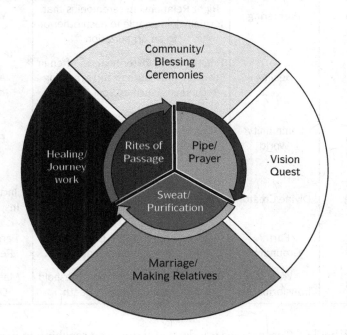

### *Ceremonies*

**Cardinal Points**

East—Visioning

South, Partnering—Making relationships

West, Dreaming—Healing and journey work

North, Community—Blessings and gratitude

**Center Directions**

Below, Earth—Grounding and purification

Above, Divine—Prayer

Center, Transformation—Rites of passage

| Direction | Focus | Ceremony | Phase |
|-----------|-------|----------|-------|
| East | Visioning | Vision Quest and other practices, both individual and collective, that foster going apart to seek inspiration and insight | No Form to Birth |
| South | Partnering | Marriage, Adoption, and Making Right Relationship ceremonies that formally join people to each other or to an organization | Youth |
| West | Healing | Practices that foster healing, often in concert with journey and dreaming techniques, such as Soul Retrieval | Adult |
| North | Community/World | Specific Blessings, Seasonal Celebrations, Sun Dance, usually done for and with community involvement | Elder |
| Above | Divine/Creator | Prayer and gratitude ceremonies in communication with the Divine, such as Pipe Ceremony | Inception, Inspiration |
| Below | Earth/Grounding | Moon Lodge, Sweat Lodge, and other purification ceremonies | Perpetual, Renewal |
| Center | Within/Transformation | Rites of passage and other threshold ceremonies: Birth to Death | Mastery to Death |

The Wheel of Ceremonies is a deep and nuanced teaching in itself, some practices learned only through apprenticeship under a Wisdom Keeper or medicine person. For some of these ceremonies, experience is unquestionably the master teacher. We cannot stress enough the importance of training before attempting to facilitate many of these rituals or perform these practices. Unfortunately, both participants and facilitators can be and have been harmed emotionally, mentally, spiritually, and physically; some have even died.

Ceremonies can range from those steeped in tradition and strict protocol to those you design for yourself. Every facilitator follows the ceremonial processes and protocols as they have been taught. These protocols include elements such as:

- Setting sacred space
- Using smoke for clearing and cleansing
- Creating an altar
- Praying for protection
- Setting intention
- Calling the circle: directions, spirits, ancestors, and helpers
- Inviting participation from those present
- Performing the ceremony, ritual, or healing work, which can include:
  - Meditation and journeying
  - Drumming, singing, chanting, dancing to raise energy
  - Purification
  - Prayer
  - Healing techniques
  - Other ritual components
  - Grounding or releasing the energy raised
- Sending ancestors and helpers home
- Closing the ceremony or the circle
- Feasting and community cleanup

Each of these steps is important and typically performed with intention and attention, regardless of whether it is noticeable to participants. The Resources section at the back of this book covers these practices in detail. In *Journey of the White Bear*, we have designed a series of ceremonies to augment the work you do in each direction chapter, with details in the Resources section to research as a foundation before performing them.

Ceremonial tools can include herbs, flowers, fruit, liquor, water, earth, fire, wands and staffs, animal medicines, jewelry (power pieces), headdresses, mirrors, crystals, other stones, feather fans, and other items. Ceremonial instruments—which can also be considered tools for certain functions—include drums, rattles, flutes, singing bowls, chimes, whistles, harp, harmonium, chants, songs, and dances. These tools and instruments are also discussed in detail in the Resources section at the back of this book. These objects will vary by facilitator based on their lineage, traditions, preferences, and the intention of the ceremony.

## Personal Initiation and Rites of Passage

Personal initiation ceremonies and rites of passage allow us to recognize and celebrate transformations that nudge us from one way of walking in the world to another. These rites encompass celebrations that mark personal milestones, such as birth, bat/bar mitzvah or confirmation, graduation, marriage or a commitment to an organization or career, parenthood, retirement, and finally dropping our robes/death.

In mainstream Western culture, however, some of these rites have either lost their meaning, or their significance rendered all but trite—think ridiculous baby shower games or roasting a retiree as he dons a gold watch. Without an initiatory rite of passage to guide someone to the next life phase, individuals can remain in stasis, wearing their old ill-fitting shoes. This can often lead to remaining in a perpetual childhood or adolescence, never crossing the threshold to adulthood or mastery or eldership at the appropriate times—not to mention never embracing the spiritual adulthood needed to and discover and pursue a life purpose for All Our Relations over a lifetime.

Initiatory rites of passage typically include three phases: 1) detaching from the old role and separating from community for a time to give space for envisioning what is to come; 2) crossing the threshold into liminal space away from a familiar home so that the divine, universal, cosmic, or spiritual might inform the initiate's next role; and 3) returning or rebirthing back into the world to take up that new role and shouldering the attendant responsibilities. Mythologist Michael Meade, author of *The Water of Life: Initiation and the Tempering of the Soul*, writes: "What initiates us also strips us down to the inner essentials and releases qualities and powers that were hidden within." In this chapter, we briefly discuss three types of rites of passage: adolescence to adulthood, adult life transition, and adulthood to eldership.

## *Adolescence to Adulthood*

Adolescence to adulthood is one of the key initiatory rites of passage that not only fosters self-discovery, but accepts the youth and sees the unique gifts they bring in service to the community, perhaps even calling the youth into service in some way even if they are not yet old enough to work a job. We cannot stress enough how empowering and healing it is to simply be seen and appreciated. This gift of initiation, held in a container by non-judgmental and mature adult leaders, moves the adolescent further through maturation by providing a space for them to make the connection to something greater than themselves, to see their importance on the Wheel of Life, and to begin to take responsibility for their actions and consequences.

Initiation encourages and channels the individuation process and accepts the adolescent's wildness, rather than leaving their maturation stunted in self-absorbed invincibility, competitiveness, greed, and childish entitlement.

- For women, this initiation traditionally accompanied menarche, the entrance to the Moon Lodge, the point at which a girl turns to womanhood and where her womb could carry a child. This point in a girl's life becomes one of great celebration and responsibility: celebration for her maturity, and her responsibility for her body to ensure future generations.

- For men, this initiation traditionally accompanied his transition to provider, warrior, hunter, and protector; the point as a teenager at which a boy turns to manhood and where his skills begin to emerge and are honed. This point in a boy's life becomes one of great celebration and responsibility: celebration for his maturity, and his responsibility to his family and people to ensure future generations.

- For men and women both, some cultural traditions included a sexual rite of passage as part of the initiation to adulthood; note, however, sexual initiation in and of itself is not the equivalent of the adolescence-to-adulthood initiations that transition an individual mentally and emotionally across this threshold.

Unfortunately, when the patriarchy, and later, colonialists, began stripping away sovereignty, personal power, earth wisdom, and individual connection to the Divine from those they conquered, they began perpetuating a cultural adolescence, an immaturity, where the conquered are dependent on the conquerors. The ripple effects of this "power-over" dynamic still apply to individuals *and* communities, and those with power-over are nearly as wounded by their fear of losing power, control, and comforts as are those who are oppressed and controlled by power-over.

Personal initiation and spiritual adulthood are the medicine that will eventually beget community healing, equality, and empowerment. This work is ours to do.

## Adult Life Transitions

Adult life transitions are those we are classifying as personal milestones, the type of milestone where, from that point forward, you walk differently in the world. You have demonstrated some form of mastery and may shoulder responsibilities and perform tasks you could not before. Often, this transition incorporates a title, and you may be addressed differently, such as a military rank or an academic or medical degree. Other times the title is religious, such as becoming a nun or pastor, or even professional, such as obtaining some licensure. This transition could mean something as earth-shattering as becoming a parent or getting a divorce, changing your name, or taking on a spirit name or even a pen name.

In some circles, this life transition comes when your apprenticeship ends and you are able to conduct a particular ceremony or ritual, such as becoming a Wiccan priest or priestess, sweat lodge pourer, or pipe carrier. True shamanic initiation, however, is a category in and of itself. These types of initiations can be those ceremonies and rituals performed by a Wisdom Keeper or medicine person after someone completes an apprenticeship; practices vary between traditions. Or the initiation can be an event that erupts as a personal healing crisis or series of visions that takes the prospective shaman to the brink of death and returns them changed; in this way we say the spirits are the initiators.

The specifics of these transitional rites of passage will vary by culture, institution, and tradition. Graduation ceremonies are one of the most familiar mainstream events that mark these occasions. Yet there remains an expansive opportunity for us to create meaningful ceremonies to honor phases of mastery, ceremonies that guide us through the gate and across the threshold in a more meaningful way *and* allow us to share our light with others.

As with the transition from adolescence to adulthood, these individualized rites of passage may include the three phases discussed earlier in some form. With the return to community, you are seen in your new skin, and witnessed by whomever you invited to share the experience. The exercise in this chapter helps you design your own ceremony to celebrate a transition important to you. Also, as an adult, it's important to note that some of these transitions take you further down the trail to eldership, discussed in the next section.

## Adulthood to Eldership

Adulthood to eldership is the initiatory rite of passage most overlooked in mainstream Western culture. This oversight is linked to a cultural obsession with youth and a perception that denigrates aging by associating it with the inevitability of decline, thus fostering the practice of shutting elders away so we are not reminded of our own mortality. Marginalized and rendered invisible, elders wither and withdraw, an untapped resource relegated to the TV room. Yet the image of the gray-haired elder is a familiar one when we see portraits of America's bewigged founding fathers, a tradition that persists in some royal courts and courts of law. Gray locks still mean a wise and noble head, useful and sought after in some parts of the world.

With the stigma attached to aging, it is not surprising many older people have a bucket of resistance to being considered an elder, which is one of the reasons why hair dye companies are so profitable. But unfortunately—and perhaps surprisingly to many readers—the suicide rate among elders is growing. Shifting our cultural perspective around elders is key to embracing our own initiation into spiritual eldership, so we can minister to the world we find ourselves in, to love more deeply, to give and receive more fully, to continue creating, learning, changing, and to be of greater service to All Our Relations into our older years.

Indigenous cultures respect and honor elders for their wisdom and cultural knowledge. They are the carriers of our history as a people, our traditions, our family stories. The Hawaiians and other indigenous tribes call their elders Living Treasures and honor a few of them publicly every year. Elders possess the wisdom of many years' experience, having seen and experienced generations of elders before them. They have much to teach us about aging, about life. Like Whale, they are our record keepers, a living history. The life stories and traditional stories of our elders are always priceless, and often impart life-changing insights.

Transitioning to elderhood can mean many things. Some definitions include becoming a grandparent or retiring from regular work; others mark it with an age, such as seventy or eighty, or in some other fashion. These individualized rites of passage may also include the three phases mentioned earlier. This gift of initiation, often held gently by nonjudgmental peers, moves the adult into their next phase of life by providing a space for them to again make the connection to something greater than themselves and to see their importance on the Wheel of Life. This initiation encourages deepening personal growth, the opportunity for healing and forgiveness, and the ability to make sense of our individual stories, integrate dualities, and embrace new perspectives.

- For women, this initiation traditionally accompanied menopause, the time when a woman is said to hold her wise blood and take her place on the wisdom councils, a time of increased responsibility for her community. Also, this time often coincided with children growing to adulthood and a woman becoming a grandmother.

- For men, this initiation traditionally accompanied a transition to leader, teacher, mentor: the time when a man began to teach the skills learned and honed over a lifetime and took his place on the wisdom councils, a time of increased responsibility for his community.

Spiritual eldership will facilitate community and, eventually, global unity. It can heal family grievances and build a firmer foundation for youth to channel their gifts. We are seeing this happening now with Grandmother and Grandfather Wisdom Societies across the planet.

## Talking Circle—Healing the War Within

*by Robin Youngblood*

I want to share a bit about my personal healing journey, because I think it's important to help each of us understand that we must heal ourselves first if we want to heal the world.

In my late twenties and early thirties, I had to take a close look at the war within myself. Part European Catholic heritage, part Native American Indian beginning on the Red Road. Now THAT'S a dichotomy!

During my mother's era, it wasn't safe to be Indian. As a blonde, blue-eyed Cherokee, she could (and did) pass as white. She made my hawk-nosed, black-haired, brown-eyed father say we were Italian, so he could get jobs. She forbade my grandmothers to speak our native languages to me and took away the medicine pieces they gave me "until I was older and could understand" (translation: she knew if I carried them, I'd talk about them—*and she was right*).

My father proudly served America in WWII. He returned an alcoholic. Nobody understood PTSD then, but, having married a Vietnam veteran who was also native, I understand my father far better now. Our people know that warriors are protectors. They don't murder and rape women and children. They protect them. They don't kill unnecessarily. My father saw things that were beyond his comprehension. He was a bitter man, a loving man, a proud man. He never healed the war within himself.

So, I had to look at what it means to be a mixed blood. My ancestors killed each other—far more on the white side than the dark. How could I reconcile that? I chose to learn more about my native heritage, and I've followed that spiritual path ever since. Eventually, I had to forgive my pioneer settler ancestors, and realize that some of them married my native ancestors, when they could have killed them.

I'm also a modern woman, a citizen of the world because of my travels. I live in a house on land I've bought. I drive a car that uses gasoline (a hybrid, but still ... ). I buy things wrapped in plastic, made from oil. I recycle, yes, but every time I open a plastic package, I pray that we will stop buying these things, and tell the manufacturers to stop using plastic. And I'm buying less.

I don't grow my own garden because I'm not home enough. I do buy organic, locally grown vegetables and eat hormone- and antibiotic-free meat—preferably, wild meat, hunted responsibly, whenever its possible.

What I do is *ceremony*. Ceremonies to honor the elements— Mother Earth, the Four Winds, the Sacred Fires, and the Waters of Life. I do ceremony whether I'm alone or with others. I do prayer ceremonies to ask for the healing of all life, and ceremonies to give thanks for all life. I believe every step, every breath, is a prayer, and I try to be conscious of it. I fail, often, and I keep trying.

I serve on several councils that bring people together to share culture, wisdom, and ceremony at Wisdom Gatherings in many parts of the world. And I share ... I share the foundational values that indigenous people around the world practice, and that they passed on to me to share with others.

Why say all this? Because I want you to understand that you likely have a war within you, too. Every one of us is indigenous to Mother Earth. We all KNOW we are desecrating her, using up and defiling the very being that gives us life.

Until each of us heals the dichotomy within and learns to live in right relationship to All Beings, we will continue to destroy life. We are born terminal, and it's death we fear most. In fearing our death, many of us numb ourselves every way we can, denying its reality. In denying our own death, we hasten it by killing off everything that keeps us alive. Not only do we do this to ourselves, we do it to our children and grandchildren. Don't think they don't see it. They know at a very young age. They're angry and they're sad. The incidence of child suicide is epidemic across all cultures now. Despair is rampant. Our children need us to heal the wars within ourselves!

I originally wrote this essay a few years ago, when I had been helping a tiny bit during the Standing Rock confluence. I was glad to see people of all nations and tribes gathering and standing at

Standing Rock. FINALLY! This is the true meaning of Warrior—we are Protectors. We are one Human Family, the only species on Earth who can stop the destruction we've created. And it's not just Standing Rock. It's the Amazon, Peru, Ecuador, Europe, Africa, and Asia. The desecration needs to STOP, so we can let the healing BEGIN— both for ourselves and for the planet. We've been forewarned by indigenous wise people for decades. Even science says if we don't turn things around now, we will create a mass extinction event, and may become extinct ourselves.

IT'S TIME! WE ARE THE ONES WE'VE BEEN WAITING FOR!

## Journey of the West

Ask your new totem or ally who joined you in the east to accompany you on a journey to seek guidance on the Life Transition threshold you most need to celebrate, the personal ceremony that would better allow you to acknowledge your path and accomplishments, as well as fully inhabit your own skin.

Trust that your guide will bring you to a place in the journey world where you'll be able to meet whomever you need to obtain this information. Honor the wisdom you receive. Ask your guides: What do you need to accept in yourself? What do you need to release? What do you need to heal? Is there a particular type of ceremony or healing they tell you is needed? A threshold to cross to a new way of being?

Prior to beginning the journey, consult the setup instructions described in Tools for Journeying in the Resources section at the end of the book. You may wish to also review the Journey World discussion in the chapter entitled Journeying with Bear.

Remember, we do not journey alone, so always call in your totem or guide before beginning. We recommend a fifteen-minute journey.

## Journal

1. After you complete your journey, use your journal to record the events and your impressions.

2. Did you receive answers to the questions you asked about fully inhabiting your own skin? What do you need to accept? What do you need to release? What do you need to heal? Is there a particular type of ceremony or healing that your guides tell you is needed? How do you begin to do that?

3. Take time to look back over the life path you've traveled. Think about where you were before you started this most recent spiral of learning—challenges you were dealing with, your understanding of self, your life situation. Consider writing a review in your journal, even it's a simple list of Before and Now observations, a list you can then reference in the future to see how you've grown over time.

4. Call in your teachers, guides, animal totem, and White Bear for council. Ask them what form your ceremony or healing should take. Meditate on what would best meet your needs. For example: Do you want to finally experience an adolescent-to-adulthood rite of passage? Is there a spirit name you wish to embrace? Are you ready for a healing ceremony? Or is there another adult life transition you wish to honor?

5. If you feel called, return to the journey world with your totem and have a conversation with your spirit guide to clarify any information.

6. Use your journal to record dreams, journeys, conversations, and other experiences during this time. Identify how these supplement or clarify your work in the west.

7. Review the Sacred Elements section at the back of this book and the information on ceremonies and healing practices: Life Transition and Giveaway, Sweat Lodge, Pipe, Making Right Circle, Prayer Ties, shamanic healing, etc. Your ceremony will undoubtedly incorporate one or more of these elements.

**Assignment**

During your life journey, you have undoubtedly attended many types of ceremonies, as well as performed certain ceremonies for yourself to help integrate and honor the teachings in this book. Although details in each ceremony differ, this simplified format is by now familiar. To honor your specific life transition, your assignment this month is to create a ceremony uniquely your own. This can take many forms; regardless of what you choose to do, it is intended to focus on your personal transformation and healing.

1. Identify the ceremony format that's right for you. Consult Sacred Elements in the Resource section for ideas. Now pray. Let go and trust.

2. If you feel called to, return to the journey world to have a conversation with your guides. How might this help you with this ceremony?

3. Pay attention to what occurs in your three-dimensional reality. What comes to your attention that might be the universe supporting your ceremony? Who walks into your life with skills or wisdom to contribute?

4. Decide whether you wish someone specific to facilitate this celebration. Or, better yet, keep things simple and design the ceremony yourself, perhaps sharing leadership.*

5. Choose a location, day, and time for your ceremony, remaining aware that many of these types of events work on "spirit time"— they start when they start and end when they end (remind other attendees of this too). Making plans before or after the ceremony is not recommended (but some of us have to learn that lesson through experience).

6. Select ceremony participants, friends, and relatives with whom you want to share this event and witness your accomplishment.*

7. Determine the best way to gift the facilitator, the facilitator's assistant, and the participants who come to support your day.*

*See the discussion on Facilitators, Participants, and Witnesses, and Gifting in the Setup for Group Meetings and Ceremonies discussion in the Resources section at the end of this book.

## *Personal Life Transition Ceremony*

Ceremony unites group members and celebrates life transition milestones, including healing. The ceremony you conduct for this chapter will be uniquely yours, celebrating YOU.

Although some of you may want to enlist the assistance of an experienced facilitator, we encourage you to dive in and plan this yourself. This is *your* rite of passage! You know how to call the circle—so text your friends, create the Medicine Wheel together, and assign each a task (a prayer, a poem, prayer ties, cleansing, drumming, a song, etc.).

Remember to review the Resources section in the back of this book that covers much of the basics you'll need to know, including: 1) the Setting up for Group Meetings and Ceremonies discussion in the Community appendix and 2) the Tools for Ceremony discussion in the Basic Tools appendix. These sections provide detailed step-by-step instructions, including a list of tools and general setup instructions.

If your ceremony includes other forms of Giveaway—either from you to the participants (typical) or from participants to you (both are optional but make for a special remembrance of the day), you may want to discuss this practice with the participants so there are no misunderstandings or embarrassment.

Consult the section on Facilitators, Participants, and Witnesses, and Gifting in the Community discussion located in the Resources section at the back of this book.

Enjoy your ceremony day!

Celebrate yourself, your accomplishments, your healing. Show your gratitude for all that has happened to bring you to this place in this moment, and for those who share this time with you. As always, when departing your ceremony location, try to leave the site more beautiful than when you found it by placing a small offering: a bundle of herbs, a flower, or a pinch of tobacco.

## *Chapter 7*

# COMMITTING IN THE NORTH

In the north, we encounter and embrace the aspects that reflect and support our journey as a Spiritual Warrior. You may find other traditions place the aspects in a slightly different manner, or that certain aspects may come to your attention strongly in a direction other than the one expected. This is all a part of the mystery of the wheel and the timeless medicine of these teachings.

## ASPECTS OF THE NORTH

| | |
|---:|:---|
| Element: | Mineral/Stones |
| Embodiment: | Mental |
| Emotions: | Gratitude/Serenity |
| Season: | Winter |
| Day Cycle: | Night |
| Moon Cycle: | New |
| Phase of Life: | Elder |
| Color: | White |
| Creatures: | Standing Ones (Trees) |
| Expression: | Rattle, Sticks, Bones |
| Way: | Mentor, Warrior |

| Place on the Wheel: | Standing in Truth |
|---|---|
| Lesson: | Wisdom/Power |
| Relationship: | Community |
| Wheel within Wheel: | Ancestors |
| Ceremony: | Seven Generations |

. . . . . . . . . . . . . . . . . . . . . . .

### Warriors—A Medicine Dream

*Robin woke from a dream of two wild geese pecking at each other.*

*Then they turned into two warriors fighting with spears, thrusting, blocking, thrusting again.*

*Then they turned into two mothers fighting over the same baby.*

*Then the scene switched. First, she was looking at seven lions sitting calmly in the middle of the road, doing nothing but enjoying the sun, yet their presence effectively blocked the drivers on the road.*

*The scene switched again, to an alpine meadow where mustangs and elk, deer, and a bobcat and a mouse all wandered and grazed freely—even the bobcat and mouse. Surrounding the meadow were camps of different tribes, some drumming, singing, dancing; some digging and gathering herbs for food and medicine; some sitting in talking circles; some in an intertribal council. Warriors from each village watched or provided assistance to those in need.*

*Robin woke abruptly with all of this still playing in her mind. She wondered if the bobcat would eventually eat the mouse, or if the mouse had a safe place close by.*

*She realized this was what we call a Medicine Dream. Usually, these dreams carry messages just for the dreamer. As she began to interpret what she'd seen, however, the spirits in the dream returned in waking time, each one urging her to share the messages. So here goes ...*

*Geese are the storytellers of the world. They fly great distances to tell us unavoidable change is happening—spring or fall is here. The change is inevitable. You can either move, as they do, or you can stay. Either way, the change of seasons is happening. These geese were arguing, pecking for one-upmanship, being "right," being top goose in the pecking order. Robin didn't hear or see the story they had told each other that created the argument. Why? Because the stories are just stories, opinions, ideas. The stories didn't matter. The arguments did. Because one had to be the winner, the right one, the one who owned the truth. That one got to move up the pecking order while the other was lowered and would have to submit. Another important aspect is they couldn't accomplish anything else. There was food all around them. They could have chosen to eat together, as the rest of the flock was doing ... but no, pecking at each other was more important.*

*Same with the two warriors. In the Haudenosaunee/Iroquois culture, "warrior" means those who carry the bones of the ancestors (heritage, cultural traditions, value systems) and Mother Earth on their backs. Doesn't sound like they're at war much, eh? Their job is to protect and care for the elders, women, and children. They hunt to feed the people. They make sure no one enters the village until they're sure they come in peace. They build the lodges and ceremonial grounds. When the women are in Moon Lodge, they bring furs and blankets to keep them warm. They cook and bring food to the women and take care of the children that week, every month. If an elder needs anything—their home needs repairs, they need wood for the stove in winter, they need medical help or traditional medicines—the warriors find and give what's needed. Do they get paid? In spiritual, mental, and emotional health, they get paid in acknowledgement and gratitude. In physical wealth, they get strong, trained bodies, adventures, the joy that comes from serving, food to keep them healthy, and the assurance that they're doing their part to keep the village safe and healthy.*

*But these men were fighting. It was obvious from their dress and position in the village they belonged to the same tribe. This was a challenge to gain authority and recognition. Again, ego. Others were watching, some cheering one man or the other. Nothing else was getting done. Some of the watchers were betting, making a game of the whole thing, until one warrior's spear pierced the other warrior's heart. Suddenly, everything became DEAD serious. The family and village were shocked. The warrior's death was a huge loss. The warrior's mother and sisters started keening in grief, loudly singing his death song, wailing and sobbing. Instead of being victorious, the villagers turned away from the killer. He'd gone too far, and the village ostracized him, at least for a time. Perhaps a karmic debt was created.*

*Then there were the two women, another village, another country, another culture, another time. They reminded Robin of the biblical story of Solomon. "Do you want me to slice this baby in half?" Each of these women so fervently believed the absolute truth that this baby was theirs and theirs alone, they might have said "yes" to Solomon. Robin didn't see the outcome. But she knew this raging argument over truth might well kill that baby. For what? Who can say they KNOW the truth, the whole truth, and nothing but the truth? We sure can't. We'd be the real birth mother who would either be willing to share the responsibilities and joys of mothering that child or give the baby away to save its life. And maybe Robin was that mother.*

—Robin Youngblood
July 2020

We are the result of the love of hundreds, if not thousands. We *all* have ancient blood. Stardust runs through our veins and lives in our bodies—minerals and water, and for those of us who have star being ancestry, even more. We are enlivened by the greatest ancestor of all, Creator, who breathes their life into us, and fills us with the fiery ember deep in our core that keeps us alive.

In the north, we connect with our ancestors to understand and activate the gifts they have passed down to us. There may be personal gifts, like a definite craving for a particular food. There are also many gifts that we receive so that we can be of service to Mother Earth and All Our Relatives. If we are on the Shaman's Path, these are lifelong gifts, talents, and skills inherited from those who came before us.

Some of us don't like certain ancestors. Perhaps abuse of some kind runs in your biological family line. There are ways to heal that, and they begin with you. Maybe you're adopted and don't know a thing about your natal family. There are ways to find out, to connect with both your biological and adopted ancestors.

In the north, what we're looking for first are the ancestors whose "job" it is to help you in this lifetime. To these loving ones, you are their inheritors, and they want the very best for you. In ancient cultures, tribal people made decisions that would affect many generations beyond them in the best way they could see. Indigenous people have a saying: "Unto the next seven generations and beyond." And there's far more to connect with and begin to understand.

## Wheel of Ancestors

As you'll see, we actually have several different lineages and relationships with all of them, conscious or not. According to the science of epigenetics, there are markers in our DNA that make us unconsciously react to trauma in the same way our ancestors many generations ago responded. Shamanic people have known this forever. We always chuckle when science finally catches up! And shamans have methods and ceremonies to help heal the multigenerational trauma that lives in our DNA. We even have a saying: when we heal something in ourselves, it heals the seven generations and more behind us, and the seven generations and more to come.

The Wheel of Ancestors works first with our blood (and often adopted) family in the east. If you've done a search on Ancestry.com or another site, you may already have learned some things about how Great-Aunt Jenny was a riveter in WWII, and Great-Great-Grandpa Jeremiah left Wales to come to America in the 1700s. That's a good starting point. But wouldn't you like to know more than names and birthdates? Good. Because you're going to take at least one journey to meet some of those foremothers and forefathers. Along the way, you can ask them to show you what lives in your DNA and learn a bit about how to use it to help yourself and others.

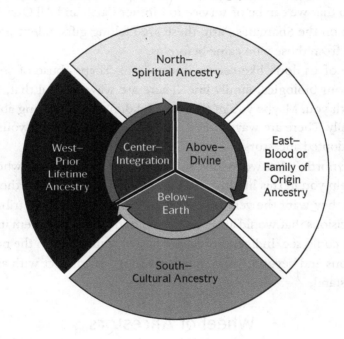

*Ancestors*

**Cardinal Points**

East—Family of Origin Ancestry (Blood or Adopted)

South—Cultural Ancestry

West—Prior Lifetime Ancestry

North—Spiritual Ancestry

**Center Directions**

Below—Earth Kinship

Above—Divine and Star Ancestry

Center—Personal Integration and Transformation

| Direction | Ancestry | Description | Source |
|-----------|----------|-------------|--------|
| East | Blood Lineage | Family of Origin (FOO) heritage which can also include adopted families and the inheritance of our race and gender | Beginning |
| South | Cultural Lineage | Socio-economic, political, organizational, religious, and often psychological inheritance | Learning |
| West | Lifetime Lineage | Inheritance from prior lifetimes, karmic and soul connections, even if from other life phases. Conscious understanding of ancestral patterning. | Dreaming/ Sensing |
| North | Spiritual Lineage | Spiritual resonance, could be different from what you inherited from your cultural lineage | Internal Beliefs |
| Above | Star Nations | Inheritance from star beings and from the Divine, of which we are all a spark | Beyond |
| Below | Mother Earth | Kinship with and inheritance from Earth, plants, animals, minerals, elements, places | All Our Relations |
| Center | Integration | The braid of lineages within, the unique tapestry you have been, are, and will be | Self |

When we move to the south, we look at our cultural lineage. Are we mastering our magic or muddling along? Have those who have lived before us bequeathed cultural values, systems, ceremonies, rituals, interests, even careers to us? What does that mean for you? If you were raised in a religion, what does that mean for you now? Do you retain some or all, or none, of those beliefs? We're going to explore that more in another section of the wheel, but it's good to take a quick look now. Do you have innate cultural talents, or have you developed a skill that reflects your cultural heritage?

Returning to the Wheel of Relationships, do you use those values when working with family and cultural dynamics?

Next, we move to the west. Many of us believe we've had many lifetimes. This is where we look at our own past lives, scanning to see which lifetimes traumatized us; where we have an unfinished karmic debt; which lifetimes were fulfilling and why; who our soul family is; perhaps even discovering a current relationship that still has karmic attachments from another life. Again, anything that needs to be healed can be. Awareness is half the "battle," and the place where our skills as Shamanic Warriors are tested. If you don't believe in other lifetimes, don't worry. We can look back at events in this lifetime to discern whether we have PTSD from a traumatic experience, what has been most satisfying in our lives, where there are damaged relationships that need forgiveness and healing. It's important to remember that we will heal on different levels throughout our lives, and that each of us has their own time schedule.

In the north, we meet ourselves at all our spiritual crossroads. Many times, in this and other lives, we've had to make decisions about what we believe, what we value, how we act on those principles, and whether what we have been taught is still useful to us in the present moments of our daily lives. Do you have a set of spiritual beliefs that fulfill you? Are you dissatisfied with some aspects of your spiritual life? Have you explored several pathways in this life? Were some of them familiar, as if you lived them in another time, another place, another culture? If so, you probably have, and there are things you can do to access that information. Are you already aware of other spiritual paths you've followed in different lifetimes? If so, are any of those systems still valuable to you? What have you discarded and what is current for you?

As we mentioned earlier, we all have stardust in our veins. Some of us may be star beings, or be descended from beings from another planet, or even another galaxy. We have the opportunity to explore this in the above on the Ancestor Wheel. Many people have never felt at home here on Earth. If you've descended from a star lineage, you may have extra bones, or have been born with a special mark, or have a special gift or insights that "normal" people don't have. A shaman might be able to tell you what solar system and planet you've inherited. People from this lineage are often indigo, crystal, or violet ray children who have special knowledge that is needed at this time.

And, of course, we are in relationship with the Divine, in all its aspects. Whether you call the Great Mysterious One God, Creator, Jehovah, YWH, Wakan Tanka, Allah, or the Collective Conscious, nearly all of us recognize that there is an intelligence in the way the universe exists. Do we experience a relationship with this essence? An inheritance? Are we developing it, and aligning with something greater than ourselves?

Below is our relationship with Mother Earth and All Our (nonhuman) Relatives. Did you know that our DNA and the DNA of a tree is very similar? And we have a symbiotic relationship with the Tree Nation: as we breathe out, they breathe in, absorbing our CO2. When they breathe out, we inhale the oxygen they've cleaned. Our kinship with the natural world— be it the Earth Mother who sustains us with everything that grows, or the animals we interact with, or the elements of earth, air, water, fire—serves us and we are here to serve it in return. All our actions create equal reactions. In this section, we examine our fears of the natural world, our desire to be one with our relatives, and our need for symbiotic relationship with all that lives. What are your values when it comes to the earth, animals, trees, insects, and elements? What are your fears? Do you respect them? Do you love them enough to change the way you live in order to support them? What is your inheritance from them?

Then we integrate all we've discovered about ourselves, our heritages and lineages, our relationships or lack thereof, in the center. We may have discovered some shame and guilt, and a need to seek forgiveness. We may be proud of ourselves. We may have learned humility. Wherever there is shadow, there is also great light. If we shine the light of love into the shadows we've discerned, we will become Spiritual Warriors, Shamanic Protectors of All Life. When we balance masculine/feminine, light and shadow, joy and suffering, we live at the core of life.

The Shamanic Warrior serves and protects both humanity and nature. One doesn't have to be a shaman to do that, but one does have to stand for all of creation. If you have psychic gifts, shamanic training, and skills, if you've been called and initiated, then the shamanic path is a lifelong road. If you've read a few books on shamanism, perhaps know a few rituals, attend ceremonies and so forth, you're a seeker, who is learning to know themselves much better. You'll also begin to understand more about why you're here at this time, and what your purpose is. Whatever your pathway, you will discern the ways you can help to co-create a better world.

## Talking Circle—Sweetgrass Calls the Ancestors
### *by Robin Youngblood*

Sweetgrass, one of the Native Americans' medicine plants, is used to cleanse. The strands of sweetgrass are braided into a bundle. In the way that I've been taught, the first seven strands represent the seven generations behind us—our parents, grandparents, etc., seven generations back—who we are and what we are is because of them. The thousands who have lived before us set the paths upon which we now walk.

The time has come to heal and connect with our ancestors. They paid a tremendous price for us to be able to speak out against injustices; we do not have the right to remain quiet. They have embedded both their gifts and traumas in our DNA. It's time to heal our multigenerational epigenetic wounds. And we need to give our forebearers our honor and respect for all the wisdom they have passed to us. Sweetgrass tells them we love and honor them and their sacrifices.

I was taught the next seven strands represent the seven sacred teachings we find on the Wheel of Relationships: Love, Respect, Humility, Honesty, Courage, Loyalty, and Wisdom. The elders tell us how simple, powerful, and beautiful these teachings are:

- Love: unconditional affection with no limits or conditions that starts with loving yourself

- Respect: due regard for the feelings, wishes, rights, or traditions of others, with consideration, thoughtfulness, attentiveness, politeness, courtesy, civility, deference

- Humility: freedom from pride or arrogance; being humble; when we truly understand the teaching of humility, that we are not any better than anyone else and you are not any better than me, that at the end of the day we are simply human beings, this is what makes this teaching powerful and beautiful

- Honesty: integrity, and honor, and being open to intimate truths; sharing from a place of vulnerability; free from fraud or deception; legitimate and truthful

- Courage: bravery; permitting one to face extreme dangers with boldness; withstanding danger, fear, or difficulty

- Loyalty: the ability to hold nonjudgmental space with and for another over long distances of time and space; a commitment to not abandon another, physically, mentally, emotionally or spiritually; facing matters together, with veracity, sincerity, candor, and genuineness

- Wisdom: knowledge plus experience, understanding when to apply a certain knowledge to a particular situation, with love and kindness; discernment in action; the quality of having experience, knowledge, and good judgment

The last seven strands in the sweetgrass braid are those of the seven generations in front of us—our children, our grandchildren, and our great-grandchildren ... including those children yet to be born. This is important because everything we do to Mother Earth will one day affect them. We have lost our way; everything we do to Mother Earth gives us everything we need to heal ourselves and the earth. We must go back to our roots and bloom, as well as assist the natural world to reclaim its balance and beauty.

There is a saying often attributed to Chief Seattle, the great Suquamish leader, or sometimes to the Amish, and used in various forms by environmentally conscious writers over the years: "We do not inherit the earth from our ancestors, we borrow it from our children."

By healing ourselves of our ancestral wounds, we clear the DNA pathways so our inheritors need not experience the pain and consequences that have been held in our lineages. These teachings need to first start from within ourselves, respecting ourselves. They tell us that the teachings need to first start from the inside.

Never forget we are the whispered prayer of our ancestors. They are waiting for us.

An alternate version of "Sweetgrass Calls the Ancestors" can be found on the Nation of Shawls Facebook page.

## Journey of the North

Prior to beginning the journey, consult the setup instructions described in Tools for Journeying in the Resources section at the end of the book. You may wish to also review the Journey World discussion in the chapter entitled Journeying with Bear.

Keeping in mind the aspects of each direction, ask your new totem or ally to guide you on a journey to the below world. Trust that your guide will bring you to a place in the journey world where you'll be able to see a Medicine Wheel with four quadrants, the Wheel of Ancestors.

Now call in seven generations of your grandmothers on your mother's side. Thank them for their Giveaway and ask them for their wisdom. See where your mother's mother, and her mother, and each mother for seven generations, stands in the Wheel of Ancestors. Do any of these women have something to say to you? Or show you? Why are they where they are placed? Do any of them need to move to another direction? Or closer or farther away? What does this reveal to you about yourself? If there are any ancestors that show themselves as something other than human, simply note them in the same manner you would the others. Thank each grandmother for showing up, then return to record your journey in your journal.

Then, repeat this journey once more, calling in seven generations of your grandfathers on your mother's side. You can work with your father's ancestors another time.

Remember, we do not journey alone, so always call in your totem or guide before beginning. We recommend a fifteen-minute journey.

**Journal**

1. After you complete your journey, use your journal to record the events and your impressions.

2. Where did your mother's mother, and her mother, and each mother for seven generations, stand in the Wheel of Ancestors? Did any of these women have something to say to you? Or show you? Why do you think they were in that place? Did any of them move to another direction? Or closer or farther away? What did this reveal to you about yourself? About your family?

3. Detail what you learned from each ancestor. How might this affect you?

4. Were any of your ancestors something other than human? If so, research what they might be, where they originated, and what that means for your lineage. What did this reveal to you about yourself? About your family?

5. Where did your mother's father, and his father, and each father for seven generations, stand in the Wheel of Ancestors? Consider the same questions as detailed in number 2, above. What did this reveal to you about yourself? About your family?

6. If you were to classify what role best fits these ancestors—Seer, Teacher, Healer, Warrior, or something else—what might it be? How does this ancestor's role mirror or augment the role you feel most resonance with at this time?

7. If you feel called to, return to the journey world and repeat the journey with seven generations of your father's mothers and fathers. Review the same questions detailed above.

8. Pay attention to what happens in your three-dimensional reality.

9. Use your journal to record dreams, journeys, conversations, and other experiences during this time. Identify how these support or clarify your ancestor work.

## Assignment

This month your task will be to create an ancestor altar.

1. Research how many of your ancestors you can directly find either through old photographs or the memories of other family members. Create a family tree to keep track of everyone.

2. What stories do you recall about your grandparents or great-grandparents? Do you know their professions? Their histories? What trauma might they be carrying due to events during their lifetimes?

3. Consider researching your family lineages further via an online source to see how far back you can access records. If you are particularly curious, you might consider a DNA analysis to track your biological ancestral lineage, which may provide additional details not known in your family.

4. Create a space in your home (not your bedroom) where you can set up a small altar for your ancestors. Place the Seven Sacred Directions and any objects you feel belong, perhaps something of your family's.

5. Remember the sweetgrass? You can create your own version. You'll need seven pieces of colored paper or yarn, each a different color. Some of you are familiar with prayer ties and prayer flags. Cut the pieces of paper or yarn into narrow strips about a foot long. Offering a prayer of gratitude and healing for the seven generations that preceded you and gave you life, weave these seven different-colored strands together until you have a fine braid. Tie off each end so the braid doesn't fall apart. Next, saying prayers for all family members in this generation, and remembering the attributes ascribed to the sweetgrass, weave the next strand of seven colors together and tie it off. Finally, in prayer for the next seven generations and all they will experience, carry, and heal, weave the final seven strands together. Take all three braids and weave them together, then place them on your ancestor altar, knowing that you have braided your family lineage and healing throughout the generations.

**Seven Generations Healing Ceremony**

This is a Seven Generations Healing Ceremony. For a list of tools and general setup instructions, see the Tools for Ceremony discussion in the Resources section at the end of the book. (See also the Calling Ceremony described in the East chapter.) In addition, you'll want to also:

- Bring items to build a small ancestor altar for this ceremony if you are holding it somewhere other than where your current ancestor altar is located.

- Remember to add representations of your ancestors, items from your home altar, photographs, or small family items.

- Include the colored "sweetgrass" braid you wove for your ancestral healing.

- Request the presence of guides and other helpers, particularly the new ally who came to you during your work in the east.

Create a Medicine Wheel in a private place, outdoors if possible. Set an altar representing YOU and your ancestors next to the center. Using your rattle, call in the Seven Sacred Directions, your protectors and guides. Now call in the seven generations of your mother, grandmothers, and grandfathers, those who dreamed you. Visualize them standing in their places, as they were in your North journey.

Stand in the center and turn around the circle, beginning in the east. Stop at each cardinal direction. Close your eyes and see the ancestor before you. Give each a gift. It could be a flower, a feather or stone, a hug, or a song … or anything else you feel called to give them. Speak your gratitude for all they've given you—both the lessons and the gifts—for the Giveaway they made so that you could stand here in this moment. Thank them for their continued love, their investment, their help. Bless them for all they have done and all they may yet do.

Next, ask each ancestor to awaken and activate a gift, a skill, an understanding, a healing in your DNA. After you accept this healing, return it to them with love. Visualize it rippling out through the Medicine Wheel to each and every ancestor, your gift to them. When the ripples return to you, pause a moment. Ground and breathe. Their healing is your healing; your healing is their healing.

Then allow this healing to ripple out again, this time to your descendants, be they physical descendants or heart descendants. Seven generations ago, our ancestors dreamed us, and now you dream for future generations. Allow the healing given to you from your lineage go forward into the world. Speak your prayers aloud for those who are yet to be born. Their healing is your healing; your healing is their healing.

Envision how these ripples—these circular energy patterns—interconnect, intersect, or even merge. Remember Black Elk's teaching: "Everything an Indian does is in a circle, and that is because the Power of the World always works in circles, and everything tries to be round … The sky is round, and I have heard that the earth is round like a ball, and so are all the stars. The wind, in its greatest power, whirls. Birds make their nests in circles, for theirs is the same religion as ours … Even the seasons form a great circle in their changing, and always come back again to where they were. The life of a man is a circle from childhood to childhood, and so it is in everything where power moves …" Sense how the healing power of this simple ritual moves across time, touching not only you, standing here in the NOW, but your ancestors and descendants.

Close the circle by releasing each direction in the reverse order that you called it in. Thank the spirits and guides for their support, including the spirits of the land where you spent this time. Leave the site more beautiful than when you found it by placing a small offering: a bundle of herbs, a flower, or a pinch of tobacco.

## *Chapter 8*

# EXPANDING ABOVE

In the above/sky direction, we encounter and embrace the aspects that reflect and support our journey as a Traveler. You may find other traditions place the aspects in a slightly different manner, or that certain aspects may come to your attention strongly in a direction other than the one expected. This is all a part of the mystery of the wheel and the timeless medicine of these teachings.

## ASPECTS OF THE ABOVE

| | |
|---:|:---|
| Element: | Space |
| Embodiment: | Ethereal/Astral Body |
| Emotions: | Lightness/Emptiness |
| Season: | Eternal |
| Day Cycle: | Timeless |
| Moon Cycle: | Void of Course |
| Phase of Life: | Perpetual |
| Color: | Indigo |
| Creatures: | Star Beings, Star People |
| Expression: | Sounding/Toning |
| Way: | Union with the Void/Traveler |

Place on the Wheel:   Openness

Lesson:   Universal Consciousness

Relationship:   Divine

Wheel within Wheel:   Cosmic Wheel

Ceremony:   Star Wheel

. . . . . . . . . . . . . . . . . . . . . . . .

Above we find Sky Father, keeper of the Great Mystery and Universal Mind or Universal Consciousness. Here lies the crack between the worlds where the present, past, and future braid together. This direction reflects no time and all time, the timeless and eternal, with a sense of lightness and emptiness that characterizes our etheric energy body. Within our emptiness lies our fullness, a single note that sings us into rapt wholeness, a reverberation in our bones that sets us free from the limitations of the physical body and the agreement of time/space and propels us into our astral bodies.

The above direction asks you to release preconceptions, beliefs, and cultural perspectives to learn something new, something outside the known. Here we experience ourselves as spirit in body, a divine spark from Creator, the Great Mystery. The Great Spirit defies definition, supersedes ideology. Opening to the mysteries, the esoteric teachings of the masters who have evolved beyond the Earth plane, connects us with that Divine essence, in communion with "those who watch us always."

Connecting with the Divine brings you into relationship with your timeless higher self, and those spirit teachers who guide you into the upper world and beyond into the void. These beings of pure spirit may be kind and compassionate ancestors, ascended masters who have moved beyond earthly incarnations, guardian angelic beings, or star masters from another constellation. Receiving guidance from Spirit ensures you remain in alignment with your sacred purpose, so that when manifesting your desires individually or collectively in the below direction, the end result is spirit-filled. Your intention is manifested in a way that may be bigger and better than you ever imagined because your goals are in alignment with your highest self, and you opened the door for Spirit to enhance your creation.

The above direction is sometimes perceived as the most difficult because you may be left wondering what there is to connect to in the invisible world beyond the physical. Yet three-dimensional reality encompasses only one facet of reality. Working with the above, you move into a deeper level of awareness, more familiarity with your astral body, more open to receiving information from other sources. The Akashic records, stored in the stars since before time began, are open to you, offering you the ability to better understand your timeless self and your sacred purpose, and perhaps that of others who come to you for counsel.

The color of the above is indigo, the shimmering blue-violet-charcoal of the night sky. Raven, with wings the color of night, appears in many indigenous peoples' myths, particularly the Pacific Northwest Coastal peoples. In some stories Raven is a trickster who steals what he wants when he wants; in others, he is a hero, making things right. In this Haida tale, the story of how Raven became black, he is both.

> Long ago, at the beginning of the world, Gray Eagle was guardian of the sun, moon, and stars. He was also the guardian of fresh water and fire. It is told that Gray Eagle hated the People so much he kept all these wonderful things hidden. So the People lived in darkness, without fire and without fresh water.
>
> But Gray Eagle had a beautiful daughter. And Raven fell in love with her. In the beginning, Raven was snow white, and he pleased Gray Eagle's daughter, who invited him to her father's longhouse.
>
> When Raven saw the sun, moon, and stars, and fresh water hanging on the sides of Eagle's lodge, he knew what he must do. He watched for his chance to seize them all when no one was looking. And eventually his chance came. He stole them, and a brand of fire also, and flew out of the longhouse through the smoke hole. As soon as Raven left the longhouse, he hung the sun in the sky. The sun made so much light that he was able to fly to a distant island in the middle of the ocean. When the sun set, he hung the moon in the sky too and all the stars around in

*different places. By this new light he kept flying, carrying with
him the fresh water and the stolen brand of fire.*

*Raven flew back over the land. When he reached the right place,
he dropped all the water he had stolen. The water fell to the
ground and became the source of all the fresh-water streams
and lakes in the world. Then Raven flew on, holding the brand
of fire in his beak. The smoke blew back over his white feathers
and changed them to black. When his bill began to burn, he had
no choice but to drop the firebrand. It struck rocks and hid itself
within them. That is why, if you strike two stones together,
sparks of fire will spring out.*

*Raven's feathers never turned white again after they were
blackened by smoke from the firebrand. That is why Raven is
now a black bird.*

(as told to Robin Youngblood)

In this story, Raven frees the gifts of water and fire to support life, and
hangs the sun, the moon, and the stars—the cosmos as we know it. As trickster, he stole these things from Gray Eagle's lodge; as hero, he gifted them
to the people, the price singeing his white feathers black. Raven is known
across cultures as a master shapeshifter, taking various forms to accomplish
his goals and moving easily between the upper, lower, and middle worlds.

Star lore brings us stories of people and animals moving to and from
the Sky World in the time when the boundaries between the worlds was
thin and somewhat fluid. In some indigenous creation myths, such as that
of the Skidi, an independent Pawnee band, Great Star created the Earth by
dropping a pebble Bright Star gave him for that purpose, but that world was
covered with water. The Okanagan also tell of a time when the Earth was
covered with water and all the creatures lived in the Sky World until Duck
retrieved mud from the bottom and it grew on the back of Turtle to form
the land.

The Iroquois tell the story of Skywoman, a pregnant woman who fell
from a hole in the sky to land on that same Turtle Island and, welcomed by
the birds and animals, planted fruits and flowers and bore children. Other

indigenous peoples hold the belief that their true home is in the stars, that their ancestors were star people who came from one of the star nations, commonly the Pleiades or Sirius. For example, the Dogon in Africa, as well as the Masai and Zulu have stories of an origin in Sirius. Australia's Original People, Maori, Hawaiian, Okanagan, Cherokee, and Lakota tell stories of the Pleiades as their origin.

Indigenous legends describe star people in many forms. In *Stars of the First People*, Dorcas S. Miller includes a Cherokee myth on the nature of stars (originally printed by James Mooney in *Myths of the Cherokee*). In this story, hunters found two strange creatures on a ridge where they had seen bright lights shining in the night. The creatures were round and covered with fine gray fur like downy feathers, which, when the breeze struck them, emitted sparks. Their heads were small and round like terrapins (turtles). These beings stayed for a week, then suddenly rose from the ground like balls of fire. Similarly, the African Kung Bushmen describe star beings as porcupines covered with tiny spines. The Dogon depict star beings as amphibious, from the same star system (Sirius) as the Egyptian Isis, as do some old stories from Mesopotamia. There are many descriptions of star people in sizes ranging from the porcupines, described above, to tall beings with blue-black skin, to giants from the Sky World in Greek and Norse mythology, as well as other mythologies. There are also stories of star beings called "walk-ins," spirit forms from other star systems who offer to take over a human body when the owner is done with what they came to Earth to do, or does not have the heart to continue their incarnation.

Robin's story of star beings came in a dream after she went to her tribe's Winter Dance many years ago.

*I went to that Winter Dance with some big questions. Why am I so frustrated being a realtor? Partly, I guess because I'm an Indian; we don't even believe in land ownership! What am I supposed to do for a living? Where am I supposed to live? And so on ... We danced four nights, and I hadn't received one bit of an answer. At the end, I went to Medicine Man and told him my questions. He told me to watch my dreams for the next four nights.*

*The first night, I dreamed a golden windowsill with a blank night sky on the other side. No movement. Second night, I saw the golden windowsill with stars shining in the night sky. Other than their twinkles, nothing happened. Third night, I saw the golden windowsill again, and an ancestor on every star, smiling, waving, whooping, beckoning. It was a little overwhelming because I didn't know why. On the fourth night, I saw the golden windowsill again, stars, ancestors (some of whom were actual star beings), and I saw myself half over the sill, my left side in native regalia, my right side still inside dressed in a business suit with a briefcase. At first, I interpreted this to mean I was supposed to leave the corporate world and climb into a fully traditional lifestyle.*

*I took the dream to the elders, who told me that a traditional lifestyle wasn't what I was being asked to do. They said I needed to learn how to dance in both worlds, to become a bridge over the barriers between ancient and modern, tribalism and colonialism, between races, conflicts, realms, and dimensions. I was really overwhelmed then! They said that to do this, I would need to understand complementary opposites and how they work ... e.g., east/west, north/south, above-up/below-down, in/out, day/night, winter/summer, spring/fall, earth/air, fire/water, masculine/feminine, and so on.*

*And **that** is the Shaman's Journey.*

The Cherokee tell how they came from the stars as the Original People who were to begin building a new world on Earth. For this tribe, the heavens were seen as the Original People's teachers, a connection to the place where the Great Spirit made his abode. Star patterns provided maps to teachings, the people's ancestry, and marked the trail to follow (once they set their physical body down) to return home to the stars and the peace they knew existed there. Not only did the Cherokee consider stars their origin, but they also believed stars held the keys to the future. With master teachers residing in the constellations, medicine and wisdom were imparted via star energies; thus, the ancestors danced in starlight, praying for their world and the teachings to guide their leaders and show the people the way to live.

Certain stars and constellations played a vital role in indigenous people's ceremonies, the rising of certain star formations signaling the changing of the year, the beginning or end to a particular ceremony or season. Some ceremonies are said to have been given to the people from the stars, such as the Blackfoot story of a woman who marries a star and lives in the Sky World, then returns to the people with sacred objects and instructions for the Sun Dance.

In the twenty-first century, there are more and more people wondering whether they too have a different planetary home than Earth, whether they might be what we call a star seed. Although the Pleiades-Earth connection is one of the most commonly discussed as an origin star system, there are also potential star seed origins on Sirius, Arcturus, Vega (in the constellation Lyra), Andromeda, Polaris, Betelgeuse and Rigel (in the Orion constellation), and elsewhere. These star seeds (labeled indigo, crystal, violet ray, or rainbow children) are sensitive, empathic, wise beyond their years (old souls), and quite intuitive. They often struggle with belonging on Earth, but strongly feel they are here for a reason. Although knowing what that reason is may not come easily, it is typically something that falls in the realm of helping Earth ascend to a new state of consciousness. For star seeds, connecting with the above direction can help tremendously in settling into their Earth incarnation and discovering their purpose.

Shaman as Traveler holds the ability to move out into the cosmos and visit other worlds, as well as see into past/future worlds. With this capability the shaman becomes a messenger across time and space, a bridge between ancient and modern times. Although similar to shaman as Seer, Visionary, or Hollow Bone, shaman as Traveler goes beyond the boundaries of Earth, dissembling time and space. These shamans become one with the NOW to step into other worlds, other lifetimes to seek information, read the Akashic records, receive guidance from the star masters on planetary councils, the ascended masters, angelic beings, and the ancestor helping spirits who live in the "other side camp," their campfires burning in the starry sky (those who have passed into spirit).

Shamanic Travelers, like Raven, can often shapeshift to be present in alternative locations in different forms. These practitioners can suspend time, tracing the trajectory of events forward or backward. Shaman as Traveler may journey for very long periods in their astral body, holding only the thinnest silver cord to bind them to the physical plane. With the information Travelers receive, like shaman as Seer, messages can come forward that can help us perceive and understand differently what's happening in our own lives, in our communities, nations, and world.

## Cosmic/Sky/Star Wheel

The wheel we bring forward in the above is the Cosmic Wheel, the Sky Wheel, or Star Wheel. This wheel perpetually spirals above, changing from dusk to dawn and fluctuating based on the seasons and where we live on the planet. We have only to step outside and look up on a clear and cloudless night.

Stars were used for navigation by seafaring peoples; star maps were used as a memory aid in teaching routes to particular destinations both at sea and on land, such as the songlines the Australian Aborigines used. The star wheel many are familiar with is the astrological zodiac, the twelve (or, more recently, thirteen) star formations assigned to birthdates within certain calendar periods based on the constellations we can see from Earth.

Star teachings represent a substantial study, held in sacred reverence by ancestral and modern Wisdom Keepers worldwide. Star people and sky people populate these teachings, bringing wisdom from beyond. From the Cherokee, Iroquois, Hopi, and Maya in the Americas to the Egyptians, Berbers, and Dogon in Africa, to the Finnish Sami, Celts, and Druids in Europe, Australian Aborigines, Polynesians, Hawaiians, and Incan civilizations around the Pacific Rim, and the Greeks and Romans of the Mediterranean, each culture held star myths based on what they saw above them as the wheel of the year turned, old stories passed down through the generations.

These stories could be seen in the skies, folklore reflected in stars and star patterns, the images superimposed on star formations. Given the fluidity between the earth and heavens for many ancient and indigenous peoples, the stories often tell how the people went to the sky or came from the sky. These were sometimes cautionary tales, sometimes gifts from the Sky People, or sometimes teachings designed to help mankind live in right relationship. Even the Christian Bible in Genesis 1:14 (New King James Version) references the stars and planets as signs: "And God said Let there be lights in the firmament of the heavens to divide the day for the night; and let them be for signs, and for seasons, and for days, and years."

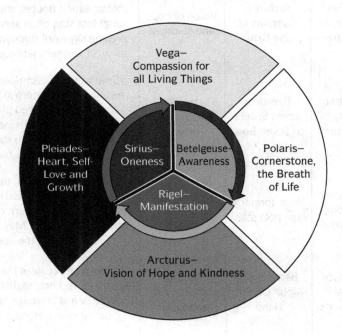

For this cosmic wheel, we include seven star nations said to hold specific attributes for the good of incarnate man on Earth. The chart to follow gives a broader definition, including the star location (see also the following bulleted list for additional details). Unfortunately, light pollution in many areas prevents us from seeing the beauty of the starry heavens or identifying the constellations. A trip away from the city can be a welcome treat to see what our city lights mask.

| Direction | Star | Attribute | Location/Description |
|---|---|---|---|
| East; Air, breath, beginnings | Polaris; North Star | Cornerstone; Breath of Life | Tip of the Little Dipper in the Northern Hemisphere. This star shows no movement opposite Earth's axis point, a stable cornerstone in the heavens |
| South; Fire, change, partnership | Arcturus; Guardian of the Bear | Vision of hope and kindness | At the hip of the Herdsman, constellation Boötes, the fourth brightest star, often seen in the evening sky April through August in northern latitudes |
| West; Water, maturity, introspection | Pleiades; Seven Sisters or Seven Boys | Heart, self-love, and growth | Seven small bluish-hued stars setting in the western sky in the spring dusk signaled planting time to many northern indigenous peoples, rising again in the east in fall as the season turns |
| North; Stone/earth, wisdom, Giveaway | Vega, formerly the pole star | Compassion for all living things | In constellation Lyra, the fifth brightest star in the northern sky (second in the northern celestial hemisphere), visible May through November in the north |
| Above; Space, universal, consciousness | Betelgeuse; Alpha Orionis Hand | Shadow Dance of Life, awareness | Betelgeuse occupies the upper left tip in the constellation Orion. Visible late fall through spring in the Northern Hemisphere. |
| Below; Organic, Mother Earth, all nations | Rigel; Beta Orionis Foot | As above, so below; Manifestation on the Earth plane | Rigel occupies the lower right tip of the constellation Orion. Visible late fall through spring in the Northern Hemisphere. |
| Center; Alchemy, mastery, integration | Sirius; the dog star | Relationship with and love for all, interdependent oneness | Sirius can be found off and behind Orion's "belt" stars in Canis Major. The brightest star in the sky, it is actually a binary star, a combination of Sirius A and B. |

Across the planet there are varied cultural interpretations of a particular star or constellation. Below we include a few notes of interest for these Northern Hemisphere stars from the indigenous peoples in the Americas and offer a brief description of the associated star nation teaching.

- **Polaris**, the North Star, is known in many places in the Americas as the Star Who Stands Still. In Paiute legend, the Big and Little Dipper (which holds the North Star at its tip) are boys who turned into mountain sheep and climbed so high on a mountain, they could not return, so one of the boys' fathers made them into stars to guide others. This star is said to represent the energy of renewal, beginning again, as with each new breath, each new course, and each new phase of life.

- **Arcturus**, guardian of the bear, is named for its placement near the Great Bear (Big Dipper) and the surrounding stars considered the herdsman's sheep. The Hawaiians call this star Hokule'a, star of joy and gladness, one of the main stars used by the Polynesians when navigating by sea across the equator to Hawaii. As a watcher and guide, this fiery orange-hued star represents the pure vision of hope and kindness, that there is another place, another way—a joyful way—and a reminder that simple acts of kindness kindle both hope and joy.

- The **Pleiades** are named after seven sisters, the daughters of Atlas in Greek mythology, who either escaped or were cast into the sky. The Cherokee call these stars the Boys, also a story of children who inadvertently escaped into the sky. These stars represent expanding self-love and growth, the choice and intention developed in adulthood.

- **Vega**, Arabic for descending eagle, part of the constellation Lyra, is one of the stars that make up a lyre or harp-shaped formation recognized across many cultures. In the Americas, among the Pawnee, Vega is recognized as one of the stars given the responsibility of holding one of the four quarters of the sky, as well as the patron star of medicine people. This star is said to represent the bodhisattva-like energy of deep compassion for all living things and the transformational power of forgiveness.

- **Betelgeuse** and **Rigel**, both in the constellation Orion, represent the hand and foot of the hunter, and often work together. Betelgeuse, as the hand, signifies soul purpose, awareness, the reason you incarnated this lifetime, and the shadow dance of life that comes with authentically living your purpose. Rigel, as the foot, embodies the "as above, so below" concept: the ability to braid matter with spirit for healing, transformation, evolution, and manifestation on the Earth plane.

- **Sirius**, also called the dog star, runs at Orion's heels across the Northern Hemisphere's winter sky. In the Americas, this star is also called Wolf Star or Coyote Star. The Cherokee also call Sirius a dog star, one of the guardians to the path of souls (Milky Way) along with Antares. As a binary star, Sirius represents the awakening of the Sacred Masculine and Sacred Feminine dancing in unity and oneness with the Great Spirit and All Our Relations.

In southern latitudes, the Southern Cross (Crux) and the two bright Pointers (Alpha and Beta Centauri) are undoubtedly the most recognizable, featuring prominently in Southern Hemisphere star lore from Africa, South America, Australia, and Polynesia.

The seven stars we mention in this chapter and the teachings and attributes they represent are just a few of the star nations invested in Earth. There may be others you are familiar with that speak to you in a profound way. As well, there may be particular planets that draw your attention—their Western names reflecting those of the ancient Greek and Roman gods and goddesses who lived in the heavens (Sky People) and, as the stories tell us, sometimes came down to Earth. All of this is the realm of Sky Father.

The planets most commonly seen with the naked eye—Venus, Mars, and Jupiter—were classified as stars by early peoples.

- **Venus** (Aphrodite, goddess of love), depending on its cycle, is called both the Morning Star and the Evening Star. Some originally thought it two stars. The planet was sometimes called Bright Star or Big Star given that, when visible, it is the brightest star in the heavens.

- **Mars** (Ares, god of war), the red planet, is often called the Great Star, Warrior Star, or Fire Star.

- **Jupiter** (Zeus or Thor, god of the sky and lightning), is also called Blazing Star or Great Star's Brother when visible at dusk.

In *Living With the Stars: How the Human Body Is Connected to the Life Cycles of the Earth, the Planets, and the Stars*, astrophysicist Karel Schrijver, a senior fellow at the Lockheed Martin Solar and Astrophysics Laboratory, and his wife, Iris Schrijver, professor of pathology at Stanford University, explain how everything within our bodies originated in cosmic explosions billions of years ago. We are literally made of stardust (carbon, nitrogen, and oxygen atoms, as well as atoms of all other heavy elements in our bodies, created in generations of stars over 4.5 billion years ago). Joni Mitchell told us this same truth fifty years ago in her 1970 song about the road to Woodstock, so for many of us being stardust isn't a new concept, simply one now quantified scientifically. This connection to star matter links us forever and always to the vast cosmos, and for those of us with star lineages, brings us closer to the garden we know as home.

## Talking Circle—What if the Atlantis Myth is True?

*by Sandy D'Entremont*

Call it pseudoscience, pre-ancient history, or science fiction, the mystery of Atlantis continues to make headlines thousands of years after its supposed demise. From Plato's writings, to Donnelly's antediluvian (pre-flood) world, to the readings of American clairvoyant Edgar Cayce, to DC Comics' superhero Aquaman, the fabled ancient civilization yet captures our attention, its location and the cause of its destruction an unsolved mystery.

In modern times, the main argument *against* Atlantis is the lack of concrete scientific evidence *for* it. Snippets of evidence compiled to date are summarily dismissed in academic and scientific circles as insufficient or mere coincidence. I suppose the same logic could be applied to many things commonly accepted in our world if we get right down to it. But that doesn't make the unseen or unproven any less real, simply less scientifically quantifiable.

Does there need to be empirical evidence to rubber stamp Atlantis as a part of Earth's antediluvian history? What if there actually *was* an advanced technological civilization that sank beneath the ocean ten thousand-plus years ago?

This is theoretically plausible and possible, regardless of scientific substantiation.

The story of Atlantis, in various permutations, is a story of a civilization whose agricultural, spiritual, academic, artistic, medical, psychic, and technological advancements far exceeded those we currently enjoy, a civilization that lasted—and prospered—for millennia. Atlantis survived a few different cataclysms, including the biblical flood, until it finally disappeared forever. The story of Atlantis is also, in part, a tale of misused power, a story of a largely self-indulgent society becoming enamored of science as their god, a hierarchical culture that enslaved "lesser" beings and held themselves "better than," a government with technological might who threatened other countries to obtain cooperation and obedience, and a powerful but reckless scientific majority whose experiments to harness atomic-like energy for economic gain abused the earth and, in doing so, destroyed their continent.

Unfortunately, this story sounds all too familiar ... and could very well be a description of mainstream Western civilization. Simply watch the evening news.

So ... what might the Atlantean myth mean for us here and now? Perhaps dramatic entertaining science fiction. Perhaps a cautionary tale.

But with the great number of Atlanteans reincarnating in the late twentieth and early twenty-first centuries as seen in the many Atlantean past life memories surfacing, we have to wonder whether the fabled Atlantis is a myth after all, or perhaps something more. We need to ask the question: Will technology in the wrong hands destroy our world again? Are we destined to repeat the same mistakes as that ancient antediluvian civilization that disappeared beneath the Atlantic? And if we *are* stumbling in that direction, hurtling toward another eve of destruction, how do we correct our course?

The answer, as with many things, begins first within: Why did we incarnate? Why now? Why this country? And what is our part, our path, our purpose, our work? Why did we make these life choices? What is the role of the others we share time with in this incarnation?

And eventually...how do I make a difference?

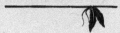

## Journey to the Above

Prior to beginning the journey, consult the setup instructions described in Tools for Journeying in the Resources section at the end of the book. You may wish to also review the Journey World discussion in the chapter entitled Journeying with Bear.

In your journey to the above, hold the intention to travel to the upper world and consult with your Council of Twelve. Allow your journey ally to guide you to a rose quartz meeting room through a space portal. Who is revealing themselves to you there? What do they want to tell you about this or any other lifetime? Have any of your council members been one of your ancestors?

Remember, we do not journey alone, so always call in your totem or guide before beginning. We recommend a fifteen-minute journey.

### Journal

1. After you complete your journey, use your journal to record the events and your impressions. Which ally guided you to the upper world? Did the route you took for this journey seem familiar or was it new?

2. Who revealed themselves to you in the rose quartz room? You may not have been able to see all twelve council members, but describe any you did see. Where are they from? What is their interest in you?

3. What did the council tell you about this or any other lifetime? How does that information influence you? How might it influence your future choices?

4. Could you tell whether any of your council members might have been one of your ancestors? If so, what was your connection with them?

5. Did your Council of Twelve ask anything of you? What was your answer?

6. If you have specific questions for your council and feel called to return to the journey world with your ally, revisit the rose quartz room. Be clear why you are returning and why it is important.

7. Pay attention to what happens in your three-dimensional reality. Use your journal to record dreams, journeys, conversations, and other experiences during this time. Identify how these support or clarify your work in the above.

**Assignment**

Human brains have two sides that work in conjunction to help us navigate our world. When these sides are working in healthy balance, we feel more alive, conscious, connected, and whole. As with the exercise in the south, you'll be writing a portion of this assignment with your nondominant hand; that is, if you normally write or draw with your right hand, use your left and vice versa. In addition, you'll be allowing your writing to follow a stream-of-consciousness: no censoring, editing, or judgment. Simply let the words (or images) flow.

1. Carve out about ten minutes of writing time for yourself each day for the next two or three weeks, preferably early in the morning after awakening, or evenings prior to sleeping. Sit comfortably and breathe deeply, allowing yourself to sink into a light meditation.

2. Each day consider the following questions, writing or drawing your response as it comes to you: 1) What were your reasons for incarnating this lifetime? 2) Why did you choose your family? 3) What has your family taught you? 4) Have you discovered some of the contracts and lessons you agreed to? 5) Are any of these contracts already fulfilled? 6) What do you want to pass on to the next generations? 7) What form do you want to pass it on in?

3. Trade off between hands each day, writing with one hand one day and the other the next.

4. Locate star charts for your latitude and season, then take a few minutes one evening (or a few evenings!) to view the night sky. What stars catch your eye? Why?

5. Research the meaning of stars and planets in different cultures. Which tradition resonates with you? Why might that be?

### Star Wheel Ceremony

This is a Star Wheel Ceremony. For a list of tools and general setup instructions, see the Tools for Ceremony discussion in the Resources section at the end of the book. (See also the Calling Ceremony described in the East chapter.) In addition, you'll want to:

- Choose a private site where you can see the stars to welcome Sky-Father-Above-Us

- Bring a portable altar, seven candles, and a small container

- Have your star charts at hand so you know what stars are with you when you perform this ceremony

- Place your writing with the answers to the seven incarnation questions on the altar and anchor it in some way so that it does not blow away in the wind

Set up your altar in the late afternoon or evening, just before dusk. Place each candle in a container so the wind won't blow it out. Place one candle in each cardinal direction. Place three candles on a small, raised altar in the center of the wheel to signify Father Sky, Mother Earth, and your Highest Self. Set your writing in the center as well.

Call in the Seven Sacred Directions, starting with the east. Call in the star nation or planet you associate with each direction and the energies they hold. Light the candles as you call in each direction. Then light the candles in the center direction. Call in all your ancestors and guides from the above direction, ascended masters, angelic beings, those from star nations. Ask them to witness this ceremony and grant their blessings and protection.

Read some of the answers to your incarnation/lessons/contract questions aloud to yourself, holding in your consciousness as you read that you *are* all that is. Review also the information you received from the Council of Twelve and allow it to sink into your mind.

Lie in the center of the circle and look up at the stars and moon if it is out. Breathe deeply as you relax completely, your eyes open to the stars. If needed, cover yourself with a blanket for warmth.

Now, close your eyes and think about the silver cord at the base of your spine, which you may have seen in your journey or your regular meditation. Allow your astral body to take hold of the cord as you gradually ascend up and out of your body. Holding the cord, look at your surroundings. Observe the stars and moon above you and your body below you lying in the circle. Still holding the cord, allow yourself to experience this state for a few minutes. Then return to your physical body and sit for a while in the state of No Mind, allowing the star nations and Great Mystery to fill your being with peace and a sense of detached observation and compassionate objectivity. Breathe deeply and feel the calmness that comes with this objectivity. Then, open your eyes when you are ready for the next step.

Consider the contracts and lessons you agreed to in this lifetime from your writing assignment. Consider also your family choice and what they have taught you. Call to mind the memories and/or life experiences you experienced fulfilling these contracts and being part of your chosen family. If part or all of a particular contract is complete, release it from your life. Remain focused on staying objective and fully present in the Now. See the significance or insignificance of your choices and experiences from this higher perspective as best you can. Bless each situation, person, thought, and emotion, asking for peace, health, and happiness to infuse each one.

Ritually cleanse your written pages using one of the methods discussed to release any holds you no longer need. Know that your spirit is now free of this contract, no longer bound.

Look around for a *wotai*, a stone memento of this experience. Place it in your medicine bag or personal bundle to remind you that you live only Now. Acknowledge yourself in gratitude for the new pathway you are walking. If possible, leave a token of thanksgiving in a nearby tree before you go (in exchange for what you have been given)—something that reminds you of the stars.

Close the circle by releasing each direction in the reverse order you called it in. Thank the spirits and guides for their support, including the spirits of the land where you spent this time. Leave the site more beautiful than when you found it by placing a small offering: a bundle of herbs, a flower, or a pinch of tobacco.

> *Note: We give great thanks to the Wisdom Keepers who hold the Star Walking teachings and are willing to disclose these teachings to those star seeds currently inhabiting human form. Our deep thanks particularly to A. Noquisi, Tsalagi, for opening her home and her heart to impart this knowledge, as well as to the other Wisdom Keepers worldwide who generously shared and continue to share these ancient teachings.*

# Chapter 9

# DEEPENING BELOW

In the below/earth direction, we encounter and embrace the aspects that reflect and support our journey as an Earth Keeper. You may find other traditions place the aspects in a slightly different manner, or that certain aspects may come to your attention strongly in a direction other than the one expected. This is all a part of the mystery of the wheel and the timeless medicine of these teachings.

## ASPECTS OF THE BELOW

|  |  |
|---:|:---|
| Element: | Organic |
| Embodiment: | Birth and Rebirth |
| Emotions: | Acceptance |
| Season: | A Full Year's Cycle |
| Day Cycle: | All Times |
| Moon Cycle: | Dark |
| Phase of Life: | Conception |
| Color: | Moss Green |
| Creatures: | Subterraneans |
| Expression: | Tears of Gratitude/Surrender |
| Way: | Earth Keeper |

| | |
|---:|:---|
| Place on the Wheel: | Initiation |
| Lesson: | The Pregnancy of Possibility |
| Relationship: | The Natural World |
| Wheel within Wheel: | Animals, Plants, Elements |
| Ceremony: | Earth Constellation |

. . . . . . . . . . . . . . . . . . . . . . . .

Mother Earth—Gaia—the Green Goddess—the Sustainer. She-Who-Should-Always-Be-Named-and-Thanked. There are many names, and many ways to understand our lovely planet as the living organic being she is. Mother Earth, below, gives us everything we need to ground ourselves, survive, and manifest our dreams.

Here, in the below direction, we become grounded. We are conceived, initiated, birthed and rebirthed, time and again, in each new chapter of our lives. Just as the Okanagan legend tells "the Earth was once a human being. Old One made her out of a woman," we too, are changed by our encounters with the Great Mysterious One. Though the changes are often uncomfortable, sometimes painful, especially when we experience and surrender to shamanic dismemberment, death, and re-membering, as we emerge anew tears of deep gratitude well up from our hearts.

What is shamanic dismemberment, death, and re-membering? Do only shamans experience it? In the old times, when we all lived in small villages, a person who was to become the tribe's shaman often became very ill, to the point of being comatose. During this time, they would see visions. They would feel as if they'd been ripped apart, tossed into the underworld, all their bones and organs scattered to the four directions. They would have to descend into the netherworlds to hunt for each part, and re-member themselves in an entirely different way. Often, they would experience death and rebirth. Myths around the world reflect this deep initiatory process.

When they emerged from this realm, they would be spiritually awakened, mentally aware of everything in their surroundings, with mind and heart connected, and heart running the show. The person's body might show marks, even scars of their ordeal, proving to others that their experience was real. They often returned with vital information for their people, and sometimes had an important vision to share.

There are many stories of the Paiute shaman named Wovoka who lived in Nevada in the late 1800s and went into a trance (comatose) state for eight days. His people thought he had died. When he woke up, he reported the vision of the Ghost Dance, with a prophecy that if the people did this dance, all would be well. At the same time he was in the Dreamtime, two shamans from Robin's tribes, Smohalla and Smolhatkin, had the same experience and saw the same dance. The Ghost Dance spread rapidly through the tribes, and it is still being danced today.

Earlier we mentioned some of Black Elk's vision; he was not the only one to receive it. Legend says Crazy Horse also had a vision of all people dancing in a circle to the Sacred Tree, the Tree of Life, in joy as all nations came together.

We believe this happens a bit differently in modern society. Because we no longer live in a tribe, because we've lost our connection with the natural world of Great Mystery, we've become skeptical of nearly anything we don't immediately grasp through our intelligence. We're not sure many of us could take the kinds of shamanic illness and initiation that happened then. So today, it seems that people experience a "breakdown" or "burnout" in one area at a time over their lifetime: spiritual, mental, emotional, and physical (not necessarily in that order). Each time they experience a dark night of the soul, a feeling of being torn apart and scattered asunder. And yet, each time they surrender and allow the Great Mystery to work with them, they emerge with a sense of being completely new and better than before. For those of us called to the Shaman's Path, we have been initiated into new levels of insight and understanding, perhaps have received new gifts and talents, and are aware that whatever we've received, it is to be used to assist and serve All Our Relations on Earth.

The shamanic Earth Keeper is one who knows the earth intimately. Earth Keepers spend a great deal of time in the wilderness with the plant, animal, and mineral people. You may find them silently meditating near a lake, stream, or ocean; harvesting medicinal plants, ancient foods and sacred seeds; observing and learning from, or conversing with, the animals who show up in the vicinity; making offerings and facilitating ceremonies for the elements of earth, air, fire and water, or for the four seasons, or the weather, balancing and healing the damage we humans have inflicted on the planet.

Additionally, the below direction brings us into deeper contact with the elemental beings who have a great deal to teach us. As mature spiritual beings composed of the elements—air, fire, water, earth—the more we understand, the more we can identify and work with all the elements inside and out, above, below, and center. Elementals can also be instrumental in healing work once you develop a relationship with them and learn their properties and scope, including their limitations.

Each element can be understood through four essential stages. Describing the stages of fire in the following paragraph, you'll be able to extrapolate, connect with, and explore the four stages of each element.

Fire's first stage is the Ember, that which sparks, enlivens, and holds space for the life of each fire. We live through the fire's ember, deep within our core. The second stage is the Fire of Inspiration (In-Spirit Initiation). This fire within us sparks imagination. Combined with Spirit's initiation, we become the activators of new inspiration. Then there's the third phase, the Heart(h) Fire, the community fire where we share our dreams, imagination, inspiration, and aspirations. This is where we attract and meet our soul family, our co-creators, and the antagonists who impel our deepest learning. Even larger is the Fire of Consumption. Some people think of the Hawaiian goddess Pele when they envision this fire, the fire of destruction (like Pele's volcanoes), which leaves room for new creation. The Fire of Consumption is necessary. We offer that which no longer serves us to the East Indian Puja, the flames that eat outmoded beliefs and release long-held disturbances like resentments and fears. Yet this fire is also dangerous. It can easily go out of control and fly across the landscape, consuming everything in its path. We've seen this in the wildfires of the last years, fires out of balance, destroying forest, animals, villages. This fire must be watched and guarded as long as it burns, to contain it continuously.

When we look at the element of water, we see its different forms as well: ice, vapor, stillness, and flow. For earth, we find sand, clay, and silt (which combine with organic material called humus to make loam), and all the minerals with their different properties. Consider what these different stages mean as you take this teaching inside your body.

Beyond the stages of individual elements, we also have the phenomena that occur when they merge. A few examples are earth + fire = lava, fire + water = hot springs, earth + wind = sandstorm, water + wind = hurricane, earth + water = mudslide, fire + wind = firestorm. Some of these combinations—the joining of opposites—can be lethal, but in other forms, they can be gifts, such as: earth + water = salty ocean with all her abundance, or simply mud for growing rice and taro; and earth + fire = smoke for cleansing and purification. In our contemporary world, we may take the elements for granted because they are an integral part of our everyday life, but they are the key building blocks of life and therefore deserve deeper consideration. The assignment in this chapter encourages you to explore them further.

In the Cherokee way, all our opposites in this world of duality can either be understood and worked with as antagonistic or complementary. Night/day, in/out, up/down, left/right—all are necessary, just as our emotional and spiritual opposites are. As shamanic practitioners, it's our job to find ways to work with all the world's opposites as complements. For example, we have found that our "shadows" are actually our best early warning systems; they show us something is out of balance, either within or without. Either way, we have the ability to restore balance by working with our complementary opposites.

## Wheel of Animals, Plants, Elements

The wheel associated with the below direction is the interdependent Wheel of Animals, Plants, and Elements.

We all know at this point that everything we do affects everything else. If a butterfly flutters its wings in Hong Kong, it may well start a hurricane in the Yucatan four days later. When corporations use destructive mining techniques, it harms the living earth, destroys animal habitat, and ruins the plants, foods, and natural medicines used by people and animals. In some areas of the world, industry has been known to enslave workers, cause civil war, and displace local indigenous populations. It's devastating! When corporations destroy the Amazon rainforest in the name of progress (translation: exploitation and profit), jaguar populations are diminished, forest animals and insects become extinct, the incredible range of plants that have provided medicine and healing to the tribes and modern medicine are gone forever. Tribal peoples are displaced and decimated, land is ravaged, and it will take hundreds of years to grow a new bio-diverse ecosystem again.

Once, we all worked together for the common good of all. The plants and animals agreed to help us survive by sacrificing themselves as food and medicine. We agreed never to take too much, and always to ask for the ones that were willing to give themselves, then to offer prayers of gratitude for all they gave us. If you ever watched the movie *Avatar*, you saw this teaching in action.

The Cherokee legend "The Origin of Disease and Medicine" speaks to this relationship:

> *The Old Ones tell us that at one time, the animals, fish, insects, and plants could all talk. Together with the people, they were at peace and had a great friendship. As time went on, the numbers of people grew so much that their settlements spread over the whole earth, and the animals found themselves cramped for space.*
>
> *The bears were the first ones to meet in a council, and the old White Bear Chief led the council. After each one had his turn of complaining about the way people killed their friends, ate their flesh, and used their skins for his own purposes, they decided to begin a war at once against man. One of the bears asked what kind of weapons the people used to destroy them. "Bows and arrows!" exclaimed all the Bears together. Grandfather Bear said, "I think we should trust it is plain that the people's weapons were not made for us."*
>
> *Had the Bear People come up with a way to protect themselves, we would not be at war with the bears, but the way it is today, some hunters do not even ask the bear's pardon when he kills one.*
>
> *The deer held the next council, under their Chief Little Deer. They decided they would send rheumatism to every hunter who kills one of them, unless he made sure to ask their pardon. They sent out a notice of their decision to the nearest settlement*

of Cherokees and told them how they could avoid this. Now,
whenever a hunter shoots a deer, Little Deer asks the spirit
of the deer if it has heard the prayer of the hunter asking for
pardon. If the spirit replies yes, everything is in balance. If the
reply is no, Little Deer follows the trail of the hunter, and when
resting in his home, Little Deer enters invisibly and strikes the
hunter with arthritis. No hunter who regards his own health
ever fails to ask pardon of the deer for killing it.

Next, the fish and reptiles held their own council. They decided
to make their victims dream of snakes climbing about them
and blowing stinky breath in their faces. They also thought to
have them dream of decaying fish, so that men would lose their
appetites and die of hunger.

Finally, the birds, insects, reptiles, and smaller animals came
together for their own council. The grubworm was the chief
of the council. They decided that each should give his opinion,
and then they would vote as to whether or not the people
were guilty. Seven votes would be enough for a guilty verdict.
One after another, they complained about man's cruelty and
disrespect. Frog spoke first, saying, "We must do something to
slow down how fast they are multiplying! Otherwise, we will
disappear from the face of the earth through extinction!" They
began to name so many new diseases, one after another. The
grubworm was more and more pleased to hear how men would
be tormented.

Then the plants, who were friendly to man, heard about all
these things the animals were doing to the people. In their own
council, each tree, shrub, and herb, agreed to furnish a cure for
some of the diseases. Each said, "I will appear and help the
people when they call upon me. The humans must remember to
make an offering, and not pick the mother plants. They must
not over-harvest what we give, because then we won't be able

*to fulfill their needs. And they must be grateful, for gratitude is everything."*

*So, this is how the medicines came to be. Every plant has a use, if only we would learn it and remember it. They have furnished the remedy to counteract the diseases brought on by the revengeful animals. Even weeds were made for some good purpose. You must ask, and learn for yourself. When a doctor does not know which medicine to use, the spirit of the plant will tell the sick person. Plant medicine people spend years listening to, respecting, and making offerings to the plant nations, in order to learn how they can help individuals who are ill.*

Once, not that long ago, all indigenous people stayed healthy by drinking medicine teas and cleansing their homes with cedar, sage, impepho (in South Africa), and other sacred local herbs. As we've experienced with recent pandemics, most "medicine" now is synthetic, but still derived from our world's plants. We no longer consult the natural world or indigenous doctors. We don't make offerings to ascertain which plant can help us, and to give thanks for all they do for us. Just as we have treated the animals, we

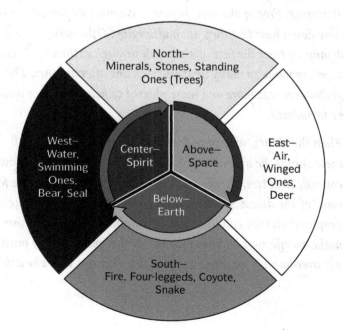

are now treating the plant nations. Because some part of our souls recognizes our abuse, we are all in grief, whether we know it or not.

In some fashion, we've been building the Wheel of Plants, Animals, and Elements throughout this book. We place certain elements in the directions, as well as members of the animal kingdom, *as a generality*. And yet, this does not need to remain static.

In moving toward deeper relationship with All Our Relations, we can change our behavior. We can make offerings of gratitude and ask these incredible beings to help us again. The first step might be an Earth Constellation, the ceremony we include in this chapter.

Placing all parties and medicines on the wheel, the constellation may look something like the diagram below. Feel free to use this in the ceremony to listen deeply to those who do not always have a voice in contemporary circles. Paula Underwood's *Who Speaks for Wolf* represents this concept as well (see the Bibliography).

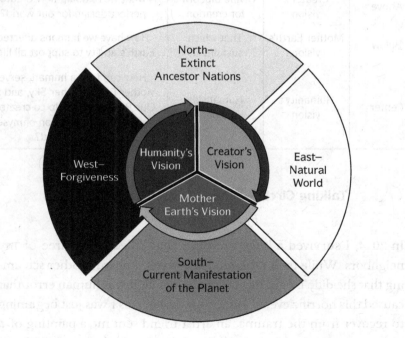

North—
Extinct
Ancestor Nations

Humanity's
Vision

Creator's
Vision

West—
Forgiveness

East—
Natural
World

Mother
Earth's Vision

South—
Current Manifestation
of the Planet

| Direction | Representing | Description | Details |
|---|---|---|---|
| East | Natural world | All beings represented | In the Earth Constellation, all species are represented, listened to, and their needs acknowledged |
| South | Current manifestation | Life as we experience it today | We heartfully examine the ways we currently affect all beings |
| West | Ho'oponopono /forgiveness | Humanity's reparation | As representatives of the human species, we ask for forgiveness for the damage we have created |
| North | Extinct nations | Those who have gone | We acknowledge, honor, and thank all those who have gone before us |
| Above | Creator's vision | Divine blueprint for creation | Is what we're doing now Creator's perfect design for our world? |
| Below | Mother Earth's vision | That which sustains us | How have we humans affected Earth's ability to support all life? |
| Center | Humanity's vision | Humans as helpers | How can I, as a human, serve Mother Earth, Father Sky, and All Our Relatives to help co-create a new and better version of myself and our world? |

## Talking Circle—When Mother Earth Speaks

*by Robin Youngblood*

In 2014, I survived a huge mudslide that killed forty-three of my neighbors. While under the mud and water, I heard Mother screaming that she didn't want this mountain to fall. It was human error that caused this horrific event. Three months later, as I was just beginning to recover from the trauma, an artist friend sent me a painting of a native woman, feather in hair, shawl dancing in the winds. When I turned it over, he had titled it *Earth Mother Dancing*. The same day, I received an email from a Cherokee elder, Dee Smith, who told us that a long time ago, my Cherokee people had a ceremony that the women offered called Dance to Heal the Earth.

I had already seen a vision of this dance, only it was no longer just for women. Over the years, four medicine men from different Sioux tribes had asked me to restore and facilitate the women's original Sun Dance. Four times I said no, because I didn't feel capable. Yet now, with the painting and Grandmother Dee's email, I knew I was being asked to facilitate a Dance to Heal the Earth.

And so the dance was born. Thus far, we have danced in the United States, several places in Europe, and Africa. We just finished our sixth dance, and reached our goal, which this year was to achieve spiritual maturity. During the pandemic, we held small, socially distanced dances in the Netherlands and South Africa, and a worldwide dance online with participants from Hawaii, Washington, Arizona, Mexico, Kentucky, Colorado, Connecticut, the United Kingdom, France, the Netherlands, Spain, and Portugal. We've learned that in order to restore balance and help Mother Earth to heal, we must find our passion and purpose, and heal ourselves enough to stand for truth, the Original Instructions and Universal Law, and to take action to live sustainably and educate others. It is an honor and privilege to work together with our dancers and Earth Keepers to understand, accept responsibility for our actions, and move into fulfilling our service to the Divine and the mother who sustains us. (If you'd like to learn more, participate or coordinate Dance to Heal the Earth in your area, please see the information in the Resources section at the back of this book.)

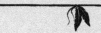

## Journey to the Below

Prior to beginning the journey, consult the setup instructions described in Tools for Journeying in the Resources section at the end of the book. You may wish to also review the Journey World discussion in the chapter entitled Journeying with Bear.

Remind yourself of the meanings of the Four Directions. Journey to the Medicine Wheel. What plants and animals are in the wheel and where? Ask each one what it has for you, and whether it is there for a reason, a season, or a lifetime?

Remember, we do not journey alone, so always call in your totem or guide before beginning. We recommend a fifteen-minute journey.

### Journal

1. After you complete your journey, use your journal to record the events and your impressions.

2. Draw a circle, a representation of the Medicine Wheel, and place the plants, animals, and elements on it as it came to you in your journey. It does not matter if this corresponds to the general animal kingdoms we associate with the directions in this book.

3. Do you talk to the animals and plants? Do you listen to the messages they have for you?

4. Do you give thanks when you eat either an animal or plant, or use its medicine? What can you do to develop a deeper relationship with both?

5. If you feel called to, return to the journey world with your ally and explore the teachings of the plants and animals and elements at a deeper level. Add any further insight to the personal wheel you drew in #2 above.

6. Pay attention to what happens in your three-dimensional reality. What plants and animals and elements show up for you over the next few weeks?

7. Use your journal to record dreams, journeys, conversations, and other experiences during this time. Identify how these support or clarify your work with the below direction.

## Assignment

Your assignment for the below direction is to explore the elements.

1. Consider the four essential stages of each element and how the medicine of these might manifest in your body. Where might they reside and how do they change you? We gave you some examples for fire, in particular, but extend this to the other elements as well.

2. Write down some thoughts on each essential stage, then rest into trance and bring these aspects inside your body. For example, considering water. What sensations do ice, vapor, stillness, and flow elicit? How does that change when the contrasts of salty, brackish, and fresh are brought in? How do these different states make you feel? Where do they live inside you?

3. What essential stages feel destructive? Which are more constructive? How can you restore balance by seeing through your opposite's perspective? What warnings are your shadow perspectives giving you?

4. Revisit the elemental combinations, both the destructive and constructive ones. See if you can think of others beyond those listed. Bring the medicines of those combinations inside your body to feel their energy. How do these different phenomena make you feel? Where do they live inside you?

5. How might these elemental combinations work together and complement each other, rather than join together in conflict? Do they need an elemental mediator (another element), and what might that be?

6. How can you, as a practitioner, make effective use of essential elemental stages and their combinations in your work?

## Earth Constellation Ceremony

This is an Earth Constellation Ceremony. For a list of tools and general setup instructions, see the Tools for Ceremony discussion in the Resources section at the end of the book. (See also the Calling Ceremony described in the East chapter.) In addition, you'll want to also bring the following:

- Portable altar

- Dried lavender, sage, cedar, and tobacco

- Four special waterproof objects and stones to represent each of the four cardinal directions

- Three crystals to represent the above, below, and center directions and a representation of your totem animal or ally for the center direction. Be sure these stones agree to be part of this ceremony

This particular ceremony can only be held outside. Find a private place in nature.

- Set protection and establish intention.

- Call in guides and other helpers.

- Begin with your grounding/stillness exercise to establish your connection to the earth.

You are going to create an Earth Constellation. An Earth Medicine Wheel Constellation is similar to a family constellation, except here All Our Relatives are represented. Animal, vegetable, mineral... we listen to them all. This ceremony is done outside, bare feet touching the earth.

Clear a circle about eight to ten feet in diameter. Place representative stones and objects at each direction's gateway. Set crystals for Father Sky and Mother Earth and center in the middle of the Medicine Wheel you've created.

Bless the objects and stones, use cedar and sage smoke to cleanse, and call in the powers of each of the Seven Sacred Directions. Call in the relation associated with each direction: east, winged ones; south, four-leggeds; west, swimming ones; north, standing ones and plant people; above, star beings and two-leggeds; below, earth and her subterraneans and creepy-crawlers; center, those who dwell in spirit.

Write the names of species of animals, plants, trees, and/or stones on separate pieces of paper to serve as proxy for a particular species' presence. Stand in the center, representing Gaia herself. Spend time in meditation before the constellation, listening to what each nation wants to say, and where it belongs in the wheel, the Circle of Life.

Step into the center of your Medicine Wheel. As Gaia's representative, you will speak first, sharing her needs and love, her wounds and forgiveness. Step to the east, and after listening, express the needs and wounds of the being(s) there. Breathe in deeply and receive what you hear and feel. Continue to follow the Medicine Wheel, standing in each direction and expressing in turn until all species have spoken.

You may experience deep grief as you listen and express. It's all right to let yourself feel it. Too many of us have learned to separate ourselves from the earth, its elements, and species, in order to not feel. This has resulted in a worldwide addiction to ignore/ance. It's time to feel. When we acknowledge that our pain and the pain of the animals, plants, and Gaia belongs to all of us, we are motivated to create change.

As you step back into the center, you will speak, representing humanity, and humanity's reactions. If you feel a need, you will then ask forgiveness and share the messages of the changes you offer to make to restore balance. You can finish by singing a song that connects you to and honors the earth, and your commitment to be an Earth Keeper.

> Note: We often sing a version of the Christian hymn
> "Sanctuary" by Randy Scruggs and John Thompson,
> substituting the word Earth and Earth Keeper where it feels
> right to do so, but you may sing any song you like.

Close the circle counterclockwise, releasing all who have come to listen, share, and protect. Bless and release your ancestors, your totem animals and guides, the stone people, and all the species you have listened to and represented. Thank them for their support, gather all the pieces of paper you used to represent each species, and burn them in a shell or bowl with a little tobacco, cedar, sage, and lavender. The ceremony is complete.

Unless you have done this ceremony in a place where you are certain that it won't be disturbed, put everything back in natural order. You can set it up again next time you come.

# Chapter 10

# EMBODYING THE CENTER

In the center/within direction, we encounter and embrace the aspects that reflect and support our journey as a Sage. You may find other traditions place the aspects in a slightly different manner, or that certain aspects may come to your attention strongly in a direction other than the one expected. This is all a part of the mystery of the wheel and the timeless medicine of these teachings.

## ASPECTS OF THE CENTER

| | |
|---:|:---|
| Element: | Magic |
| Embodiment: | Alchemical |
| Emotions: | Detachment |
| Season: | NOW |
| Day Cycle: | Dreamtime |
| Moon Cycle: | Blue |
| Phase of Life: | Mastery |
| Color: | Rainbow |
| Creatures: | Those Who Come and Go |
| Expression: | Whale Song |

| | |
|---:|:---|
| Way: | Weaver of Light, Sage, Be-ing the Medicine |
| Place on the Wheel: | Between Worlds and Times |
| Lesson: | Integrated Connection |
| Relationship: | All Our Relations |
| Wheel within Wheel: | Wheel of Integration |
| Ceremony: | Integration Movement |

. . . . . . . . . . . . . . . . . . . . . . .

In the center, the within direction, we find ourselves: all we've been, all we are, all we are yet to be, together in the NOW. The center direction represents the merging of our higher self with our earthly self, the very best of us, united within and without. In this place of integrated connection, we view our own evolution and transformation with the objectivity of detachment and the medicine of compassion, able to assess the levels of mastery we've reached during this cycle of learning.

The element of the center is one of magic, changing consciousness at will. The color we find is that of a rainbow, an alchemical song of shades and tones twisting together in strands of light and sound that carry the medicine of your essence and anchor you to Earth. In this place we have the choice to stand between worlds and times, both physically incarnate and in spirit, the perspectives of both moving through our awareness to bring greater understanding. We are bigger than our bodies, more than our minds, deeper than our hearts.

Coming to rest in the center we bring our solo vision from the east and our work in partnerships in the south. We hold the intra-cultural, multi-generational healing we experienced in the west, a time of reflecting with White Bear, and notice the family and cultural dynamics as they change for the better. Then, we merge the strength of our lineages in the north. Invoking the power and presence of the above, Great Mystery, we ground our manifestations on the altar below, on Mother Earth. Now we stand ready to integrate all we've experienced, re-membering ourselves, re-collecting the pieces of our journey, bringing the medicine of our lessons full circle into our awareness to place on the Wheel of Mastery so we can live what we have learned.

Visualizing ourselves in harmony and balance, we can see our connection to all directions and teachings. We sit at the center of the wheel, infinity symbols (8) linking east and west, north and south, above and below, passing through our hearts. The Blue Road where vision meets dreaming and releasing what no longer serves us; the Red Road where vulnerability meets integrity. We align sky to Earth where universal consciousness touches the Earth plane, which, when grounded, allows us to manifest our dreams, visions, and life purpose. The holographic wheel expands to encompass our past, present, and future, generations that walked these roads before us and those inheritors yet to come. To exist quietly in the NOW, in the heart of the center, fully present, we intentionally pause to balance our physical, mental, emotional, and spiritual bodies, knowing we are a simple spark of the Divine finding our way home.

The center of the circle sits equidistant from all the other points, none greater or lesser than the other, which is one of the potent medicines of the circle, the Sacred Hoop of All Our Relations. As Black Elk taught: *the Power of the World always works in circles.* With indigenous teachings, humans are equal to, not above or below, all of creation, and often considered caretakers and Earth Keepers, rather than seated in dominion.

Legend tells how the drum came to sit at the center of the village circle. The Abenaki of the northeastern US and Canada's maritime provinces tell a version of this First Drum story, but the version recounted here is the one Robin learned years ago.

> *A long time ago, Creator was looking around at all he/she had created, and was very proud of it all ... except those silly humans! He/she was exasperated by their constant bickering, counting coup, warring, etc. Why couldn't they just live in peace?*
>
> *Suddenly, Creator heard Woom! off in the distance. It got louder and closer, until the sound was right next to Creator. "Who are you?" Creator asked. "Don't you remember? I'm the*

*Spirit of the Drum, one of the first ones you created." Creator nodded. "Oh, yes. I remember. Why are you here now?"*

*The Spirit of the Drum explained that she thought she could help the humans. If she placed herself in the center of each village, the tribes could sing their deepest heart and prayer songs to the heartbeat of Mother Earth. If there was an argument, or a celebration, or something that needed to be communicated throughout the village or nations, she could share their voices through their drumbeats and songs.*

*Creator thought a moment, visualizing how it would be, then agreed. "You shall live at the heart of each village, then, and help the people to follow the rhythms and alignments of life in a good way."*

*And so it is that every indigenous people have the drum.*

(as told to Robin Youngblood)

The story of the First Drum is a story of the center, the heart of the people, set there by the Divine, Great Mystery, the Creator. And yet, this story is not only about the drum; it is a story of community, and aligning with Father Sky, Mother Earth, and each other, for when we unify and harmonize, we can truly listen and find solutions.

As a spark of the Divine, we too are each a powerful drum, fashioned of skin, stretched on a frame of bones. A creature of earth, air, water, and fire, our hearts beating in rhythm beneath the wide sky. As a matter of fact, the first drum we hear is the heartbeat of our mother in the womb. We are born of stardust and moonlight, golden sun and fresh wind, ocean and mountain, a universe within us. Around us. Ever unfolding.

Growing into and embracing spiritual adulthood means we take responsibility for what we create and destroy. We learn the communication skills to support our partnerships. We heal our wounds, release our past. And we live our purpose. Every moment, every day. Every step a prayer, every breath a prayer. With attention and compassion. In harmony and alignment with all that is, in order to co-create wholeness and unity. Open heart and mind. Unattached to outcome. For the good of All Our Relations. As best we can.

The mysteries of Spirit and the paths to mastery are yet awaiting our discovery, a matter of seeking with intention and preparing ourselves to find the treasured wisdom we desire. One day at a time.

In this old story told in many ways, Creator in their infinite wisdom and love placed certain treasures where only we can find them, and only when we are mature and ready.

> One day Creator gathered all of creation and said, "I want to hide something from the humans until they are ready for it. It is the knowledge they create their own reality."
>
> The eagle offered: "Give it to me, I will take it to the moon."
>
> The Creator shook his head, "No, one day they will go there and find it."
>
> The salmon whispered, "I will hide it on the bottom of the ocean."
>
> "No, they will go there too."
>
> The buffalo promised, "I will bury it on the great plains."
>
> The Creator frowned: 'They will cut into the skin of the earth and find it."
>
> Then, Grandmother Mole, who lives in the breast of Mother Earth, and who has no physical eyes but sees with spiritual eyes, said: "Put it inside them."
>
> And the Creator nodded, "It is done."

(as told to Robin Youngblood)

We all come from the Source, every one of us—some say the Goddess or the Creatrix, others say the One God or the stars. To that Source we are bound to return once we fulfill our contracts, complete our chosen incarnations, and drop our robes, our physical bodies. Introspection and integration are key to making sense of what we learn, and they bring the teachings into full awareness, weaving them into the fabric of our being—all bodies, the mental, emotional, spiritual, and physical. This is one of the reasons that movement is so important to bringing the other bodies into balance. In this chapter, we explore this attribute more fully.

In the center, we find shaman as Sage, the Weaver, one who lives the medicine, one who *is* the medicine. Becoming a shamanic Sage is the result of developing a deep competence in shamanic skills, able to grasp exactly what modality, or combination thereof, is needed at any moment. These shamans are adepts who become masters of the four elements: earth, wind, fire, and water. Their astounding work can defy time/space agreements and accomplish unexplainable healings. Some would even call their works miracles.

Shaman as Sage is Be-ing, embodying the Shaman's Heart. The Sage is one who has been be-coming for many years. The process is to BE, BE-come, BE-aware, and eventually BE-cause. To be causal and intentional in every moment, acting wisely from the storehouse of knowledge, processes, and methods one has learned over a lifetime.

The shaman Sage is one who has reached spiritual maturity through pain and promise and experience over many years. To know the way forward through the lessons of the past, combined with the reality of the present, and to see the possibilities of the future and the potential effects of each choice. To become a Sage, one has accumulated the wisdom and capabilities of the Spiritual Warrior, Seer, Teacher, and Healer. This phase of shamanic expertise is the same as the fourth essential phase of the elements. A shaman Sage can be both creator and destroyer, prophet and seer, healer and trickster, warrior and peacemaker, all depending on what is called for and guided by Spirit and helpers in each moment.

Today, we are all being initiated, time after time, death and rebirth, until we reach the prescient stage of spiritual maturity. The gifts, insights, and healing that take place in working through this book are all meant to bring you to the point where you can offer yourself in service to All Our Relatives from an inner state of knowing, wisdom, compassion, and love. If you're reading this book, you are being called to take your place as a servant leader, to help guide us into birthing a new Earth. We will all be better for your process.

## Talking Circle—Being the Medicine

### by Robin Youngblood

Many years ago, Beaver Chief and I were watching a community dancing to the drums. We watched one student in particular. He was decked out in every piece of traditional regalia he could find or make—feathers, bones, beads, knife, bells, turtle shells. And he was dancing like a peacock, preening his feathers for all to see and acknowledge.

After a few minutes, Beaver Chief turned to me, folded his arms and solemnly said, "Someday, he's going to learn to BE the medicine, rather than wear the medicine." We both chuckled gently, knowing this young man would soon find himself dis-membered, dying, rebirthing, and re-membering himself in a whole new way. He would become the caterpillar, shedding all his cells (shells, bells, whistles), in order for his imagination cells to create the shaman he would become.

And he did.

Once you shed all cultural, societal, and structural trappings, you become authentic, embodying the divine blueprint of the soul through its many lifetimes. In this state, you begin to manifest your visions and life purpose.

There is an oh-so-simple formula: sound + light + movement = manifestation and creation.

Those who have reached the heights of these practices, the shaman Sages of the world, can manifest in the blink of an eye. That's what we call a miracle.

The rest of us are still practicing.

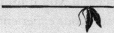

## The Shaman's Toolkit

Every shaman has a medicine bundle. The bundle is sacred, and it is only opened when a particular tool or medicine is needed. Each person's bundle is unique. One may have a rattle and tuning fork, special crystals, and herbs that person knows how to work with. Another's bundle might have colored materials the shaman uses to represent certain types of healing, plus river stones that have "told" the shaman how to use them. Another may carry several different plant medicines, essential oils, a feather fan, and a written celestial chant the shaman has been given to move energy. All these tools are both symbolic and imbued with the energy of life. They are living beings, capable of transmitting messages and transmuting energies. We list some of these tools and descriptions in our Resources section at the back of this book for your information.

In his book *Grandfather*, Tom Brown, Jr. tells of a time when his teacher, Grandfather, who had taught him how to use all his tools, called him out to the desert and told him not to bring anything. When he arrived, Grandfather gave him a list of things to do that required *magic*. Tom objected. How could he do what was asked of him without his drum, feathers, rattle, herbs, etc.? Grandfather listened, then told him to do them anyway. Once finished, Grandfather explained that we only need the tools until we know we no longer need them.

After years of practice, we may use our tools more because *others need to see them* rather than because we need them. And all of our tools were essential helpers as we learned. We ask the tools which ones want to come with us to do whatever work we're called to. If none want to come, we do our work anyway, knowing the will of the Creator works through us. This is not egoic. As you will find, it's actually quite humbling to open ourselves as true *Hollow Bones* for the Mystery to work through.

## Wheel of Integration

The center direction represents the embodiment of integrated connection. To fully experience this connection, you must complete the spiral journey and assimilate the teachings and your experiences. Over the course of this study, you have learned more about yourself and the Medicine Wheel: traveled the spiral path and dreamed with White Bear, journeyed with your allies to discover sacred wisdom, delved further through inquiry and written exercises, and observed how this learning affected your three-dimensional reality. Throughout the teachings in this book, you are working on four levels:

spiritual, physical, emotional, and mental. When all levels are engaged, healing, learning, and transformation occur.

As humans, both creators and destroyers, we have all experienced how, when we bring something from imagination to the Earth plane (three-dimensional reality), our creation may not be what we expect, and we may feel disappointment or frustration in ourselves or in others. Or we may choose to ignore what we've created and abandon responsibility for it. The experiential teachings we've given you in this book are designed to help you not only grow further into spiritual adulthood, but also to fine-tune that manifestation process and work in partnerships and with universal energies for the good of All Our Relations.

Below you'll find a summary of the properties of each direction so you can view the wheel as a whole and begin to assimilate the teachings deeper into your physical reality. This is part of the work in the center direction, to embrace the Wheel of Integration—whatever that is for you—and bring it into full consciousness. Full consciousness means living what you learned and touching this wisdom in your daily life. Remembering metaphysical teachings when coping with the modern technical world is challenging; it takes full presence and an introspective conscious practice to observe yourself without judgment as you integrate this knowledge into a life practice.

| Aspect | East | South | West | North | Above | Below | Within |
|---|---|---|---|---|---|---|---|
| **Element** | Air | Fire | Water | Stone | Space | Organic | Magic |
| **Emotion** | Excitement | Passion | Grief/Joy | Serenity/Gratitude | Emptiness | Acceptance | Detachment |
| **Embodiment** | Spiritual | Physical | Emotional | Mental | Ethereal/Astral | Birth and Rebirth | Alchemical |
| **Season** | Spring | Summer | Autumn | Winter | Eternal | Yearly | NOW |
| **Day Cycle** | Dawn | Noon | Dusk | Night | Timeless | All Times | Dreamtime |
| **Moon** | Waxing | Full | Waning | New | Void | Dark | Blue |
| **Phase** | No Form | Youth | Mature | Elder | Perpetual | Conception | Mastery |
| **Color** | Yellow | Red | Black | White | Indigo | Dk Green | Rainbow |
| **Creature** | Winged Ones | Four-Leggeds | Swimmers | Standing Ones | Star People | Subterraneans | Those Who Come/Go |

| Aspect | East | South | West | North | Above | Below | Within |
|--------|------|-------|------|-------|-------|-------|--------|
| **Expression** | Breath | Drum | Water/ Silence | Rattle | Toning | Tears of Surrender | Whale Song |
| **Way/ Shaman** | Visionary/ Seer | Teacher | Healer | Spiritual Warrior | Traveler | Earth Keeper | Sage |
| **Place** | Inspiration | Growth | Balance | Truth | Openness | Initiation | Between |
| **Lesson** | Illumina-tion | Trust | Dreaming | Wisdom/ Power | Universal Mind | Pregnancy, Possibility | Integrated Connection |
| **Relation-ship** | Self, Solo | Partner | Family | Commu-nity | Divine | Natural World | All Our Relatives |
| **Wheel** | Co-creation | Relation-ship | Ceremony | Ancestors | Star | Animal, Plant, Ele-ment | Integration |
| **Ceremony** | Calling | Making Right | Healing/ Cleansing | Seven Gen-erations | Star Wheel | Earth Constellation | Integrative Movement |

With this in mind, let's revisit the basic steps of manifestation.

**Inspiration:** When imagination inspires ideas, which become conscious

**Intention:** Identifying, clarifying, and stating your dream, vision, or desire

**Calling:** Visualization, guided meditation, or ceremony to open to the "ima-ginal cells" of possibility, and to additional information from Spirit

**Passionate purpose:** Connecting with and committing to your heart's desire, with integrity, diligence, and caring

**Disciplined application:** Exploring deeper by asking questions, observing your world, beginning to do the work

**Creation:** Midwifing your desires to assist them to birth in the here and now

**Initiation:** Birthing your dream, the first physical manifestation; your own newfound experience combined with your personal understanding of your creation

And this is not the end of the process. Follow-through and consistency are necessary to allow your creation to continue to grow.

Perfecting this manifestation process *and* allowing room for Spirit to improve and improvise your creations is a lifelong practice. Improvement and mastery take dedication and discipline. (Remember, the two ways to initiate life pattern changes are intensity and *repetition* ... something that takes both commitment and discipline.) As you take each step in the manifestation process, you must acknowledge the result of your work—whatever that is—and take responsibility for the outcome.

Spiritual truths are not just in your head or in your dreams or in your heart; you continually manifest/create/destroy on the Earth plane (three-dimensional reality). Every day. In this way, you are consistently mirroring your own unique belief system back to yourself.

> *A friend recently told Robin she knows people traveling the highways of Turtle Island from west to east and north to south on walkabout. Many grandmothers and others are and have walked the sacred Great Lakes, Lake Okeechobee's inland sea in Florida, the Mississippi River, the Salish Sea in Washington State and Canada, and many other places around the globe. Those who do this walk in prayer and self-reflection, asking for guidance about themselves, their purpose and missions, and how to help Mother Earth and All Our Relatives.*

> *The Australian tribal people have a rite of passage, a spiritual awakening event, usually undertaken by teenage boys and girls and lasting up to six months. So do the Apaches. This purposeful "walkabout" is a spiritual, physical, mental, and emotional testing of one's strength, stamina, perseverance, and inner guidance. It can come in many forms. The truth is simple; it's the microcosm of our mortal journey home, a means to expedite the learnings of pre-chosen lessons and agreements we co-created with Great Mystery, our ancestors, and guides before we incarnated. We are here for a purpose no one else can accomplish. The walkabout is the journey to step up! As the Hopi tell us, We are the ones we've been waiting for!*

In some ways, our challenge is greater than previous generations, our ancestors who lived in simpler times. Few of us have the luxury of sequestering in the wilderness for any extended period to learn and pray and meditate and discover deeper levels of spirituality. We must work within the construct of our current reality: traffic, internet, media, financial obligations, offices, and telephones included. Information and demands can come at us from all sides, making life full, if not overwhelming. Family and work commitments can fill the better part of any day. In this environment, it becomes all too easy to separate spiritual work from physical reality and neglect the important integration step in the center/within direction.

Yet without integration, the teachings don't thrum in your blood. They don't inform your daily physical, mental, emotional, and spiritual processes. The change you might initiate—for yourself and others—dissipates like fog, leaving only a memory. For you to live the medicine, like the Sage, you need to become the medicine. We encourage you to take this time to deepen your understanding of the synergistic aspects of the wheel and work with your physical body to bring this cycle of learning full circle.

After completing the movement exercise and ceremony outlined in this chapter, you will be ready to journey for inspiration for your new Medicine Shield in the next. For some of you, this exercise and crafting project will feel familiar, and yet, since you are changed, so your shield will reflect those changes.

## Journey of the Center

Prior to beginning the journey, consult the setup instructions described in Tools for Journeying in the Resources section at the end of the book. You may wish to also review the Journey World discussion in the chapter entitled Journeying with Bear.

We all have a passion, an interest that engages us in a deep way, a sacred purpose we were born into this lifetime to pursue. Your objective in this journey is to have a conversation with your guides and helpers and ancestors to help remind you of what you are passionate about, to help you determine your sacred life purpose.

Keeping in mind the aspects of each direction, ask your totem or ally to guide you into the journey world. Trust that your guide will bring you to a place where you'll be able to access each direction in some way to ask/discover what Creator, Mother Earth, and all beings are asking of you; what sparks your passion; what reminders they provide that resonate with your own heart's desire. You could find yourself visiting with other allies or beings during this journey, or simply be brought to a place where what you seek will become obvious. When you return, follow the steps you took, thanking all whom you interacted with and who provided insight and wisdom.

Remember, we do not journey alone, so always call in your totem or guide before beginning. We recommend a fifteen-minute journey.

### Journal

After you complete your journey, use your journal to record the events and your impressions.

1. Based on your journey, make a list of things you're passionate about. Find the common denominator among them. Reduce that to one sentence, beginning with "I am here to." Now you know your life purpose, and guess what? You can, and probably are, doing it anytime and everywhere. Or perhaps you find you wish to make some changes.

2. If you feel you need more information, return to the journey world with your ally and ask questions. Be clear in your intention.

3. Pay attention to what happens in your three-dimensional reality. Use your journal to record dreams, journeys, conversations, and other experiences during this time. Identify how these support or clarify your integration work.

### Assignment

This month your assignment is to create and experience your own Medicine Dance, a private ceremony that helps you both integrate these teachings and embody the powers of creation.

1. Begin by choosing a location where you will not be disturbed, preferably outside in nature, or in an uncluttered interior space that holds reminders of the outdoors.

2. Thoughtfully assemble sacred objects or stones to represent the teachings from each direction.

3. Read the Integration Ceremony instructions through a few times.

4. Dance and sing the wheel outlined in this exercise every few days this month. Observe how your process changes and who or what shows up to join you.

5. Reflect on the questions noted in at the end of the ceremony in your journal.

### Integration Movement Ceremony

Focused intention is one of the keys to manifestation; maintaining this focus all the way through the process helps shepherd our creations into fullness. As you walk the Medicine Path with White Bear, in the center you consciously work to incorporate what you've learned into your body to ground your intention. One of the best ways to integrate knowledge more completely into your physical being is to create your own Medicine Wheel dance and song.

Read the assignment steps before beginning. In addition to the items listed in Tools for Ceremony in the Resources section, you will also need:

- Drum or rattle

- Other instruments or tools that seem appropriate

- Bowl of water to place just inside the west gate

- Gift for your ancestors

- Journal

- Water and a light snack, such as fruit

Next, create a circle as you've done before. Purify the area by cleansing with sage or sweetgrass in a sunwise (clockwise) circle about six to ten feet in diameter.

Using your drum and/or rattle, call in the powers of each direction for protection. For example: the Visionary Eagle of Co-creation in the east, one of the four-legged teachers you feel close to in the south, healing allies in the west, and your kind and compassionate ancestors in the north. Call in the aspects of each direction that feel right to you, and place the sacred object you brought to represent the direction at the circle's perimeter. As you call in the aspects, take a few moments to feel the essence of what the direction means to you, what strengths and wisdom the direction represents, what you've learned in your work there.

Set your intention. In the center, ask the powers of Father Sky, Mother Earth, and your higher self to help you release all that no longer serves you. Again, call in the aspects of each center direction. Place the sacred objects for the center directions in the middle of your circle, with plenty of space for you to also sit in the center. Finally, call White Bear to sit with you and guide you.

For a few moments sit with your back to the south. Look at, or visualize with your eyes closed, the objects you have brought to represent each direction. Think about the aspects of each direction as you have called them in. Take a few moments to feel how each direction works within the wheel: the role it plays, the strengths it brings, the wisdom it holds, the lessons taught. Consider now how the wheel works as a unified whole.

- Vision and illumination enter the wheel in the east. Your solo journey begins here.

- Growth and movement in trust, innocence, partnerships, and loving balance exist in the south.

- Dreaming, analysis, healing, and maturity through introspection reside in the west and you are able to interact and accomplish in a communal setting.

- Wisdom and power in integrity and truth are found in the north where you stand for the world.

- Connection and alignment with the Great Mystery abides above.

- Grounding, sustenance, and release in surrender to the Source resides below.

- Manifestation and serendipitous alchemy resonate in the center, the NOW.

Identifying who, what, when, and how for each step is not totally necessary. Depending on the individual, each cycle of learning moves along a slightly different path. Know that the wheel exists for you as a tool, as do the wheels within wheels in each direction, and that with experience, you are understanding more and more how it all fits together. We hope you continue to use these tools for the rest of your lifetimes.

Now leave the wheel, start your drumming track, and re-enter by the east gate. Move to the center and listen to the heartbeat of the drums. Stretch to relax your body: touch the earth with your hands, drawing her clear moss-green energy upward through your body and chakras (energy centers) and out through the crown of your head. Reach toward the sky, sensing the white-gold light of illumination and inspiration enter through the crown of your head, send it all the way through your body and out your feet. Visualize the twin flames of the Earth Mother and Sky Father, the Sacred Feminine and the Sacred Masculine, melding together in union in your heart. Remember, light is a part of the formula for creation, so visualize the spectrum of light and color as you dance what's new that wants to emerge in you.

Now begin to quietly hum or sound a tone that comes purely from that heart. At the same time, begin to move your body to the rhythm of the drums. This is not a known dance, but rather an opportunity for you to express your internal dance. Feel free to dance with a rattle or a feather fan, jangles, or a drum. While in movement, visualize any limiting beliefs you want to release. Allow your body and song to lead you. Feel your power and the emotions moving through you. Dance them. Sing them. If you have words, feel free to use them, but vocables *(ah, ee, eh, oh)* often work better. Remember, you are master of your emotions and beliefs, and movement can shift these. Remember too, as Black Elk says, *"the Power of the World always works in circles,"* so do not be surprised if something unexpected comes into your mind or you find yourself doing something unplanned. Simply follow the energy and go with it.

Using gentle but powerful movement (another component of the formula of creation), dance circling the wheel as many times as feels right, then step out of the circle by the west gate, thanking Great White Bear, the totem for west, for her healing. Rest briefly. Drink some water. Acknowledge the power in your dreaming and in pure creation.

Next, enter the wheel at the south gate. Here you step forward with trust, asking for the power of new beliefs, new learning, passionate purpose and co-creators/partners, and knowledge of your life purpose to manifest in your life. Once again, visualize the twin-colored flames from earth and sky dancing in your heart.

Then begin to hum or tone and allow your voice to express this new way of being. Let your body begin to flow with the pulse of this expanded, transformed you. Feel the heartbeat of the drum, the joy of transformation and growth, then evoke this feeling in your dance and song. Picture the way your life is changing in partnership with Spirit. Know that with movement you are creating new cellular memories that will pave over the old pathways in your spirit, mind, emotions, and body—new patterns to replace the old. Holding your intention close to your heart, move and dance your passions and purpose in order to continue creating that which you most deeply desire. Intention is the second step of manifestation.

Dance circling the wheel as many times as feels right, then leave the circle by the north gate, thanking your ancestors and any totems of north for helping you sacrifice your old ways to the wisdom of the new, yet ancient, knowledge you have gained. Rest briefly. Drink some water. Eat some fruit or another snack. Acknowledge the power of transformation moving in your blood and the support of your ancestors, and the new partners who are going to show up.

Enter now through the gateway in the west. Reach down and scoop some of the water from the bowl you've placed there. Sprinkle the water over yourself, to cleanse your body, from hair to feet. While doing so, set your intention to heal and release what no longer serves you. Begin to feel the places in your brain and body that have been frozen, stuck in the past. Begin to let them move. This isn't a mental exercise, no need to think. Just experience.

In this west round, allow yourself to express your dreams in vocables (*ah, ee, eh, oh*). Sound is also a part of the formula of creation. As well, your sounds may turn into a keening grief as you release the pain of all that has blocked you—that's just as important as claiming your deepest desires. Let the emotion flow. Allow whatever your body needs to do, whether you end up screaming or in fetal position. Remember, what comes up is on its way out!

Dance circling the wheel as many times as feels right, then leave the circle by the east gate, thanking your ancestors and any totems of west for helping you sacrifice your old ways, and heal through the wisdom of the new, yet ancient, knowledge you have gained. Rest briefly. Drink some water. Eat some fruit or another snack. Acknowledge the power of transformation moving in your blood and the support of your ancestors, helpers, and the community that upholds you, in this and other dimensions.

Now enter through the gateway in the north. Raise your hands in gratitude to your ancestors, then place the gift you've brought to honor them on the ground near the gate. Let them know you're ready to receive and activate the gifts that run through your DNA. Set your intention to receive your most authentic self. Begin to feel that which wants to move in you. Respond and let yourself move, sound, see, hear, feel. Allow whatever your body needs to do to activate what wants to emerge. Shake it up, baby! This is your time to be fully YOU.

Dance circling the wheel as many times as feels right, then leave the circle by the south gate, thanking your ancestors and any totems of north for helping you activate and acknowledge all you have gained. Rest briefly. Drink some water. Eat some fruit or another snack. Acknowledge the power of transformation moving in your blood and the support of your ancestors, helpers, and the community that upholds you, in this and other dimensions.

In this last round, visualize the Medicine Wheel as a sphere with three intersecting figure eights (the symbol for infinity), two horizontal and one vertical, with your body, your heart, as the connecting center. The eight that links the east and west, Illumination and Healing, is the Blue Road of Spirit, which teaches you to shed light on that which is in darkness, embracing your own shadows in order to transmute pain and embrace healing. The second horizontal figure eight, north and south, connects in your center as the Red Road of Physical Reality. On this path you unite the wisdom of your ancestors through your DNA and the work you are here to do. This is true power—to stand in integrity *and* to be vulnerable. The vertical figure eight is the strong alignment and sustenance you receive from above and below, visualized as twin flames in your heart. Together, all the directions converge within your expanding heart, a heart opening to a new way of walking on the earth in sacred service. The Shaman's Heart.

Once again, visualize the colors of the spectrum of light. Dance with them. Sing and use those vocables *(ah, ee, eh, oh)*. Shout your needs and intentions to the universe with joy! You have now completed the formula: light + movement + sound = manifestation and creation. Know that you WILL receive what you've envisioned and asked for.

Step into the wheel one final time, and dance elongated infinity symbols east to west, north to south and back again, four times. Then, stand in the center; swoosh your arms high for above and brush the earth for below, again for four times. Feel how these energies move through the center of your body, passing through your heart. You are one with all that is.

Dance circling the wheel as many times as feels right, then leave the circle by the east gate, thanking each direction and all your allies for their protection and wisdom. Release the directions and, if needed, collect the sacred objects you brought to form the circle.

Now, rest again and consider the following questions. Note your responses in your journal.

1. What colors and pictures did you see as you danced this Movement on the Wheel exercise? What songs came forth?

2. What dance steps meant the most to you? How did your dance change as you moved through the different directions?

3. What old beliefs and patterns were you aware of releasing? How do you feel now that you've let go?

4. What new beliefs, teachings, and intentions are you dancing into your life? Into your heart? Are you surprised? Can you feel where they've landed in your body? Are they growing as you move?

5. What sensations did you feel in your heart as the energies moved through you? Did you sense something different when dancing the infinity symbols?

Envision, dance, and sing the wheel outlined in this exercise every few days this month. Notice how your dance and chant changes as the old transforms into something new. Perhaps you'll dream, or a verse will emerge, or a choreography that feels cohesive. Pay attention to what occurs in your everyday life and examine how you participated in creating these events in your reality.

Observe without judgment or attachment. Then let it all go. Remember the simple formula for creation.

Sound + light + movement = manifestation and creation.

This is what you are doing when you perform this ceremony. On the last day of your Integration Movement Ceremony, try out some new questions when you dance the directions:

- In the east ask yourself, "What is new in me that wants to emerge today?" Then let your body move in whatever ways it wants to.

- When this feels complete, step back to the center, then move to the south. Ask "What do I need to know to fulfill my purpose today?" Whatever comes, just honor it and give thanks for life.

- Then, return to center and move to the west. "What needs to heal and be released in me today?" There could be tears, laughter, howling. Honor what comes.

- Finally, move to the north, and ask your ancestors what they want to awaken in your DNA today. Dance.

Know that anytime you begin to feel out of sorts in the coming months, you can ask yourself any of these same questions and dance your responses, learning from your body as you move, feeling the connections to the wheel, your spirit allies, your ancestors and teachers.

Consider the questions Angeles Arrien proposes in the forward to Gabrielle Roth's *Maps to Ecstasy: The Healing Power of Movement*: "If you came to a medicine person complaining of being disheartened, dispirited, or depressed, they would ask one of four questions. 'When did you stop dancing? When did you stop singing? When did you stop being enchanted by stories? When did you stop being comforted by the sweet territory of silence?'" As vibrational beings, dance and sound and imagination and silence are medicine that feeds our spirits, calms our minds and hearts, enlivens our souls. Know that you can always come back to this Medicine Wheel dance exercise like an old friend and feel your connection to all that is.

After you perform this dance for the last time, collect everything you brought. Leave the site more beautiful than when you found it by placing a small offering: a bundle of herbs, a flower, or a pinch of tobacco.

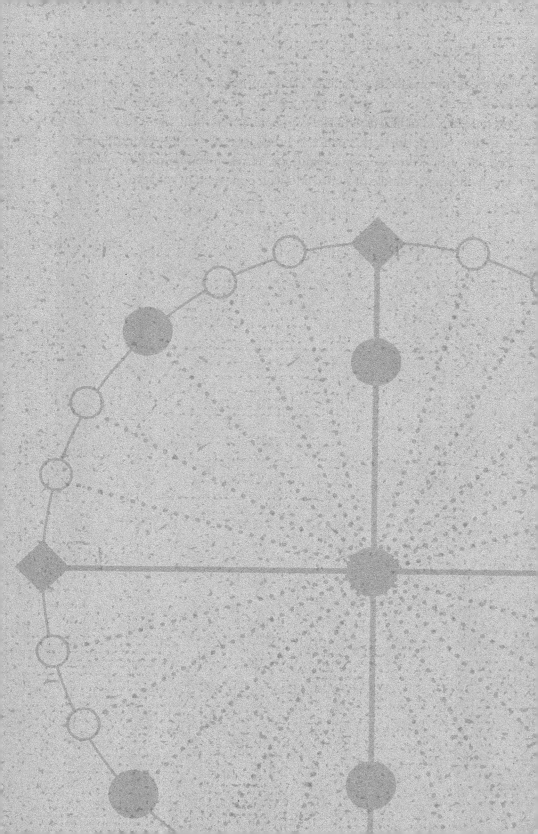

## Chapter 11

# BREATHING DEEP

So, you've traveled the spiral path with White Spirit Bear, journeyed around the Medicine Wheel and into the wheels within wheels to step into the center. What now?

US Congressman and civil rights activist John Lewis wrote, "Ordinary people with extraordinary vision can redeem the soul of America." Remember that we are not ordinary, and we are never done. In his eighty years, John Lewis may have needed to pause occasionally, but he never quit. The reverberations of his work were felt around the world. His last message may have been directed toward his homeland, but it applies throughout all cultures and societies.

This might be a moment for you to pause, to breathe. Yet life may be calling you in other directions. You may want to simply take a break, stop the intensity of learning, return to everyday life, delve into more normal pursuits. Alternatively, you may feel an urgency, a pull, to run further, fill yourself with new teachings. Or, amongst any of those pursuits, you may be deciding you need to stand firm for something, help dislodge old concepts, perhaps replace them with new systems based on ancient values. Before making any decisions, we recommend that you continue to take some integration time and recognize where you've been.

Like White Bear, you need time to dream and reflect, to practice introspection. Native peoples recognize rest to be an important and much needed step to fully understand messages from the spirit world. For certain ceremonies, such as the Sun Dance of the North American Plains tribes, participants were required to withdraw from worldly pursuits for four days before the ceremony and for an additional four days after. As the messages you receive live inside you, and the universe shows you more day to day, you can better discern the nuances of the teachings.

Without rest, there can be no renewal. One of the silver linings the cloud of 2020 brought with the COVID-19 pandemic is that we got to pause, throughout the world, and take measure of our activities. We saw air pollution dissipate in some areas within three weeks because we weren't driving. We saw animals return to natural habitats they hadn't been able to visit for years because of human trash and activity. Some of us got to know our children in a new, more intimate way. And we had to bury our loved ones, which taught us—especially in America—that entitlement doesn't always make a difference. We've had a year out of time to reflect on our current values and decide what really matters to us.

Substituting action—or diversion—for reflection draws your attention away from the power of the teachings and your experiences. Filling your attention with something new, or incessantly talking about your experiences to others, allows the power to drain away. As the Christian Bible tells us, on the seventh day God rested. When involved in this level of personal learning, you need to find balance: time to allow the teachings to percolate so a deeper understanding can rise; time to stand on the foundation of what you know and gather strength for the next task or teaching. Rest and fill yourself with energy, love, and strength so you can be clear enough to make the next decisions on your path and Giveaway again.

When you breathe deep and take pause, you can better integrate your experiences and begin to practice what you have learned. You remain open to the messages and teachings all around you to flesh out the truths. In our practice, we like to honor the teachings by crafting a Medicine Shield. This shield will reflect your walk with White Bear, your ancestors, and allies these last months, the task before you in this final chapter.

## Journey of the Medicine Shield

Prior to beginning the journey, consult the setup instructions described in Tools for Journeying in the Resources section at the end of the book. You may wish to also review the Journey World discussion in the chapter entitled Journeying with Bear.

Keeping in mind the aspects of each direction, ask your totem or ally to guide you on a journey to the below world. Trust that your guide will bring you to a place where you'll be able to access each direction in some way to discover what to place on your new Medicine Shield (although you may already have an idea). You could find yourself visiting with other allies or beings during this journey, or simply be brought to a place where what you seek will become obvious. As you return from your journey, follow the steps you took on your way out, thanking all you interacted with who provided insight and wisdom.

Remember, we do not journey alone, so always call in your totem or guide before beginning. We recommend a fifteen-minute journey.

### Journal

1. After you complete your journey, use your journal to record the events and your impressions.

2. Note the elements shown to you for your new Medicine Shield, drawing or describing each one in as much detail as you'll need to reconstruct it later. Were any of these given to you as gifts in the journey world? Did this surprise you? Why?

3. If you feel you need more information on a particular element or direction, return to the journey world with your ally and ask questions. Be very clear about your intention for returning.

4. Based on your journey, make a list of things you'll need to craft your Medicine Shield. Depending on the model you choose, your supplies will differ substantially.

5. In general, your shield should be made in a round shape and incorporate the quadrants of the Medicine Wheel. You may draw your shield with colored pencils, pen and ink, or paints—or any media you choose. Or you can craft your shield from a wooden hoop with rawhide stretched inside, using natural objects for decoration, such as feathers, bones, wooden beads, stones, leather, or other materials. It's entirely up to you.

6. Pay attention to any other objects that come into your three-dimensional reality during this time and catch your eye. Do these mirror one of the teachings you are assimilating? Do they also belong on your Medicine Shield? It's possible you may want to make a three-dimensional shield, or a series of shields, one to represent each direction. Sit with this in the dreamtime and know you'll be shown what you need to do.

7. Use your journal to record dreams, daydreams, and other experiences during this time. Identify how these supplement or clarify your work.

### Assignment

This month you will create a Medicine Shield to help you integrate what you learned on this cycle around the Medicine Wheel. This is a Seven Sacred Directions Shield, and you may find it integrates symbols, colors, and images from all directions. Don't worry if you feel you lack artistic ability; your shield can be very simple, or more complex, as we discuss on the next page.

1. Approach your shield crafting in a sacred way, calling in the directions, lighting a candle, etc. Call on the strength and wisdom of White Bear to be with you while you work to create this powerful tool.

2. If you choose to draw your shield, start by sketching a circle perhaps the size of a dinner plate. Place your hands (one at a time) in line with the quarter-sections on the circle. Trace your hands: right hand in the east, left in the west, right in the north, left in the south. Then color these representations in the colors of the directions.

3. Next, on the right side of your shield, create a section to represent your experience of the east, vision and co-creation. Add symbols, drawings, colors, and shapes that depict what you learned about yourself when you worked with the material in that chapter.

4. Continue around the circle, letting your symbols reflect what you learned in each quadrant: Partnership in the south, Healing and

Ceremony in the west, Ancestors in the north. In the middle of the shield, put images or drawings symbolizing your work with the above, below, and center directions.

You may want to draw with your nondominant hand. This kinesthetically challenging exercise opens your creative mind. And, if your creativity prompts you to make a shield different from the models suggested, follow that impulse. There is no right or wrong center shield. Simple or complex, this Medicine Shield will be a lasting record of your journey with White Bear. Move with the spirit of your own creative force. Let your shield proclaim your freedom and power, and above all, your joy!

### Additional Shield Crafting Tips

For those who wish to tackle a more complex shield format, we invite you to consider alternative constructions. The diagrams here are intended only as beginning ideas.

1. A three-dimensional shield to reflect the holographic dynamic of the wheel (below) as you danced in your Integration Movement Ceremony.

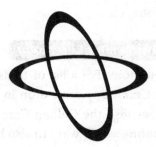

2. Miniature individual shields of different colors or materials (right) to illustrate all directions and their connection via the sacred spiral.

3. Or different sculptural configurations as Spirit speaks to you.

One thing to remember as you craft your shield: we are always spiraling in to the center to learn (there's even a song by that name), and spiraling out to our partners, community, and world. Note the spirals placed between each of the seven direction shields. In some form, paper, wire, drawing, you may want to represent the spirals on, in, or hanging from your shield, to help you remember that we are always moving. "Stuck" is an illusion in a way. We can stop moving in one area, but there will always be movement in others.

Additional shield ornaments could include items such as beads, feathers, bones, animal fur, fabric, leather, shells, antlers, stones, metal or wire, mirror, macramé, paint, herbs, ribbon, etc.

### Shield Awakening Ceremony

This is a Shield Awakening Ceremony. For a list of tools and general setup instructions, see the Tools for Ceremony discussion in the Resources section at the end of the book. (See also the Calling Ceremony described in the East chapter.) For this ceremony, you'll want to also bring the following:

- Portable altar

- Four special waterproof objects to represent each of the four cardinal directions

- Crystal to represent the above direction, a round flat stone for the earth, and a representation of your totem animal or ally for the center direction

- Dried lavender and tobacco

- Journal and blanket
- Drum or rattle
- Center Medicine Shield
- Staff to be placed into the ground in the middle of the Medicine Wheel (or other alternative if doing this ceremony indoors)

We recommend this ceremony be held outside in a private place in nature. If you wish, use the same private outdoor area you used in the exercise outlined in the Center chapter.

- Set protection and establish intention
- Call in guides and other helpers
- Begin with your grounding/stillness exercise to establish your connection to the earth

Clear a circle about eight to ten feet in diameter. You can build a small lean-to structure with sapling poles if you want a shelter (this is best if you wish to stay overnight). Hunt around for some moss or branches and use them to create a bed within your circle. Place your blanket there.

Place representative objects at each direction's gateway. Set the stones for Father Sky and Mother Earth at the head and foot of the Earth Bed. In the traditional Okanagan way, the head of the bed is in the west, the place of dreams, and the foot in the east, the place of new vision. The stone for the earth is the stone that is fairly round and flat. Remember to place your totem animal or ally representation in the circle to hold the center.

Now enter the Medicine Wheel by the west gate, calling in your totem animals and your ancestors as protectors and guides. Carry the lavender and tobacco, your journal and a pen, your Medicine Shield. Sit down on the Earth Bed and use the tobacco and lavender to surround yourself with a circle of protection—just sprinkle the individual herbs around your immediate area.

Next, stand in the center of the wheel and raise your Medicine Shield above your head. Call in the powers and colors of each cardinal direction, starting with the east. Call in the relation associated with each direction: east, winged ones; south, four-leggeds; west, swimming ones; north, standing ones and plant people. Offer your Medicine Shield toward each directional gate as you call forth the aspects of these directions. Acknowledge and give thanks for the lessons you have learned through each doorway. Be specific and take your time. It is important to tell the spirit world what you have received. Ask the ancestors and the powers in your shield to be your guides and protectors.

After you call in the cardinal directions, place your staff into the ground and hold your shield above your head and call in the center directions: above, star beings and two-leggeds; below, earth and her subterraneans and creepy-crawlers; center, those who dwell in Spirit. As you call in the center direction, bring your Medicine Shield down to heart level. Welcome your totem animals and spirit helpers, your color, song, and dance. Call in the teacher-guide White Bear to stand with you in the center of the spiral path. Tie your Medicine Shield to the staff with a prayer for the spirits to awaken it this day.

Cue your drumming track and, using your drum and rattle, complete the dance/chant exercise you practiced on numerous occasions in the center. Honor yourself, the Seven Sacred Directions, and your Medicine Shield as you complete this ritual one last time. As you dance, ask the essence of each symbol on your shield to enter it and awaken its power.

When you are finished, remove your shield from the center staff and lie down in the Earth Bed; place your shield on your chest. Feel the camaraderie of White Bear in the center. Visualize the spiral path you traveled. Feel the power of your Medicine Shield and the work you have done. Allow your mind to drift into a meditative state or a daydream, with the purpose of seeing the things you came to this lifetime to accomplish: for yourself, your family, your community, All Your Relations on Earth, and the world. If you feel you need to release some sadness, it is okay to shed tears.

When you finish, gently remove the shield, sit up, and write these things down.

Now just lie on the earth and enjoy the sensations of sun and sky, fresh air, soft grass and moss, and the ground beneath you. When you feel complete, cleanse your shield with sage and sweetgrass smoke, turning again to each direction as you do so. Then, bless and release your ancestors, your totem animals and guides, and any others you have called to join you. Close the circle by releasing in reverse order each direction you called, and thank each for its support.

Unless you have done this ceremony in a place where you are certain that it won't be disturbed, put everything back in natural order. You can set it up again next time you come.

You have awakened your Medicine Shield. Know it is now charged with the powers with which you have been working and will provide you with blessings and protection. Consider hanging this new Seven Sacred Directions Medicine Shield in a special location, perhaps above your altar to remind yourself of who you are, what you've learned, and the spirits and guides who stand beside you.

## Talking Circle—Reflections

### by Robin Youngblood

The twentieth century has been called the marathon age of invention by some—and many inventions were absolutely life-changing. Revolutionary. Future impacts aside. Yet the fact remains: these "discoveries" were first imagined, dreamed in the minds of humans. Given that premise: *We have the ability to dream and create wondrous, healthy, and healing methods and technologies, as well as those that harm and destroy, AND the ability to consider the impacts.*

Until the last five hundred years, many decisions were made by connecting the heart to the mind and looking as far ahead as possible to see what effect any invention would have on the human family and the natural world around us. Indigenous peoples made decisions by consensus, unto the next seven generations. If we couldn't envision positive effects for that long, we didn't make that decision.

Truth is, humans have invented many responsible energy systems—solar, wind, Tesla turbines and electric cars, high-speed commuter trains running on hydroelectric power, solar roadways, etc. Here in the US, we've been the LAST to use these wondrous technologies. Why is that? Fear of the unknown, fear that we will lose privileges and entitlements, fear that we won't be able to handle the changes we create. Fear that companies founded on old technologies will lose money? And why isn't there more government funding for further R and D for developing sustainable energy sources?

But there is some progress afoot. Recently, the US government stepped in on the #NoDAPL pipeline issue, finally recognizing that sovereign tribal governments need to be heard and laws need to be revised. In December 2020, President-elect Biden appointed Congresswoman Debra Haaland (D-NM, Laguna Pueblo) as Secretary of the Interior, the first Native American cabinet secretary in US history.

*We are all indigenous to Mother Earth*! If we want to pass a habitable planet to our children and grandchildren, we need to start co-creating the new, better, more balanced world we all really want.

What we are seeing in these turbulent times is that the Four Brothers, representatives of the four races spoken of in the Hopi prophecies, are coming together from around the world to restore right relationship to All Beings. Because Native Americans hold the responsibility for Earth, we are the ones who had to focus the intention for healing our mother. And first, we have to heal the divisions between us and release historical wounds so we can stand united. This happened at Standing Rock. From the place of healing and peace, we can move forward in unity. Honoring each tribe's diverse culture and wisdom, we stand together. From this place of power, our black, white, and yellow brothers and sisters join us. In focused, unified prayer and ceremony, we can and will co-create and restore balance to Mother Earth and All Our Relations.

Just as people of all nations gathered at the Standing Rock pipeline protest, we are gathering worldwide to eradicate systemic racism, endemic poverty, and human trafficking. We need to protest the use of pesticides, GMOs, antibiotics and growth hormones, oil, fracking, carbon emissions, etc. We can, and are, doing this through our social networks; it's worked with #NoDAPL and to elect new leaders. We will no longer allow police brutality, vote manipulation, lobbyists with big money influencing governing officials, Big Oil, Big Ag, Big Pharma, dictatorial governments, fraudulent cover-ups, and business that lacks integrity and responsibility.

As we each acknowledge our personal responsibility, we create collective responsibility. We are holding *ourselves* accountable for the politicians we elect, for their policies, and, through teachings such as those in *Journey of the White Bear* and our unique individual paths to our Shaman's Hearts, we are ascertaining the ways we can personally help to change our world.

Together, we are ONE. Working in common unity, we have the ability to manifest a new and better world for all. And we have an opportunity for a new beginning in the east to co-create the world we really want—balanced, full of beauty and grace, fueled by wisdom, love, and joy. This is a good time to sit together around the Medicine Wheel, listen to each person's perspective, agree on common needs that respect all beings, and find ways to meet them.

Many years ago, Black Elk too saw we would have the potential to restore right relationship to All Beings in a new way. His prayer has been passed down for many generations:

> *For All People: It is true that many of the old ways have been lost. But just as the rains restore the earth after a drought, so the power of the Great Mystery will restore the way and give it new life. We ask that this happen not just for the Red People, but for all people, that they all might live. In ignorance and carelessness they have walked on Ina Maka, Our Mother. They did not understand that they are part of All Beings, the Four-Legged, the Winged, Grandfather Rock, the Tree People, and Our Star Brothers. Now Our Mother and All Our Relations are crying out.*
>
> *They cry for the help of All People.*
>
> —Black Elk—Oglala Sioux

The next cycle in humankind's evolution is at our doorstep. What we choose to do with it is the question.

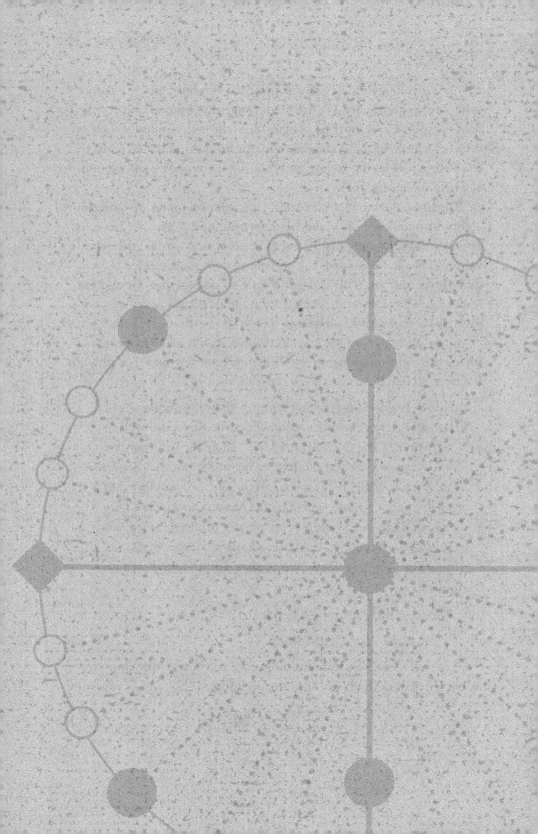

## *Conclusion*

# CIRCLING AND CYCLING

As we described in the beginning of this book, the *Journey of the White Bear* is circular and evolutionary, taking you deeper when you are ready. Consider the image of a helix: each revolution brings you back to the same place on the spiral, but at a slightly higher level. We cycle the wheel again and again as we evolve, learning something new each time.

After resting, you will stand ready to envision your next adventure on your spiritual path. As your next cycle of learning begins—whatever it might be—you now possess a deeper understanding of how to use the Medicine Wheel's principles, and how to bring these teachings forward to touch others. You have the ability to stand fully present in the balanced center, holding tremendous power.

A few years ago, after making a life-changing career decision, Sandy received a vision.

> *I journey through a long stone tunnel where luminescence*
> *gleams on the cave walls creating windows to stories in pasts*
> *and futures, of those who have come before and those who*
> *are yet to come. At the end of the tunnel lies Grandmother*
> *Ocean, and my guide and I swim to the northwest to a pine*
> *forest island. When we arrive, it is dusk and we join a dance*
> *ceremony around a Sacred Fire. A dance where bear medicine*
> *reigns: where people dance to become bears, and where bears*
> *dance to become people. They are dancing their dreaming,*
> *circling first one direction, then another. There are bears of all*

*sizes and colors, and one by one they step away from the circle to travel forth out into the world. It is a sensing and a knowing they have, what direction to take, what right action is for them: their Original Instructions. When the sun rises, the few remaining bears also go, swimming. They are bears of many colors, and yet in their heart, they are all bear people, connected as one, dispersed throughout the world to share their dreaming.*

*I remain on the island, with the large elder White Bear, who walks with me to the shoreline as the sun gleams on the horizon. She directs me to the ocean depths surrounding the island coastline where a warren of caves glow with phosphorescence. I seek one cave in particular—the cave where my contracts are stored. She says I will know it when I see it. And now, I understand. I am looking for a part of my soul, and that completing a contract —or dismantling it—will allow me to don my true skin again and re-member my Original Instructions.*

*Finally I find the cave and remove a scroll. I take it to the surface. White Bear opens it and reads it: my agreement to conform, to become a partner to one who needed healing as part of a karmic debt (although, she confirms, some things only God can heal). Trying to fulfill this contract created experiences that resulted in soul loss for me. White Bear pauses in introspection, then asks if I am ready for this contract to be complete. I nod. With one claw, she tears it down the middle. I do not have to carry this woundedness any longer. My commitment to that contract, that way of being in the world, is done. What I experienced partially shaped me this lifetime. There is no erasing it; there is only moving forward.*

*Then White Bear tells me I must now retrieve my bear heart. My wild heart. I return to the vaults under the sea and remove the soft heart from the chamber where it's been stored all these many years. When I bring it to the surface, I hand it to White Bear, who slices my chest and places the translucent blue organ inside. She puts it on the right, an accompaniment to my physical heart. I hug it into my chest for a long time, embracing this part of me now returned after being missing for so long.*

In Sandy's story, her teacher, White Bear, led her to release herself from a contract she'd fulfilled and find her missing bear heart. In this same way, your own spirit animal allies or ancestors may lead you to a glimpse of what is next for you in the journey world!

## The Next Adventure

To move into the next cycle, the next adventure, you have only to peer into the wilderness of your heart's desire and your soul's purpose. Define your intention, in the way you've been taught, and begin in the east again pursuing your vision.

While you have barely scratched the surface of some of the subjects we present in this book, you now have a stronger foundation. There are many fine teachers all over the world stepping forward to share their wisdom and opportunities to explore traditions on this path. Robin teaches courses both online and in workshops throughout the world. You have only to ask. We also encourage you to find a local spiritual community, with whom you can gather and share medicine work.

As you already know, your intention, decisions, priorities, and experiences determine what happens next: where you go, what you do, who you meet. Of course, Spirit has a hand in that, too. Wherever you are on the path is where you belong. No right or wrong answers, only choices, including the choice to rest from continuing any spiritual work at this time.

Whatever you decide, your guides, allies, ancestors, totem animals, spirit teachers, and White Bear are with you. We find it incredibly interesting how Spirit works: if you take a few steps in a direction that supports you highest purpose and All Our Relations, the universe often does the rest of the work. Amazing things fall into place in a manner both synchronistic and synergetic. Other people move through your life as if by design, some staying, others leaving. Dreams and journeys provide answers to age-old questions. Opportunities suddenly appear from sources not only unlikely, but never imagined. And, of course, the lessons needed for your personal spiritual evolution do not stop, regardless of whether you are actively pursuing any particular teaching.

Because wherever you go, you're the first one you meet.

At times it can be difficult to know right action, and it may be best to yield to the universe flowing around you; allow the river to be the river. Know you have the ability to choose your response. Detaching from outcome is always recommended. Remember the lesson Creator hid in your heart: you—both the individual and the collective—create your own reality. Your internal state is mirrored in what you see around you.

In embodying the Shaman's Heart, you'll know whether each new decision supports your highest good and the good of All Your Relations. If you feel conflicted, call on the wisdom of White Bear, on your allies, power animals, and spirit teachers: ask them to help ... or to simply listen when you need a friendly ear. Pay attention to the wild instincts in yourself. But remember that together, we can do so much more than we can do alone. As natural co-creators, our only choice is whether we will create harmony and balance, or chaos and destruction.

Once you've developed spiritual maturity and the ability to maintain balance in your inner work, the world begins to change with you. And thus it is in the dance of life.

*Techqua Ikachi!* Blend with Mother Earth and celebrate life!

Thank the Great Mystery for the beauty in the world. Trust that your life lessons and experiences were planned before your birth. Thank All Your Relations for the blessing to continue your earthwalk, the opportunity to learn and experience life on our beautiful planet. Gaze into the eyes of White Bear and know there is always a place for you. Look at your Medicine Shield and re-member who you are.

Thirty years ago, Robin wrote a poem that ends thus:

> *Don't push the river*
>
> *Let it flow from the Source*
>
> *All good things come slow*
>
> *They don't need to be forced*

Aho Mitakuye Oyasin! All Our Relations!

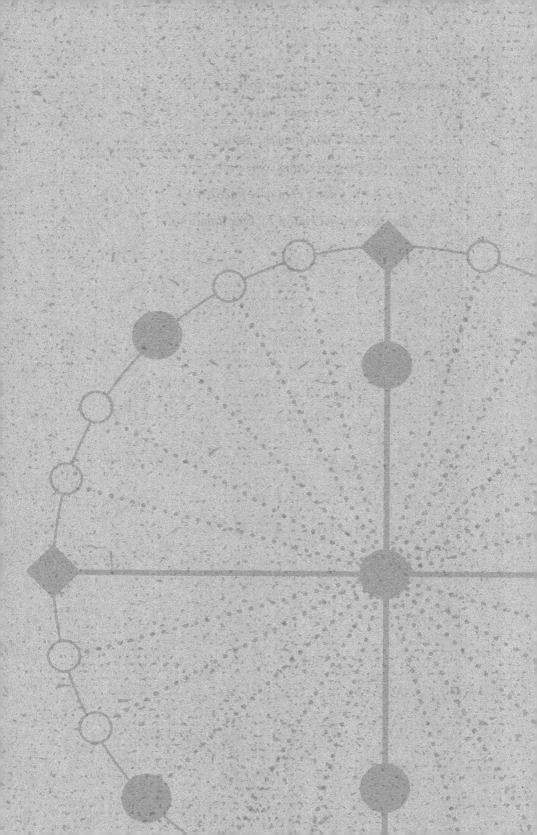

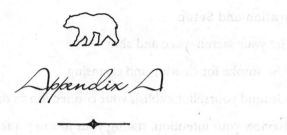

# BASIC TOOLS

This section provides a set of checklists and tool descriptions to augment the discussion from the Preparing for Study chapter and to support your work throughout this book.

## Practicing Visualization and Journeying

Visualization and journeying are key techniques that allow us to obtain information from non-ordinary reality with its lower, upper, and middle worlds, sometimes called the astral plane or dreamtime. You'll use these visionary practices often in the work you do in *Journey of the White Bear*. For a complete discussion of the journey worlds, see the chapter entitled Journeying with Bear. The section below offers a checklist to follow.

### *Tools for Journeying*

**Objects**

- Journal
- Journey (drumming) track or CD, such as those distributed by the Foundation for Shamanic Studies Journeywork® Series
- Cedar or sage to burn for ritual cleansing
- Candles with matches

## Preparation and Setup

- Set your sacred space and altar

- Use smoke for clearing and cleansing

- Ground yourself: establish your connection to the earth

- Review your intention, stating your journey question clearly

- Envision a circle of light around you and say a prayer for protection

- Call the directions; light the altar candles if you are using them

- Request the presence of your guides and other helpers

- Cue your drumming track, keeping in mind your journey question, then go

Remember to follow the path you took into the journey on your return, thanking all you met on your quest.

### *Preparing for Ceremony*

For each ceremony, you'll assemble the tools needed and prepare the space you wish to use. In addition to the discussion in the Preparing for Study chapter and the details included in the Ceremony Design discussion in Appendix B, the section below offers a condensed checklist to follow.

### *Tools for Ceremony*

Check your local bookstore, gift shop, or music store—or even internet sources—to locate these items.

## Ceremonial Objects

- Items needed to create your altar, detailed for each ceremony

- Cleansing: use different types of herbs for different ceremonies and purposes

- Colored candles, any size; tealights work well

- Matches or lighter

- Journal

- Drumming track (for certain ceremonies)

- Drum (optional)

- Rattle: can be as simple as dried beans or small beads in any hand-sized container

See individual chapters for the items needed for specific ceremonies.

## Basic Setup for Ceremony

- Choose a private indoor or outdoor site for your ceremony.

- Build a Medicine Wheel using a representation for each of the Seven Sacred Directions (see the one described in the Co-creating in the East chapter).

- Put the environment in order and have your journal at hand.

- Set sacred space.

- Use smoke for clearing and cleansing.

- Review your intention.

- Say a prayer for protection.

## To Call the Circle

1. After cleansing yourself and the space where you'd like to do your work, ground and hold your intention clearly.

2. Stand in the center and using your hand or a sacred object draw an imaginary circle of light around the perimeter of the area. (You may also use cornmeal, ash from a ritual cleansing, or sea salt to physically draw the circle perimeter.)

3. Turn completely around the space.

4. Some practitioners use a statement to enforce this act. This can be very simple, such as "I call this circle of protection for this sacred space. Let only that which is beauty, truth, and love enter here." Even simpler: "Highest truth, greatest good, only love, harm to none." Tailor this to your individual needs.

5. Once complete, the space is ready for you to call the directions, etc. for your personal work and ceremony.

Consecrated in this way, the space will remain a sacred refuge for as long as you wish to use it. Similarly, you can perform a ritual of protection for yourself anywhere, anytime by visualizing yourself surrounded by a bright white light of protection, and calling on your guides to watch over you. See the section below on guides and helpers.

## Using Medicine Tools

Within your practice, there will be tools that you'll grow to depend on, form a relationship with, and use on a regular basis. Not all tools are for all practitioners; some may use only a few. In this section, we list some of the most common medicine tools.

## Drums

The drum is the heartbeat of Mother Earth. The drums we use most often in our work are single-sided hand drums, and, in larger gatherings, double-sided mother drums on a stand that can be used by multiple people at one time. Different animal skins on the drumhead create a different harmonic vibration and bring the medicine of the animal totem into play in the role of Helper Spirit. Many drums are created in special ways to carry the balance of the masculine and feminine, which in turn balances the energy of the person/people being worked on in healing or simply dancing. Different drumbeats evoke different states of being.

### Sacred Drum Rhythms

1. Calling the ancestors, guides, and helpers; creating the sacred space, the energetic container for the circle: a slowly repeated single beat

2. Inviting the ancestors', guides', and helpers' participation in the ceremony: heartbeat, aligning everyone to the One Heart, the rhythm of Mother Earth's pulse

3. Calling inspiration, the fire that ignites creativity: trinity—three rapid beats, pause, repeat. Masculine/Feminine/Child; above, below and center

4. Calling the powers of the Four Directions; the elementals; the Wheel of Life; wind, fire, water, earth: four beats, pause, repeat

5. Combination of #2 and #3: call in, invite participation, ignite co-creation

6. Two #3s really ignites the fire—passionate communal co-creation to manifest or release energy

7. Combination of #3 and #4: calling and honoring all Seven Sacred Directions; implanting the energies of all into our own beings

8. Continuous rapid beat: used for shamanic journeys; unifies the alpha and beta states; joins us to the plant kingdom and provides protection when working with the major plant spirits; also unifies the intention/prayers for All Our Relations. Used to unwind or close ceremonies, releasing All Beings to their own realms and dimensions

Crafting your own hand drum is a wonderful way to connect with the medicine of the Giveaway animal whose skin you are using to create a sacred tool.

## Rattles

Rattles shake things up! These tools change and move energy. Any type of rattle or shaker can be used to clear chakras (energy centers in the body) and disperse stuck energy. Gourds with seeds or seed beads inside produce a really soft, easy sound. Rawhide, shell, and antler rattles generate a more distinctive, hard sound. We've even seen a mint box or a plastic water bottle filled with small stones or beads used in a pinch when a medicine person was called on to do a spontaneous healing and didn't have their usual tools available.

## Flutes and Whistles, Songs and Chants

There are many ways medicine people call the ancestors, guides, and spirit helpers. Spirits pay attention to the sound current, as well as spectrums of light and color. Certain medicine people are gifted with the use of the flute, whistles, drums, rattles, songs, and chants to call in specific helping spirits. This is a special gift.

Indigenous people come from oral traditions; traditions without "copy-right" laws. In practice, if a medicine person gives you one of their songs, it's important to refer to them when you sing it to credit the source. Songs are often "caught" by medicine people—from the spirits, or the ethers. Thanking the person or tribe that gave one the song is respectful.

## Bells

The tinkling sound of bells calls the helper spirits and can also be used to banish negative energies around body orifices and chakras. Bells were first used by the Romany (Gypsy) peoples in India. Our Northwest Shakers use bells in rituals. The teaching is that the settler colonists "forgot" the correct use of the bell, and our people are holding it until modern culture remembers what it is to be used for.

## Feathers

Feathers are used primarily for cutting energetic cords, cleansing, and healing work. Eagle and hawk are best for this. Owl, heron, swan, vulture, or even turkey feathers can also be used. For non-Indians, turkey or duck feathers are best because they are legal for anyone. Feather fans are also used for ritual cleansing with smoke and dance.

## Hollow Bones

As we discussed in the East chapter, the medicine person is often called a "Hollow Bone," meaning they are channels for spiritual energy, information, and healing. Many medicine people actually keep a hollow bone (usually a bird leg bone) in their tool bag, to use for "sucking medicine." This technique is used when a person exhibits signs of being "hit" and implanted with an energy object (usually a feather, bead, piece of bone, etc.) meant to curse them with illness. The medicine person will perform a ceremony to extract the object, cleansing themselves and the client, then using the hollow bone to suck the implant out. Others may not be able to see the implant on a physical level, but the client will often feel it being extracted.

"Sucking doctors" can be found throughout the world's indigenous peoples. These practitioners can often remove tumors and other physical ailments by sucking them out of the patient's system.

## Candles

Candles are often used to mark the directions on an altar, to hold a prayer, or to use for burning/releasing ceremonies. As outlined in the Cleansing section, they can also be used to "light up" a person, brushing candlelight from the feet upward to the head (no downward motions). This practice releases negative energies, smooths the aura, and fills the etheric body with light.

## Calling Staff

Many medicine people use a staff to "call" the ancestors, spirit guides, and helpers and to create/consecrate the sacred circle (sacred space) needed to conduct ceremony. Staffs can be large or small; use animal skulls, crystals, feathers, bones, etc. These are very personal tools, typically decorated with symbols of a medicine person's personal protection and the medicine they walk with.

## Talking Stick

Protocols are important to native peoples. The way things are done conveys respect: respect for self, each other, and the spirits. Whenever people call and sit in a circle, the facilitator will use a talking stick to create order. The rule is, "He or she who has the stick talks." No cross talk. No interruptions. The leader may hold the talking stick while teaching, then pass it around for each person's comments. When participating in a talking circle (discussed in Honoring Sacred Ceremonies in the Resources section), it's typically respectful to introduce yourself, then mention your lineage or direct ancestors, as they've been called into the circle and are watching and listening to our spoken and unspoken prayers and needs.

## Medicine Bundles

Medicine bundles store personal medicine objects, plus the sacred tokens (symbols) given to a specific person, ceremony, or tribe to use for particular purposes. Each medicine person has their own bundle (sometimes a few), typically wrapped in leather and/or red cloth. The bundle includes their "tools": sage, cedar, sweetgrass, lavender, osha, and whatever other herbs they might use, plus stones that carry certain energies or symbols, perhaps a rattle, hollow bird bone, etc. Different bundles are assembled for specific ceremonies—a pipe bundle, a sweat lodge bundle, a bundle for vision quest, and so forth. Ceremony bundles are passed to a medicine person when they are experienced enough to receive permission to perform a ceremony.

## Medicine Bags

There are many types of medicine bags, and most medicine people own several. A personal medicine bag will be filled with sacred tokens from experiences such as vision quests—symbols that represent the gifts and lessons received. Medicine people may also carry medicine bags filled with tobacco, cedar, sage, etc., which they will use in ceremony. Pipe carriers will also have a special pipe bag. Some medicine people own and wear "power pieces," jewelry they have made, or that has been gifted to them, with special blessings placed within it. These personal items are sacred and carry the protected (and protective) energy of the wearer. *Please always follow protocol and refrain from touching these items unless explicitly instructed to do so by the owner.*

## Psychedelic Plant Medicines

Psychedelic plant medicines are not to be taken lightly and are to be used ONLY when the plant spirit itself calls, and then only in ceremony facilitated by a truly qualified medicine person. We cannot express this CAUTION strongly enough. We've personally observed several people fall "over the edge" with these medicines, never to return—either through insanity or suicide.

*Plant medicines are spirit beings and they demand respect.* To "play" with them recreationally, overuse them, or take them without proper intention, invocation, and protection is asking for trouble. On the other hand, if a plant spirit calls you, you will know it. The medicine can be quite enlightening, helpful in curing addictions and releasing negative energies and entities ... but only if done with great care and respect.

# COMMUNITY

At our core, we are tribal peoples, gathering in groups for both survival purposes and companionship. We all have a family, a village, a tribe: even if it's embodied only in our pets, the plants that share our homes, or the trees outside our door. As human beings, we are drawn to—need to—share our earthwalk with someone who loves us. Although many of the exercises in this book can only be done alone, sharing your experience in some way often deepens it, makes the journey less lonely, and can help support you if you find yourself stuck in an uncomfortable stage.

## The Tribe

Children were taught differently in tribal environments than we are taught as Westerners in modern culture. The great outdoors was our schoolhouse and teachers were aunties and uncles. Usually by the time a boy was six or seven, he would be assigned to a skilled craftsman, usually an older relative, who could teach him the skills necessary: hunting, fishing, and perhaps the martial skills of a warrior/protector. A boy might also begin to learn a trade, such as crafting arrowheads. Girls learned the art of basketry; how to sew hides, barks, and rushes for clothing, temporary shelter, or tipis; and were trained in the skill of finding, identifying, and preparing herbs for medicinal and ritual purposes.

Some boys learned to mix medicine; some girls became warriors. These individuals were "twin spirits" *(berdache)*, who carried the spirit of both man and woman, and were considered sacred, often training to care for sacred items used in tribal ceremony. Sometimes a dream of the thunder beings would proclaim an individual as *heyokah*, the sacred clown, who taught the people by doing things backward. Each youngster, no matter their calling, received a mentor to kindle the gifts given to the child at birth or through dreams and visions. This way of teaching was, and still is, quite different than our modern methods that feel so limiting and unsatisfying to so many.

Storytelling was another teaching tool employed by our ancestral tribal peoples. Children began to hear stories at birth, and, over time, the tales were expanded. Teaching was a circular process—yet another representation of the spiral. The storyteller would lead the children within, to the kernels of truth found in the story, then out again to the larger picture, how the truths could be applied in life. Teaching was always underlined by hands-on experience.

Each story incorporated a multitude of layers and meanings, and the children learned what was most pertinent to their life experiences. By adulthood, they had gleaned much from each tribal story or legend. This is archetypal learning, something that often goes unaddressed in our current culture. In today's schools, ancient myths such as the Greek tragedies are studied more for structure than content, without mention of the transformation of the characters and the lessons learned. As a people, we miss much by touching only the surface, for an oft-repeated myth challenges our minds to find the hidden significance within the narrative.

## The Value of the Village

Each person who studies the *Journey of the White Bear* will have a different set of experiences. What might be profound for one may be less important for another. Sharing these experiences deepens your connection with your community/tribe and village. While the written exercises in these chapters were developed for someone working alone, if you anticipate an exercise will bring discomfort, please find someone who can witness and support your work. You and your study partner can exchange places, so each receives encouragement and feels seen. Also, you can connect with Robin, who offers online courses, including the Shaman's Path, based on the teachings in *Path of the White Wolf.* We're also developing curriculum for *Journey of the White Bear.*

As a society we have forgotten how to live together in nurturing support of each person's unique purpose. Unfortunately, without support and sustenance we might wander aimlessly, forgetting our purpose entirely; or become caught up in fulfilling someone else's purpose. As a result, we sometimes find ourselves trapped in jobs we despise, feeling we must in order to survive. We participate in activities that drain our energy, and form partnerships with those we may really not want to be with because we feel there is no other choice. We spiral downward into ambivalence, depression, despair—sometimes even committing crimes against ourselves and others.

But there is an alternative. This societal flaw that ignores or denigrates an individual's sacred purpose can be repaired by creating your own village, a tribe of friends, or a *tiyospaye,* an extended family. This family, which you choose, can be more supportive and fulfilling than your natal family. And that is exactly what happens with each of Robin's small online group courses.

If you decide to study the teachings in this book with other like-minded individuals—and we recommend you do if the opportunity presents—we suggest a group of no more than seven, with each person holding one of the Seven Sacred Directions. Power increases exponentially with connection, concentration, and consolidation. As has been written and proven: "Wherever two or more are gathered, I (the Great Mystery) shall be there." You may prefer a mixed group, or one composed of all women or all men, depending on your orientation. Consider which environment will best support your growth. This group should include those who wish to delve deeply into the mysteries of themselves, and who are willing to embrace the expansion that will unfold with their heartfelt participation. You might choose to elect a pathfinder to guide certain portions of each chapter's lesson, but remember, that person is more a facilitator/servant to the group rather than a leader.

## Setup for Group Meetings and Ceremonies

If you choose to study with a group, the first activity might be to choose a site to build a Medicine Wheel and a group altar. An outdoor setting is best to connect with nature, but an indoor area will work if it is relatively empty and large enough to comfortably hold the group—and for locales where the outdoors may not be private enough or the weather presents challenges. Set up the sacred space needed with three separate areas: 1) group altar, 2) Medicine Wheel, and 3) village entry, including a gateway into the Medicine Wheel and the altar. The altar here is the group shrine, not the altar within the Medicine Wheel.

### Ceremony Design

Ceremony is formally defined as an activity prescribed by custom, ritual, or religious belief that unites group members and celebrates accomplishments or milestones. We discuss ceremony in the chapter entitled Healing in the West. In addition, in the section entitled Honoring Sacred Ceremonies, we've listed common ceremonies that typically follow a set pattern. This pattern is then adjusted and expanded by the facilitator in accordance with the way they were taught.

There are a few differences between ritual and ceremony, as practiced by native peoples: generally, rituals are contained within ceremony, and there may be several ritual components in a complete ceremony. You will be conducting private or small group ceremonies for yourself or your tribe based on the recommendations for each chapter lesson. These ceremonies celebrate completion of the teaching, provide a final component needed to bring the lesson to closure, and provide a way to physically integrate each teaching. The imagery and the emotions they evoke are powerful and transformative, elevating your understanding.

For group gatherings, set up ceremonies simply or elaborately, as you desire. Spirit dwells in spontaneity, so the more spontaneous you can be, the better. If a question arises, move into silence for a moment—the Great Mystery will speak to you in the pregnant pause of possibility.

Ceremonies can range from those steeped in tradition and strict protocol to those you design for yourself. Every facilitator follows ceremonial processes and protocols as they have been taught. These protocols include elements such as those we list below and on the following pages. For the ceremonies we outline in *Journey of the White Bear*, consider these steps:

- Setting sacred space (discussed in the Preparing for Study chapter).

- Creating an altar (discussed in the Preparing for Study chapter): this can be begun before the ceremony begins, and can continue into the ceremony, if appropriate.

- Calling the circle. If performed outside, spread cornmeal around the perimeter of the Medicine Wheel or circle while inviting in all the helping spirits of those present.

- Invoking protection for the group: include an opening prayer.

- Setting an intention (discussed in the Preparing for Study chapter).

- Calling in the directions: use drum and chant, song, or prayer to acknowledge the powers of each direction (as noted in each chapter) as they apply to the reason for the gathering.

- Summoning the ancestors and helpers of each person present: each individual can do this, silently or aloud, as he or she leaves the village area and steps into the Medicine Wheel circle to participate in the ceremony. If it's a group ceremony, the pathfinder should ritually cleanse (smudge) each person at this time as well.

- Performing the steps or activities for each ceremony in the chapter (or for the intention of the gathering). Sometimes there will be a visualization included, particularly for the ceremonies we introduce in the chapters in this book. See the pertinent chapter for guidelines; it is important to follow the formula outlined, as each one builds and expands on the previous.

- Closing the circle. The chosen facilitator or pathfinder releases the ancestors, helpers, and powers of each direction with drumming and prayer. Leave an offering of beauty as a sign of respect and gratitude for what you have received.

- Sharing food, as desired, and community clean up, as needed.

## *Creating a Ceremony for the Tribe*

Ceremony bonds members of the group and confers on each participant the power of the whole. Each of you will contribute in many ways to the success of this practice. We include some tips here for creating a monthly ceremony for your study group tribe or *tiyospaye* (extended family) as you explore the teachings in this book.

1. Before the ceremony, and each time the tribe comes to Council to share a lesson, each participant should choose an item to bring for the altar. The altar item should be specific to the teachings of the direction, such as a representation of the animals found in your work, or the element the direction explores.

2. Place the altar away from the Medicine Wheel, facing the direction in which you are working. Make the altar area beautiful: it is the shrine of All-Who-Have-Come-Before-You, the ancestors, animal nations, star beings, and Creative Mind.

3. The group will meet in the region set aside for the village. This section is removed from the Medicine Wheel and altar. It is a circular area where people can sit to discuss the chapter and share individual work completed before coming to the gathering.

4. When it is time to begin, the pathfinder invites the tribe to proceed to the altar, find a comfortable position, and revisit the journey from the current study chapter.

5. The pathfinder will need to appoint someone to bring and operate the CD player and/or drumming track; stay aware of anyone who needs support through the journey; and identify one or two group members to assist in whatever ways are needed.

6. When the journey is finished, the tribe can spend a few minutes sharing experiences and any insights received when doing the assignment for the chapter earlier in the month.

7. When this is complete and the group is ready for the ceremony, select members to take on the different roles incorporated in the ceremony: someone to drum and call in the Seven Sacred Directions, someone to light candles, etc.

8. Depending on the ceremony, each group member may take a turn performing the specific ceremony prescribed for the direction—or the process could be done simultaneously, all group members at once, if appropriate. If done individually, allow each person to take as much time, make as much noise, experience as much emotion, and move around as much as he or she needs to. If, however, someone seems to be drifting out of control or too far off topic (this won't happen often), the pathfinder and helpers have the responsibility to take that person aside, if appropriate, and offer gentle words, prayer, and chants to calm him. It is important to encourage the person and let him know that release through ceremony is a part of healing. It is also important to remind him that he has a choice about whether he wants to stay in the past story of his life or let it go. You may wish to recommend a more conventional method of counseling or support in addition to the work with the wheel, especially for someone who has been deeply traumatized.

9. If performing the ceremony one at a time, when the first group member has completed his turn, the village welcomes him back with loving support. Then the next person enters the Medicine Wheel, and the process begins again, until each person, including the pathfinder, is complete.

10. Consider building in some sharing time after completion to discuss the experience—as we say, to tell the healing stories—especially if the ceremony format is one where everyone performs the ceremony simultaneously.

11. Once you have experienced this sustenance and healing for the soul, nourish the body in comfort, love, and community celebration. Bring delicious food for a feast after the ceremony. This step is essential. We can't tell you how many times we've been told to feed the people. Enjoy sharing bread with each other. Feast, laugh, and express your joyful exuberance at the completion of this rite of passage.

# Facilitators, Participants, and Gifting

This section provides some additional discussion on the benefits and protocols for working with ceremony facilitators, choosing participants and witnesses, and the practice of gifting.

## *Facilitators*

Your community may hold someone with experience in the type of ceremony you want to hold. Discuss your situation and ask for help creating and performing your ceremony. If you choose to engage the facilitator, do not expect to retain control over all parts of the ceremony. This leader will have their own way of doing things, according to the way he or she was taught. You'll have the great opportunity to learn as you observe the way in which the facilitator goes about their business. (For example, if you ask someone to pour a sweat lodge or conduct a pipe ceremony, you would not tell them, what prayers to pray or what songs to sing, etc.) Discuss what you envision for the ceremony, but do not get attached to details. Follow the facilitator's directions with respect.

If you cannot locate an experienced facilitator, you may decide to plan your own simplified ceremony based on those referenced in this book—particularly the Life Transition and Giveaway Ceremonies—using the core steps we outline (see the discussion in the chapter entitled Healing in the West). After all, you know how to call the circle—so text your friends, create the Medicine Wheel together, and assign each a task (a prayer, a poem, prayer ties, ritual cleansing with smoke or another method, drumming, a song, etc.). Bless the power of community to help you celebrate!

## *Participants and Witnesses*

When inviting participants and witnesses to attend a personal ceremony, choose those who are supportive of your chosen path and will be able to share your joy in this type of forum. Discuss particular tasks you want them to do for you with the facilitator or as part of shared facilitation, such as calling directions, saying prayers, and other ceremonial practices. Review the ceremony format and remind them what to bring.

As we mentioned earlier in the chapter, ceremony bonds group members, the ripples of one person's experience touching another's, often conferring on each participant the power of the whole. Each participant brings their own medicine to the gathering, regardless of whether they acknowledge it. One medicine that participants share is standing as witnesses to each community member's transformation. We cannot stress how important witnesses are as a part of this process. Those who participate in your ceremony not only acknowledge your accomplishments in the moment and see you in your new skin, but they can also help you remember your achievements when you feel discouraged. We all encounter moments in life when we need help remembering how much we've grown and changed!

## Gifting

An energy exchange occurs anytime you give or receive goods or services, including ceremony. If the dynamic balance of giving and receiving is not maintained in one area of your life, other areas tend to fall out of sync. Gifting your ceremony facilitator and those who support you not only shows appreciation for their work and attendance, a contribution to your growth, but also maintains this energetic balance.

Some facilitators are quite clear what they expect to receive—not always money—but others leave it more free-form. Then it becomes up to you to determine how valuable their service was. Either way, the ceremony is not complete without gifting.

Often it's okay if you aren't able to give money. There are other ways to gift people who offer you spiritual teachings and services. Balancing energy exchange, or bartering, is an age-old alternative to a financial gift, especially if funds are short. Our ancestors conducted most business via bartering: farmers traded chickens for herbal remedies from the local healer, who then traded feather pillows to someone else for potatoes. In modern times, currency or cash replaces bartering, but currency is also an energy exchange. As one of Robin's teachers liked to say, "It's called *currency* for a reason! It's a current of energy, just like electricity. And just like any other current, it needs to flow. When one stops the flow, one is unable to fully receive what's been given." Money/currency is also energy exchange, and it, too, can get out of balance.

In many native circles gifting takes the form of tobacco, which symbolizes respect for the teacher's wisdom. But as many native teachers will tell you, "Tobacco does not pay the rent or the phone bill." Hint: include a monetary donation with the tobacco if you can. At some gatherings, you'll find a donation basket in a convenient place so that participants can offer money to cover expenses, such as firewood, or to reimburse the facilitator's travel expenses.

Tithing is another common form of balancing energy exchange. This word comes from a Christian practice that usually involves giving a percentage of your income to the church. We encourage you, however, to think about tithing in a slightly different way. You can keep your energy exchange dynamic in balance by tithing *to the source that nurtures you spiritually*—whatever that source is: the earth, yourself, a medicine teacher.

In lieu of money, gifts can be simple: a crystal or other stone, sage or sweetgrass bundle, a book, or a beautiful plant. More elaborate handcrafted gifts such as drums, rattles, jewelry, baskets, or beadwork are entirely appropriate and treasured.

## Honoring Sacred Ceremonies

The ceremonies outlined in this section are typically group rites, although some can be practiced solo. Group ceremony can be created for almost any occasion, provided you show consideration for the participants and their respective belief systems and ensure group safety. Until you have formal training and a history of experience under your belt, we do not recommend you facilitate ceremony for any groups except your study group, and especially with people you don't know. Group ceremony energy dynamics can be unexpected and unpredictable. You do not want to be reckless and end up responsible for someone getting hurt. People can be and have been injured physically, mentally, and emotionally. We cannot stress this enough: it can be dangerous to use medicine tools and rituals without understanding the ways these powers can impact and influence others.

In a similar vein, we recommend that you find out about the facilitators and their experience before you participate in any event they lead. Although you have protection tools, choose events and facilitators carefully to ensure you do not put yourself in a potentially unpleasant or uncontrolled situation.

## Medicine Circle

This is one of the first events attended by most people when stepping onto the Red Road. A Medicine Circle, or Sacred Circle, is called when two or more people wish to come together for a specific intention, such as prayer, healing, witnessing someone's rite of passage, or an invitation to join in Council. To initiate Sacred Circle is to set intention, clear the space, call in the ancestors and the directional powers for protection and guidance, and set the boundaries and guidelines that must be honored during the time that the circle is meeting. Once a circle begins, it is disrespectful to interrupt or intrude; you must wait for an invitation, and if you don't receive one, you should leave.

## Council Lodge

This Sacred Circle of Peers is called to discuss needs, problems and solutions, resources, and the events for a community. Guidelines for the Medicine Circle apply here. A council lodge is typically conducted by selected elders, equal numbers from both genders if a mixed community. Depending on the reason for gathering, this circle may last for days and is served and witnessed by the community at large. Many other rituals may be performed over the duration of the council. Decisions are by consensus, not the vote of the majority, so unresolved agenda items are tabled for the next council lodge. Interestingly, these pending issues often either disappear or resolve themselves between meetings.

## Prayer Ties

Sometimes called tobacco ties because each one is filled with a pinch of tobacco, prayer ties are made with small squares of cloth in the colors of each direction. These ties are then connected together about two inches apart with a piece of string. Cut cloth in a three- or four-inch square, then fill it with tobacco as you pray for your intention according to the direction of that color: in the east you might pray for illumination about your intention; in the south you might ask for trust that your needs will be met, and so on. Prayer ties are usually made for sweat lodge and vision quest, but occasionally a tie, or string of ties, in any color is created to set on an altar to hold intention for a prayer. In addition, sometimes other herbs are included, such as lavender, sweetgrass, cedar, sage, cornmeal, rose petals, and, in some traditions, salt as a crystal to focus intentions.

## Seasonal

Indigenous people worldwide celebrate the change of seasons, offering gratitude for the blessings of each yearly phase. Often these ceremonies are performed at the quarter marks of the year: equinoxes and solstices. Spring rituals may include planting (corn is one of the main staples for eastern Native American tribes); summer may be a ritual offering to the sun; fall is a harvesting ritual where gratitude is expressed to and for all the bearing plants; and winter's rituals may include the dreamtime. Each tribe or community develops its own rituals as part of the overall ceremony, and with repetition these ceremonies become part of the common tradition.

## Blessing Ceremonies

These include baby blessings, house blessings, and event blessings. The medicine person calls in the powers of the Seven Sacred Directions, and uses smoke to cleanse the people and the area of the event; calls in the ancestors and spirit guides responsible for the participants; and asks blessings and protection for all that happens to them now and in the future, releasing all that has happened in the past.

## Moon

There are many practices for "drawing down the moon." In some cultures, the moon is called Grandmother, married to Grandfather Sun. She is his reflection and controls the ebb and flow of the tides of life. Her power is needed for new plant growth, and for women on their menses (also called a woman's "moon-time"). Grandmother Moon nurtures both individual and collective energies. Most tribal people dance at the full moon, and in many societies the women gather at the dark of the moon to bury their menstrual flow and the placenta from childbirth, as well as plant new corn and other crops.

## Moon Lodge

In villages where women lived and worked together, most women's menses came at the same time each month, following the cycle of the moon. In some tribes, the women came together in the Moon Lodge for the duration of their menses, to share crafts, stories, and teachings. Moon time is often said to be the time of a woman's greatest power, and this sacred circle was a time for prayer, as well as discussion of community needs. Women are at their most vulnerable during their moon and are also most susceptible to the opening of the crack between the worlds. The Moon Lodge was a time for deep introspection and communication with other worlds. In some traditional societies, the men cooked and took care of the children during a woman's moon.

Today, women are sometimes taught to be ashamed of menses, sometimes called a woman's "curse." This attitude can foster sickness and pain. When women understand their true heritage and the gift of life they hold within, much of the pain and discomfort of menstruation disappears. Women in Western culture have also seen the benefits of setting aside sacred time during menses and receiving the gifts of women's spiritual community with each other.

### Life Transition and Giveaway

These are often called Rites of Passage Ceremonies, such as those we discuss in the Healing in the West chapter. In tribal cultures, specific events trigger the need for an initiatory experience witnessed by the community. This experience helps a person make a transition to the next phase of life. A new birth is occasion for such a ceremony, as is first menses for a young woman or the beginning of adolescence for a young man. Other life transition events that call for ritual are weddings, the loss of a loved one, and entering the Lodge of the Elders.

Entering the Lodge of the Elders is a personal honoring ceremony that marks an important life transition in traditional indigenous cultures that value elders and their contributions. This occurs for women when they begin to hold their wise blood and take up a more formal teaching/healing role in the community (Western culture calls this menopause). For men, this occurs when their experience and wisdom are sought more often than their physical ability, announcing their passage into sagehood (Western culture calls this retirement).

Community rituals are an important facet of indigenous culture that have, for the most part, been all but lost in the modern world. In Western culture, birthday parties, graduations, retirement parties, baptisms, and bar/bat mitzvahs serve a similar purpose, but often lack much depth.

A significant element in a Life Transition Ceremony is the Giveaway. Generally, in our present Western culture, witnesses/guests offer gifts to friends and loved ones to celebrate their life transitions. In traditional cultures, the opposite occurs; the person in transition gifts others as a means of shedding the old to make way for the new—a transformation in every facet of life.

Giveaway, while central to the Life Transition Ceremony, holds a role in almost every Native American ceremony: from the Interior Salish tradition of Winter Dance, the Northwest Coastal people's Potlatch, the Pueblo clan's Kiva ceremonies, the Plains tribes' Sun Dance, to an intertribal Pow-Wow. The power of Giveaway is universal. In Japan, people give gifts to others on their birthday, rather than receiving gifts. This is a form of ceremony as well.

## Marriage (Tsa Ya Su Ye Ta)

For the Cherokee Wedding Ceremony, each of the lovers is wrapped in a separate blue blanket. The medicine person first calls in the Seven Sacred Directions, ancestors, and spirit helpers with a chant. Then the officiant cuts the cords from all prior relationships with an eagle knife feather, asking each person if they are ready and willing to forgive and release all past relationships. Then the couple stands together and a large blue blanket is wrapped around them to signify their union. The medicine person recites several prayers of union, then offers the couple the Cherokee Wedding Vase, a double-sided vase. The groom gives the drink to the bride, and the bride offers the drink to her husband. The couple exchange their vows (and rings, if they choose), and the medicine person pronounces them married. If the couple wants, they can have two members of the bridal party hold a broomstick horizontal a foot or so above the ground. Once the couple "jumps the broomstick" they are considered truly married. (If the bride ever breaks the broomstick, the marriage is considered finished.)

## Making of Relatives

In traditional societies, the Making of Relatives (adoption) was not taken lightly. When one adopts a new sister, brother, child, grandchild, parent, or grandparent, it's for life. That means one has all the same responsibilities to and for that new relative that one does with one's birth family. When one "makes a relative"—or, as the Hawaiians call it, *hanai*—one also takes on their natural family, just as when one takes on a lover, one also becomes in relationship to all the other lovers that lover has had.

## Making Right Circle

A Making Right circle or Forgiveness ceremony is called specifically to promote healing between two or more people who are in disagreement (see the Ho'oponopono discussion in the chapter entitled Balancing in the South). Often, an elder mediates this circle. Once the circle is set, prayers spoken, and the intention defined and agreed upon, each person is offered time to tell their viewpoint of the event in question without interruption. The mediator's purpose is to make sure each person is allowed to speak freely, ask additional questions for clarification, then offer suggestions for possible solutions to the problem. Before the circle ends, each person is asked whether he or she is ready to embrace the other in healing and reconciliation. Each expresses what they need to be forgiven for, and what they need to forgive. Once the expression has been completed, the medicine person "feathers" each person with an eagle knife feather, cutting away the past; asks each person if they are willing to forgive and release all past harm; and blesses the person for the present and future generations. Once amends are made, the elder prays for the healing of all concerned, asking the ancestors and personal guides to help them find the truth of their connections to themselves and each other.

## Vision Quest

This visioning ceremony has been held by indigenous peoples throughout the world since time immemorial. In Okanagan life, children who reached the age of puberty are sent alone into the wilderness over a one- or two-night period to find their *tamanohwis,* or guardian spirit power. The Sioux call it *hanblecya,* crying for a vision, while Australian Aborigines call it Walkabout, a quest they send young adolescents on to cross the threshold into adulthood. Vision quest is the way tribal people seek their life purpose. It's also the way many become acquainted with their personal spirit helpers, guides, and totems.

In the general form of vision quest, a petitioner travels alone to a preferred spot in nature (one where you will not be disturbed by other humans), casts a sacred circle, sometimes divesting themselves of clothing and other accoutrements (often no tents allowed!), and usually fasts, although many people today take water with them. The intention is to simply "be" in silence and prayer within the circle, often without eating, for up to four days. While some people attempt this ceremony on their own, it is preferable (and recommended) to ask a medicine person to "put you on the hill." This facilitator will pray with and for you before and during your time away, tend a sacred fire for your strength, support your intention, and offer a sweat lodge for your purification when you return. He or she can then assist you with interpreting any signs, dreams, visions, or encounters you experienced.

## Lineage-Specific Ceremonies

Occasionally, medicine people may offer someone a personal ceremony, or if you are apprenticed to a medicine person, at some point you may be gifted a bundle and altar to perform a ceremony for others. When inheriting a ceremony in this way, it is important to follow the ceremony the way it is given, until such time as the medicine person informs you that you are ready to design your own ceremony. Since mixing medicines from different ceremonies often confuses things rather than clarifying them, at the very least, one should ask permission before including new and different vibrational energies (crystals, plant medicines, etc.) into a ceremony that has been taught and handed down in a particular way.

## Naming Ceremony

Names are important. Consider what your parents went through weighing names to give you. Whether you like your name now, or feel it's a good "fit," your parents had a special reason for giving you your birth name. In indigenous societies, names may be given or acquired at several stages of a person's life. You receive a name at birth, and another when you reach puberty and begin the journey as a young adult; a name given in ceremony at a rite of passage ritual, welcoming you into adulthood.

One may receive a name for a deed of courage, an important life transition, a new phase of life. Sometimes one may receive a name directly from the spirit helpers during a vision quest. Occasionally, a name will come in a dream or a shamanic journey. Or an elder will see something in you that needs to be revealed, or needs to grow, or needs to be recognized and honored. Traditionally, an elder or community council will create a ceremony to gift you a new name. Before the ceremony, the elders will ask you if you accept this name and are willing to take it on and grow with it. A tall order!

### Keeping of the Soul Ceremony, the Chi Bai

There are many ways of doing this ceremony. When someone dies, it takes time for their soul to transition to the other side camp. Relatives grieve, rightly so. And sometimes, a soul gets "lost" on its journey. The one who "Keeps the Soul" agrees to pray for that person's transition and arrival home, for a specified length of time, in a specified way. At the end of that time, there will be a ceremony and a Giveaway. The family will give away many of the possessions of the deceased, releasing their attachments at the same time.

There are many other reasons for carrying grief in today's world—wars, mall/school shootings, natural disasters, etc. The experienced medicine person can work with groups and individuals to connect with their personal grief, as well as the common grief experienced by all humanity, in an effort to accept, forgive, release, and lift us all into the next level of love and acceptance.

### Shamanic Healing Work

Beyond journey work to seek information and healing for a client or group, some of the common shamanic healing practices are power retrievals and soul retrievals, both of which require training to perform.

- Power retrieval accesses medicine from non-ordinary reality to be brought forward and given to the healee

- Soul retrieval seeks the lost soul or essence and brings it back to the client

Other advanced shamanic healing work includes dispossession (extracting unwanted entities) and psychopomp (ushering a soul to the next life).

## Pipe

Many tribes believe in the sacredness of the pipe and tobacco. The Sioux pipe was given to the tribe by White Buffalo Calf Woman many centuries ago and is now carried by nineteenth-generation caretaker Arvol Looking Horse. Sioux pipes are called *chanupas*, and are always made from caitlinite, which is found in the sacred quarries of Pipestone. Other tribes have pipes made of clay and different types of stones. A few use antler, but these are usually tourist pipes and are toxic to smoke. If you have one, please do not use it as anything other than ornamentation.

It is a huge responsibility to be a pipe carrier, and one that must be authorized by a Native American elder. Robin, who carries both a Sioux Sun Dance Pipe and her Okanagan great-grandmother's pipe, tells us that pipe carriers must go anywhere that prayer is requested, whenever someone calls for the pipe. It is taught that whatever you pray for with the pipe will be given to you, so you'd better watch what you pray for!

If you have not been trained in the use of the pipe, please do not buy one in a store and think that you can make up your own ritual. If you already have a pipe and have not been trained, find someone who can teach you. They will pray with you and help you to determine if the Way of the Pipe is for you. Until then, you may not know enough to be able to use the pipe as a carrier for all the people.

## Sweat Lodge

This is the Ceremony of Purification. In the Okanagan way, the sweat lodge is called *Quilsten*, and the poles of the lodge are Creator's ribs. When the people enter the lodge, they enter the heart of the Creator. The floor of the lodge represents the womb of the Mother, and the union of the Father and Mother is the Divine Marriage. This is the place to pray for the realization of your heart's true desires. In the Sioux way, the ceremony is called *Inipi*.

This ceremony should only be led by someone who has been initiated in the way of the tribe with which he or she associates, and who has been trained through apprenticeship to pour water. Many things can happen in a sweat lodge, because people come to a lodge to do deep healing work. A well-meaning but inexperienced leader would not have the wisdom to take care of all the participants, and the outcome could be unpleasant, even dangerous. Therefore, it is very important to find out who is leading a sweat lodge and what their qualifications are. If a leader doesn't ask if new people are present who have not sweat before and does not present teachings about their lodge protocols before you enter, we recommend that you carefully consider whether you wish to participate inside the lodge. You can always pray around the fire. If you know the leader and are comfortable with their energy and ability to respond to anything that may arise, then do attend. Each lodge is different, and each lodge experience is an opportunity to commune with Spirit and emerge reborn.

## Dance Ceremonies

Commonly, each tribe or tradition holds dances at certain times of year. Each dance holds a specific intention, sometimes both personal and group. If you are invited to attend one of these dances under the mentorship of an experienced attendee, this is a fabulous opportunity to learn about these traditions and experience something quite profound. Many dances are ceremonial, with defined protocols, and require preparation. Some examples include:

- Sun Dance of the North American Plains tribes
- Winter Dance of the Pacific Northwest peoples
- Cherokee Stomp Dance
- Naraya (Dance for All People) inspired by the First Nations of the Great Basin/Plateau (originated with Shoshone/Paiute peoples)
- Earthdance, Global Peace Movement
- Star Dance
- Dance to Heal the Earth
- Pagan Fire Dance, Moon Dance, and Dragon Dance
- And many others

# Self-Designed Ceremonies, Elements

In some traditions, people design ceremonies as they are called to do so; for example, ceremonies to each of the four elements at certain times of year. On the next page we list some ideas, knowing that, with the instructions given in the Healing in the West chapter and in this section, you will design your ceremonies by asking for and listening to your spirit helper's guidance.

North—Tree/Stone Nation—Dragon. Earth Ceremony. Paint stones for offerings, drum for journey to Dragon to learn what each can do to help Mother Earth. Also, Earth Weaving Ceremony, similar to the Water Ceremony detailed below.

East—Air/breath of Spirit—Eagle ceremony. Make a feather mandala as an offering to Eagle and air together, then do a journey with Eagle to soar above, to see the bigger vision and each person's part in it.

West—Water ceremony—Swimming ones. Ask each participant to bring a small bottle of water from their home territory. By this time, you will have collected sacred water from many places you've traveled to. Each person offers a little water from their own bottle into a large, beautiful water bowl. Add water from the lake, stream, or ocean you all have met at. Bless the water in the bowl, then offer a few drops of the mixed water back to each person's water bottle, explaining that its now sacred water. Offer the remaining water to the nearest body of water, with a water song. People can drum, rattle, etc. Talk about the beautiful landscapes where the ocean meets mountains, and the air is so pure. Make a sacred fire (a candle will do if fire isn't allowed) together and explain how the elements work together.

South—ceremony to Phoenix and Fire. Create a sacred fire together and honor the four fires: the ember that keeps us alive; the fire of inspiration that helps us grow and create; the hearth/heart fire we gather around in family and community; and the fire of creation and destruction, which we must learn to keep watch over and control. Then ask each person to write a wish/prayer for themselves and the world and offer it to the fire. Everyone can drum, sing, and dance around the fire as well. It's always wonderful and fun to dance your power animals.

# GLOSSARY

---

**Aho Mitakuye Oyasin!** Lakota term for All My Relations.

**Akashic records** Chronicles of the universe that have been stored in the stars since before the beginning of time; the history of Earth and all Earth beings.

**All [My] Our Relations** All Earth's children: winged ones, swimming ones, four-legged animals, plant and tree people, creepy-crawlers, stone people, our ancestors, and our descendants—seven generations back and seven generations forward. All known and unknown, all within sacred connection, the interdependent whole of the families of Mother Earth.

**Arcturus** Guardian of the bear, this star is located in the constellation Boötes (the Herdsman), named for its placement near the Great Bear (Big Dipper) and the surrounding stars considered the herdsman's sheep. The Hawaiians call this star Hokule'a, star of joy and gladness, one of the main stars used by the Polynesians when navigating by sea across the equator to Hawaii.

**Atlantis** Ancient island nation depicted in Plato's dialogues and other works. Controversy yet reigns as to whether the land was purely fictional, mythical, or actual, but insufficient empirical evidence to scientifically prove its existence.

**Betelgeuse** Star located at the tip of the constellation Orion. Visible late fall through spring in the Northern Hemisphere.

**Big Oil, Big Ag, Big Pharma, Big Banks** Refers collectively to the largest corporations in select global industries that wield economic power and political influence, particularly in the US where these groups maintain a staff of paid representatives (lobbyists) to influence government policies.

**Black Elk**  Deceased Lakota holy man whose remarkable visions have been an inspiration to many.

**Blue Road**  Line connecting the east and west directions that symbolizes the union of spirit and matter, where illumination/vision meets dreaming/healing; the Blue Road of spiritual attainment. (See also *Red Road* and note that some practitioners position these in reversed fashion.)

**Ceremony**  In this book, the ceremony at the end of each chapter is a way to integrate each of the lessons; it helps us embody the teachings in everything we do. For a list of common ceremonies, see section Honoring Sacred Ceremonies in the Resources section.

**Chakras**  Seven energy centers within the human body, as described in Eastern philosophies; these are spirit, mind, throat, heart, will, creative center, and root.

**Circle**  A spiritual gathering with a specific intention. The intention may be prayer, healing, witnessing someone's rite of passage, or an invitation to join in Council. To initiate sacred circle is to set intention, clear the space, and call in the ancestors and the directional powers for protection and guidance.

**Co-creation**  Collaborative process that involves parties from diverse departments, backgrounds, and sources to innovate, develop, share ideas, and brainstorm improvements collectively, rather than individually.

**Color**  Indigenous people believe that the vibrations of color have potential healing power. Colors are also symbolic of the phases and directions of our lives, and they correspond to our chakras (energy centers).

**Council of Twelve**  Metaphysical beings who guide incarnated souls as they grow and develop on the Earth plane.

**COVID-19**  An acute respiratory illness in humans caused by a coronavirus that is capable of producing severe symptoms, even death, particularly in older people and those with underlying health conditions. Originally identified in China in 2019; became a global pandemic in 2020.

**Creatures**  In Native American traditions and many others, the animal tribes were considered to be people, with nations of their own. Many stories speak about the time when animals talked, and they relate ways that animals offered to help foolish humans to live in balance on the earth.

**Dance to Heal the Earth**  Sacred Medicine Dance gifted to Robin Youngblood, a profound ceremony that aligns you with Mother Earth and Father Sky, reconnects you with your ancestors to open the Sacred Medicine Bundles within yourself, and connect deeply to your core being and to the Tree of Life. This dance has been held in several locations in the US, Europe, and Africa.

**Day cycle**  Time of day/night to which a particular direction is linked.

**DDT**  Dichlorodiphenyltrichloroethane, commonly known as DDT, was first promoted as an agricultural pesticide in 1946, after WWII.

**Dismemberment**  A shamanic archetypal journey where the journeyer is literally ripped apart, pieces scattered, to be re-membered again in an entirely different way. This is an initiatory process unique to every practitioner, with a rebirth to a different way of being.

**DNA**  Deoxyribonucleic acid; the substance from which human genes are fashioned and the transmitter of inherited characteristics.

**Dreaming**  An altered state where the dreamer experiences alternative realities existing outside our everyday time and space limitations.

**DSM**  Diagnostic and Statistical Manual of Mental Disorders, a handbook used by health care professionals in the United States and much of the world to diagnose mental disorders.

**Earth Mother**  Mother Earth is the womb from which we come. She is found below the Medicine Wheel, the supporting foundation providing All Our Relations and each of us with all that we need to live.

**Element**  The element is the rudimentary physical principle used to describe each direction. Generally, Westerners consider only four elements: earth, air, water, and fire. Asian traditions use two more, wood and metal, and African tribalists call on the element of the mineral peoples (stones).

**Elementals**  Spirits that personify the four elements: earth, air, fire, and water. This term is sometimes applied to other nature spirits such as dryads, gnomes, nymphs, and others. Elementals can be instrumental in shamanic healing work and energy work once you learn their properties and scope, understand their limitations, and develop a relationship with them.

**Embodiment**  The embodiment is the way that we humans experience the aspects of each direction. Eastern peoples usually associate five or six of these attributes in their personality matrices. In this book, we use seven.

**Emotion**  The pervasive feeling often associated with a direction.

**Epigenetics**  The scientific exploration of our genetic material, which in part concludes that we each have unique markers in our DNA that represent the joys, traumas, and reactions of our ancestors encoded in us. Until we begin to recognize, acknowledge, honor, and heal the traumatic patterns of our ancestors, we cannot change these reactions.

**Expression**  A physical way of putting our beliefs into action and giving them creative form.

**Father Sky**  Above the wheel lies the realm of time-without-time: Sky Father, the keeper of Great Mystery. This is where we find the sun, moon, stars, and the great unknown of the void.

**Four-legged**  Animal kingdom; those who walk on four legs.

**Giveaway, gifting**  Practice of tithing, or of compensating those who nurture your spirit. Giveaway is an important component of many ceremonies (see discussion in Honoring Sacred Ceremonies).

**GMO**  Genetically modified organism. Organisms whose genetic makeup has been altered in a laboratory to encourage select characteristics or biological traits.

**Great Mystery**  That which is without definition, the unknown; and yet the creative source from which we come and of which we are an integral part.

**Grounding, grounded**  Act of finding stillness and becoming fully present, undistracted by outside thoughts, worries, or concerns.

**Guides**  Beings that seem to be watching over you and sharing wisdom with you. These helpers are called by many names: guardian angels, totem animals, personal guides, your own higher self, imaginary friends, relatives no longer of the Earth plane (ancestors), your own previous incarnations, gods or goddesses, etc.

**Hanblecya**  Sioux term for "crying for a vision" with humbleness. Also called vision quest.

**Heyokah**  Name given to those individuals whose visions impel them to see life and situations in contrast to the majority. They may actually seem backward; they may act or say the exact opposite of what they mean. Heyokah shows us alternative perspectives, most often in a humorous manner—like the trickster Coyote—so we can cleanse ourselves with the medicine of laughter and learn something new.

**Higher self**  Also called our essence, what some call the oversoul; the part of us that is spirit in body.

**Hollow Bone**  Visionary or seer.

**Ho'oponopono**  Hawaiian method of conflict resolution and problem-solving used to set relationships right. Also called a making right or forgiveness ceremony.

**Hopi**  Native American tribe from northeastern Arizona whose mythologies and prophecies were brought forward to modern peoples by Thomas Banyacaya.

**Infinity symbol**  Mathematical symbol in the shape of a horizontal figure eight. Also called a lemniscate. Spiritually, the symbol represents endless possibilities or forever.

**Inipi**  Purification ceremony given to the Lakota people by White Buffalo Calf Pipe Woman; also called Sweat Lodge. The Okanagan name for Sweat Lodge is Quil'sten, and the stories and traditions are somewhat different than the Lakota.

**Integration**  The act of assimilating what we've experienced, bringing it within ourselves to a deeper understanding.

**Intention**  The act of consciously and clearly setting your mind to your objective. The simpler and more concise you can get it, the better.

**Journaling**  Maintaining a written record of your life experiences. In spiritual work, this record may include your journey experiences, dreams, excerpts from books or songs that resonate with you, and the teachings you encounter.

**Journeying**  A form of meditation/visualization that entails traveling to the middle, upper, or lower worlds, held to the earthly plane typically by the beat of the drum. Drumming assists participants in reaching and maintaining an alpha state more receptive to altered realities; journeyers are signaled to return by a change in tempo.

**Kermode**  A subspecies of black (North American) bear that lives in British Columbia, Canada with very light, almost white, fur (not albino). Also called the White Spirit Bear.

**Lakota**  A tribe of peoples, also called Sioux, who live in the Dakotas.

**Lesson**  Each direction illustrates a certain set of lessons that will carry forward throughout our lives, or for this cycle of learning.

**Liminal space, liminality**  Threshold state in rites of passage where participants are no longer who they were when they began the rite, but not yet transitioned to the new status they will hold upon the rite's completion.

**Medicine**  Gifts from Spirit with which all beings are endowed; these manifest in a unique and special way for each of Earth's children.

**Medicine bundle**  Sacred package or bag containing items that hold special meaning or power; usually the gifts of Spirit, teachers, or Earth herself.

**Medicine person/teacher**  Sometimes called shaman. A medicine person helps others with healing, transformation, and understanding.

**Medicine Shield**  Image or article that integrates special symbols and designs which hold special meaning or power; usually the gifts of Spirit, teachers, or Earth herself.

**Medicine Wheel**  Circle of stones, found in many places in North America, Canada, and around the world. These circles were placed with care on sacred ground by indigenous peoples. The wheel was used for ceremony and ritual, and was known to have great power to initiate change and healing. The stone wheel represents the Wheel of Life, encompassing all that is, and illustrates the connection of every aspect.

**Moon cycle**  It has been understood for centuries that a woman's menstrual cycle is associated with the phase of the moon. If women live together in community, they will eventually experience their monthly cycles within a few days of each other. Even the oceans ebb and flow with the cycles of the moon.

**Moon Lodge**  Women's ceremonial retreat time. In villages where women lived and worked together, most women's menses came at the same time each month, according to the cycle of the moon. The women came together in the Moon Lodge for the duration to share crafts, stories, and teachings. This moon time is the time of a woman's greatest power, and this sacred circle was a time for prayer and discussion of community needs, as well as a time for deep introspection and communication with other worlds.

**Mother Earth**  See *Earth Mother.*

**Non-ordinary reality**  Also called the journey world or the otherworld. Composed of the upper, middle, and lower worlds with various portals into and levels or dimensions within each. See journeying.

**Okanogan/Okanagan** Native peoples who inhabit the central Columbia Plateau of British Columbia and Central Washington. Words like Okanagan, Colville, etc., are umbrella terms for many interconnected tribes of various names within the Okanagan Valley of what is now central Washington and British Columbia.

**Original Instructions** Core purpose and way of being for each different species in the web of life, including humans, as given by the Divine, the Creator, or Great Mystery.

**Other Side Camp** Dwelling place of those who have passed on from the earthly plane and wait for us in the spirit world.

**Phase of life** Just as the sun and moon have cycles, so do we. We begin at birth, move through childhood and adulthood, and into our elder years. Each stage is unique and has its own learnings.

**Pipe** Sacred ceremony and implements given to the people by White Buffalo Calf Woman (to the Lakota) many centuries ago; it is now carried by nineteenth-generation caretaker Arvol Looking Horse. Sioux pipes are called *chanupas* and are always made from caitlinite, found in the sacred quarries in Pipestone. Many indigenous tribes received sacred pipes in many different ways. Some of these legends are accessible via tribal internet sites.

**Place on the wheel** We always return to the place of beginning. This is our truth. But truth without experience is weak. We must journey around the wheel, stopping in each sacred direction, in order to strengthen our ability to stand in our truth.

**Pleiades** Loose cluster of stars in the direction of the constellation Taurus. Named after the Seven Sisters of Greek mythology, these stars appear to be surrounded by a keen nebulosity that shines by their reflected light.

**Polaris** The North Star, known in many places in the Americas as the Star Who Stands Still. In Paiute legend, the Big and Little Dipper (which holds the North Star at its tip) are boys who turned into mountain sheep and climbed so high on a mountain, they could not return, so one of the boys' fathers made them into stars to guide others.

**Prayer bundle**  Medicine bundle used to represent certain prayers, often used with prayer arrows.

**Psychopomp**  One who guides souls from Earth to the afterlife. Often depicted as angels, or anthropomorphic entities such as crows or horses, this role is a shamanic specialization that helps usher those who have recently died into the arms of their ancestors.

**PTSD**  Post-traumatic stress disorder. A condition triggered by experiencing or witnessing a terrifying event. Symptoms include vivid flashbacks, nightmares, anxiety, and extreme distress at reminders of the trauma long after the event.

**Re-member**  To reassemble that which has been dismembered or torn apart.

**Red Road**  Line connecting the north and south directions, the joining of creativity and ancestral wisdom, where vulnerability meets integrity; where our ancestral gifts inform our life passion and purpose; the Red Road of the physical plane. (See also *Blue Road* and note that some practitioners position these in reversed fashion.)

**Rigel**  Star located at the bottom right corner of the constellation Orion. Visible late fall through spring in the Northern Hemisphere.

**Rites of passage**  Celebrations that mark personal milestones over the course of a lifetime, such as birth, bat/bar mitzvah or confirmation, graduation, often marriage or a commitment to an organization or career, parenthood, retirement, and finally dropping our robes/death.

**Sacred Feminine/Masculine**  The Sacred Feminine represents the nurturing, intuitive expression; the pause to consider and weigh before action; the internal intuitive, reflective, dreaming principle. The Sacred Masculine represents rational thought and expression; the drive to design and build something external; the active, doing principle.

**Sacred Hoop**  The energy that encompasses all beings and Earth; the circle of life that holds all that is and All Our Relations.

**Sacred space**  The environment within which you can do spiritual work; it includes creating an environment, a place that is blessed, and it allows you to focus on the work at hand.

**Sacred Tree**  Sometimes called the Tree of Knowledge, World Tree (axis mundi), or Tree of Life. Connects the upper and lower worlds as portrayed in various mythologies (Yggdrasil in Norse mythology) and spiritual belief systems.

**Seasons**  Seasons have been astrologically related to the directions of the Medicine Wheel since time began. Tribal astronomers often used Medicine Wheels to determine the changing of the seasons.

**Seven Generations**  Native American philosophy that asks mankind to consider whether decisions made today would benefit those seven generations into the future.

**Seven Sacred Directions**  The four cardinal directions—east, south, west, and north—as well as the three center directions—above, below, and within.

**Shadow**  Also referred to as shadow aspect or archetype in Jungian psychology. Represents those parts of us, beautiful *and* challenging, that are not yet accepted or that remain unknown, unconscious.

**Shaman**  Siberian word for someone who journeys into non-ordinary reality to serve community by acting as a healer or medicine person. This term is often applied to any medicine person, regardless of tradition. One traditional practice of shamanism includes entering a dreamtime/vision state through drumming, chant, and/or dance.

**Sirius**  Also called the dog star, this bright binary star runs at Orion's heels across the Northern Hemisphere's winter sky. In the Americas, this star is also called Wolf Star or Coyote Star. The Cherokee also call Sirius a dog star, one of the guardians to the path of souls (Milky Way) along with Antares.

**Sky Father**  See *Father Sky.*

**Smudging**  The act of ritually cleansing an object, an energy field, or an area such as a room. Personal cleansing is often done to prepare for inner work or ceremony. A common way of cleansing is to use the smoke from herbs such as sage, cedar, or sweetgrass burned loose in a fired earthen bowl or a shell, or as a tied bundle. Pass the smoke through your energy field, your front torso, your backside, the soles of feet, and above your head. Focus your attention on cleansing; use a prayer or sacred words if you wish (silently or aloud).

**Spiral path** Circling the Medicine Wheel, a series of cyclical teachings, that we continue, in some fashion, throughout our lifetime.

**Spiritual Warrior** One who serves and protects those who cannot protect themselves, both humanity and all of nature.

**Standing ones** Ancient trees, who have stood for longer than any other living being.

**Standing Rock** Sioux Indian Reservation with land in North and South Dakota where the Dakota Access Pipeline (DAPL) was rerouted in 2016 and the site of protests to protect tribal waters. These protests drew hundreds of participants from many indigenous nations—even those from many other countries, as well as a contingent of US veterans—standing together in peaceful solidarity with the Sioux to prevent pipeline construction. The events of this protest were finally widely publicized, despite the fact the pipeline was completed. The tribe sued and a federal judge sided with them in 2020; as of this writing the case is currently continuing in the US Federal Courts.

**Star beings, star people, star nations** Those who come from the sky and beyond. Many indigenous peoples have stories of beings who came from star nations.

**Subterraneans** Those who live below the earth; they aerate the soil, enrich the humus, and fertilize the plant people.

**Sun Dance** Four-day renewal rite of endurance, sacrifice, and thanksgiving; held in the summer among many northern Native American tribes.

**Sweat lodge** See *Inipi*.

**Talking circle/stick** Group gathering that uses a talking stick to acknowledge speakers one by one until all have been heard.

**Time**  The time of day or night is important because each phase of the sun/moon dial carries with it a certain type of power. These powers can be called upon to aid us in our endeavors.

**Tiyospaye**  Lakota word that describes our own village tribe of friends and/or family; an extended family; our tribe of affinity.

**Totem animals**  Also called power animals, totem animals act as our guards and guides.

**Tsalagi**  Cherokee peoples.

**Turtle Island**  Native name for North America; derived from creation stories recounting that mud from the floor of the great oceans was placed on the back of a great turtle.

**Two-legged**  Those who walk on two legs, used to refer to humankind.

**Vega**  Arabic for descending eagle, this star is part of the constellation Lyra, and one of the stars that make up a lyre or harp-shaped formation recognized across many cultures. In the Americas, among the Pawnee, Vega is recognized as one of the stars given the responsibility of holding one of the four quarters of the sky, as well as the patron star of medicine people.

**Vision quest**  See *Hanblecya*.

**Vocables**  In music, a syllable or sound without specific meaning, such as *ah, ee, eh, oh*, etc.

**Walkabout**  Australian Aboriginal male rite of passage from adolescence to adulthood in which boys live for up to six months in the wilderness. A form of vision quest.

**Way**  Pathway we follow in learning about the powers we can receive through each direction.

**Wheels within wheels**  The concept that each Medicine Wheel contains secondary wheels in each direction.

**White Buffalo Calf Pipe Woman**   White Buffalo Calf Pipe Woman brought the gift of the sacred pipe and other ceremonies to the Lakota (Sioux) peoples. Throughout time her story has been told to remind the people of the sacredness of life and that we must walk the earth in a good way, in balance with All Our Relations.

**Wisdom Keeper**   Sometimes called shaman or medicine teacher. A Wisdom Keeper holds a set of teaching for their tribe, often part of a family lineage or an apprenticed arrangement.

**Wotai**   Cherokee term for small sacred stone that represents protection and connection to one's helping spirits.

**Wovoka**   Paiute shaman who brought forward a Ghost Dance movement based on a prophetic vision. Smohalla and Smolhatekin of the Columbia River tribes had the same vision at the same time.

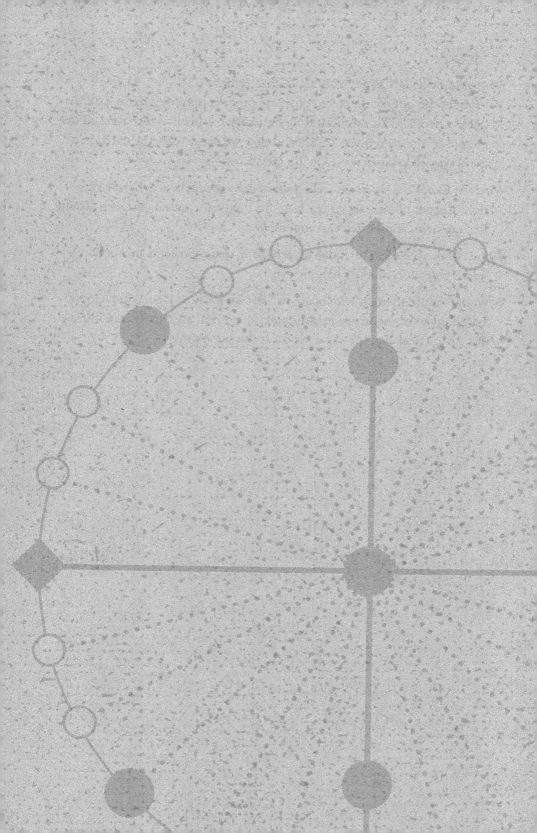

# BIBLIOGRAPHY

Brown, Jr., Tom. *Grandfather: A Native American's Lifelong Search for Truth and Harmony with Nature*. New York: The Berkeley Publishing Group, 1993.

Eliade, Mircea. *Rites and Symbols of Initiation: The Mysteries of Birth and Rebirth*. Spring Publications Inc., 1958.

Harner, Michael. *The Way of the Shaman*. New York: HarperCollins Publishers, 1980.

Hubbard, Barbara Marx. *Conscious Evolution: Awakening the Power of Our Potential*. New World Library, 2015 (revised edition).

King, Serge Kahili. *Urban Shaman*. New York: Atria Books, 1990.

Lewis, John. "Together, You Can Redeem the Soul of our Nation." *The New York Times*, July 30, 2020. Retrieved from https://www.nytimes .com/2020/07/30/opinion/john-lewis-civil-rights-america.html.

Meade, Michael. *The Water of Life: Initiation and the Tempering of the Soul*. Seattle: Greenfire Press, 2006.

Miller, Dorcas S. *Stars of the First People: Native American Star Myths and Constellations*. Boulder: Pruett Publishing Company, 1997.

Mitchell, Sherri (Weh'na Ha'mu' Kswasset She Who Brings the Light). *Sacred Instructions: Indigenous Wisdom for Living Spirit-Based Change*. Berkeley: North Atlantic Books, 2018.

Mooney, James. *Myths of the Cherokee*. Garden City: Dover Publications, 1996 (revised, original 1900).

Neihardt, John G. *Black Elk Speaks: Being the Life Story of a Holy Man of the Oglala Sioux As Told Through John G. Neihardt (Flaming Rainbow)*, Lincoln: University of Nebraska Press, 1961, also New York: Washington Square Press, 1972 (originally published 1932).

Roth, Gabrielle. *Maps to Ecstasy: The Healing Power of Movement.* San Francisco: New World Library, 1998.

Schrijver, Karel, and Iris Schrijver. *Living With the Stars: How the Human Body Is Connected to the Life Cycles of the Earth, the Planets, and the Stars.* Oxford, UK: Oxford University Press, 2015.

Underwood, Paula. *Who Speaks for Wolf: A Native American Learning Story.* Georgetown: A Tribe of Two Press, 1983.

Youngblood, Robin Tekwelus, and Sandy D'Entremont. *Path of the White Wolf: An Introduction to the Shaman's Way.* Phoenix: Phoenix Publications, 2014 (original 2007).

## *Recordings*

Harner, Michael. Journeywork® Series CDs. Mill Valley: Foundation for Shamanic Studies, 2010. Available at https://www.shamanism.org/products/audio.html.

Youngblood, Robin Tekwelus, and Sandy D'Entremont. *Path of the White Wolf: Seven Sacred Meditations.* Phoenix Publications, 2007.

## *Other Online Resources*

Discussions such as Honoring the Sacred, Healing Global Multigenerational Trauma, Towards Healing Systemic Racism, Indigenous Social and Restorative Justice, the Circle of Courage, and the Medicine Wheel of Mastery are available at these internet sites:

sacredearthcouncil.com

churchoftheearth.org

churchoftheearth.org/teachings/7daysofrest

7days-of-rest.org/storytellerslodge

ubiverse.org/welcome.html

Storyteller's Lodge Facebook page

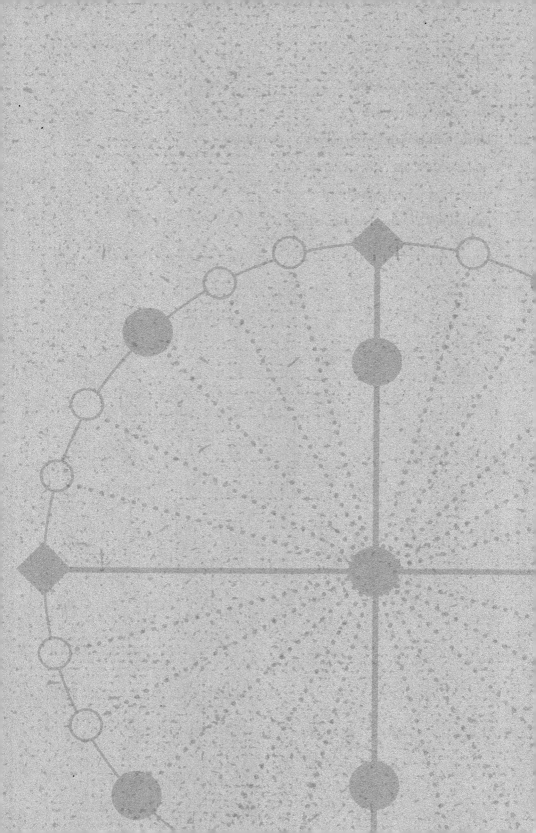

# RECOMMENDED READING

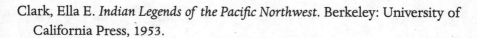

Clark, Ella E. *Indian Legends of the Pacific Northwest*. Berkeley: University of California Press, 1953.

Essene, Virginia, and Irving Feurst. *Energy Blessings from the Stars: Seven Initiations*. Santa Clara: S. E. E. Publishing Company, 1998.

Hilbert, Vi (taq W seblu, Upper Skagit Elder). *Haboo: Native American Stories from Puget Sound*. Seattle: University of Washington Press, 1985.

Medicine Eagle, Brooke. *Buffalo Woman Comes Singing*. New York: Ballantine Books, 1991.

———. *The Last Ghost Dance: A Guide for Earth Mages*. New York: Ballantine Books, 2000.

Sams, Jamie. *Dancing the Dream: The Seven Sacred Paths of Human Transformation*. New York: HarperCollins, 1998.

———. *The 13 Original Clan Mothers: Your Sacred Path to Discovering the Gifts, Talents, and Abilities of the Feminine Through the Ancient Teachings of the Sisterhood*. New York: HarperCollins, 1993.

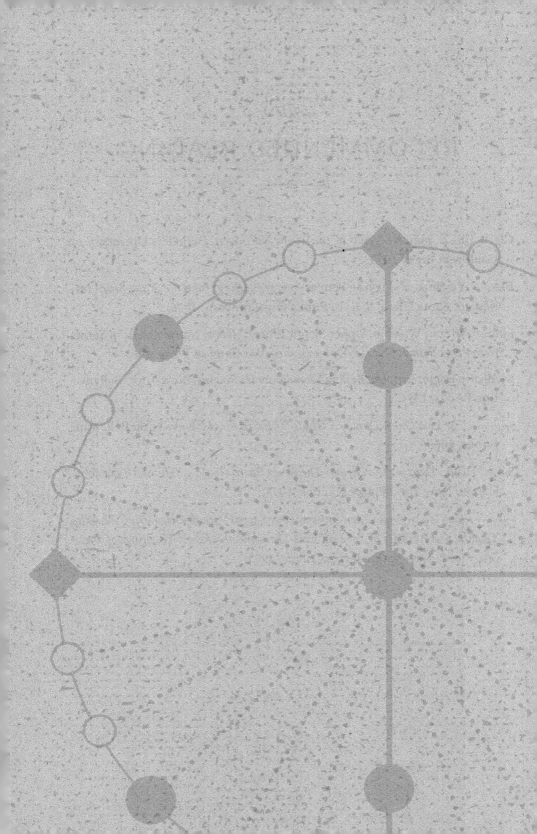

# ACKNOWLEDGMENTS

———◆———

We owe a debt of deep gratitude to those who taught us to walk the path of beauty. For many years Robin followed the Sun Dance Way and her own people's Winter Dance. Many thanks to Martin High Bear, Sun Dance Chief, a man of great strength, vision, and wisdom. Robin gives her most humble gratitude to Grandfather Frank Settee, Okanagan/Anishinaabe/Cree Sundance Intercessor, for adopting her as his sister in ceremony on Maui in 2010. Sandy and Robin learned the healing songs and ceremonies with Northwest Coastal Salish teachers and healers Fred Beaver Chief Jameson and Johnny Moses. Hopi messenger Thomas Banyacya shared the prophecies and taught us to be humble. Siberian Shaman Grandmother Mingo, Grandfather Misha, and his niece, Nadyashta Duvan shared the teachings of the Kamlanya. Our thanks also to our students and the communities where Robin teaches in North America, Hawaii, Europe, Australia, New Zealand, Asia, and Africa, including a big thank you to all the wonderful Dance to Heal the Earth (DTHTE) community circles around the world.

Robin has been deeply touched by the Huna teachings of L'au Lapa'au, Henry Awae, Aunties Pua, Mahealani, Nahi Gutzman of the Hawaiian Nation, and by Hinewhirangi, Nga Tai, and Raina Ferriis of the Maori Iwis. Peruvian Shaman Don José and Aboriginal elder Gagadju shared the wonders of the plant medicine world. Among Robin's wonderful women teachers are her mother, Charlotte, and her adopted mother, Edythe Wildshoe Hardman; her grandmothers, Lucille Raymond (Okanagan) and Cubal Youngblood (Tsalagi); great-grandmother Salmiac (Okanagan), who transmits from the Other Side Camp; Karen Timentwa, her grandmother, Mrs. Lum (Okanagan/Sioux), and Sahn Ashinna (Navajo/Blackfoot).

Sandy has been blessed with the opportunity to learn from the incredible women teachers who travel to the Pacific Northwest for the annual Women of Wisdom conference, including inspirational teachings from Brooke Medicine Eagle, Nicki Scully, Jamie Sams, and Ruth Barrett. Sandy also sends her deepest gratitude to Wabun Wind and Dawn Songfeather Davies, who held up the sign to the Red Road many years ago; to her women's community for their heartfelt teaching, support, and encouragement; to A. Noquisi (Tsalagi) for sharing her sacred traditions; and to Audrey LaRue, whose fabulous master's thesis launched Sandy into partnership with White Bear.

And lastly, we send our sincere appreciation to the team at Llewellyn Worldwide for producing this book in all its beauty.

Tsonkwondiyonrat! (We are all One Spirit!)

## *To Write to the Authors*

If you wish to contact the author or would like more information about this book, please write to the author in care of Llewellyn Worldwide Ltd. and we will forward your request. Both the author and publisher appreciate hearing from you and learning of your enjoyment of this book and how it has helped you. Llewellyn Worldwide Ltd. cannot guarantee that every letter written to the author can be answered, but all will be forwarded. Please write to:

Robin Tekwelus Youngblood and Sandy D'Entremont
⁒ Llewellyn Worldwide
2143 Wooddale Drive
Woodbury, MN 55125-2989
Please enclose a self-addressed stamped envelope for reply,
or $1.00 to cover costs. If outside the U.S.A., enclose
an international postal reply coupon.

Many of Llewellyn's authors have websites with additional information and resources. For more information, please visit our website at http://www.llewellyn.com.